S0-AEG-690

THE SOVIET AIR AND ROCKET FORCES

ALSO BY ASHER LEE

The German Air Force
The Soviet Air Force
Air Power

THE SOVIET AIR AND ROCKET FORCES

EDITED BY

Asher Lee

Theodore Lownik Library
Illinois Benedictine College
Lisle, Illinois 60532

FREDERICK A. PRAEGER, Publishers
NEW YORK

BOOKS THAT MATTER

Published in the United States of America in 1959
by Frederick A. Praeger, Inc., Publishers
15 West 47th Street, New York 36, N.Y

All rights reserved

358
.40947
L477s

Library of Congress
catalog card number: 59-7394

Printed in Great Britain
© 1959 in London, England, by George Weidenfeld & Nicolson Ltd.

CONTENTS

ILLUSTRATIONS

ACKNOWLEDGMENTS

The photographs are reproduced by kind permission of the follow-
ing: those on pages 120 (top) and 152 (below), the Associated
Press; 120 (bottom) and 121 (centre and bottom), *Aviation
Magazine*; 153, the Camera Press; 152 (centre and bottom),
Planet News; and 120 (centre), 121 (top) and 152 (top), the Press
Photo Combine.

INTRODUCTION

THERE WAS A time when the Soviet Union deservedly held the blue riband for inaccessibility and for military security. Information about Soviet air and rocket developments was hard to come by and the most a writer could do was to be usefully speculative. But since the outbreak of the Korean War in 1950 information has been much more freely available. Samples of the *MIG 15* jet fighter engaged in that war have been examined and flown by Western pilots. From them one learnt something firm about Soviet jet engine progress and general work in metallurgy. At the annual Soviet Air Force days of the 1950s there has been unexpected public display of the latest jet fighters, bombers, helicopters and transport planes. Indeed one could today produce a large illustrated collection of authentic pictures of post-war Soviet aircraft which would in themselves give the aeronautic specialist clear pointers as to when the Soviet Union first developed swept-wing fighter and bomber designs, air to air guided missiles, large jet engines in the 15,000 lb thrust class, airborne radar and many other technical facets which provide trends in the over-all air potential of the Kremlin's armed forces. Then there has been the testimony from hundreds of German air engineers who have themselves been engaged in Soviet electronic factories, aero-engine development centres and experimental and operational rocket firing areas.

A further most valuable source on which one has been able to draw is the 'Institute of the USSR' where there are hundreds of ex-Soviet citizens, most of whom have served in the Soviet armed forces, some of them as officers in the jet-atomic age. Further evidence has come in a steady stream from the flow of refugee pilots, radar operators and aircraft mechanics from Poland, Hungary and Czechoslovakia who have escaped from their Communist rulers in the last ten years after being trained to use Soviet air equipment.

It would of course be idle to pretend that sources of raw information are adequate on all or even most subjects concerning Soviet air and rocket power. One would for instance like to know exactly how many atomic weapons, bombs and rockets there are in the Kremlin's stock-pile, broken down into the various categories of intercontinental ballistic missiles, tactical artillery rockets, atomic shells, etc. However even this information would not necessarily be a guide to Soviet air and rocket potential which hinges so much on US air defence and attack weapons, US intelligence and counter-intelligence and of course on Soviet military leadership and training.

I believe this book has drawn on most of the available information on Soviet air and rocket forces. Its authors are drawn from the United States, Britain and Germany. In addition ex-officers of the Soviet Defence Forces have contributed both directly and indirectly to the text. Brief biographical details about them are given in an Appendix. After a general introductory chapter the first ten thousand words or so deal with the early period of development before the Second World War from 1917–41. We have been fortunate to get an intelligent experienced Soviet officer to cover this ground and to write authoritatively on this crucial formative period, which was marked by extensive practical tests of Soviet air equipment and personnel in war theatres in Spain, Finland and on the Chinese-Manchurian border areas. George Schatunowski is a trained scientist and a bomber navigator with Soviet Air Force experience. Another ex-Soviet officer, Boris Kuban, has had active military cum political service in the USSR and has since achieved a growing reputation in Britain as a lecturer and writer on Soviet political and military affairs. There are two chapters, about ten thousand words in all, dealing with the operations in the Second World War. The first period from June 1941 to Stalingrad is covered through the eyes of an experienced senior *Wehrmacht* Air Staff Officer, General Walter Schwabedissen. The second, written by Peter Williams, editor of the *Royal Air Force Flying Review*, covers the period of Soviet success and air superiority from early 1943 to the summer of 1945. The parachute and airborne troop operations of the Second World War are covered by J. M. Mackintosh in his chapter on this Soviet military arm. He is in my view one of the most scholarly and precise of present day writers on Soviet military affairs.

There are three chapters which cover the human and personnel side of the post-war Soviet Air Force. Two of them, dealing with Communist politics and the routine daily life of air and ground crews, have been compiled by Boris Kuban writing from detailed first hand experience on these subjects. The third chapter on technical education and air training has also been compiled by an ex-Soviet Air Force Officer, George Schatunowski, whose authenticity and balance of viewpoint I have learnt to respect.

But in the final analysis, present Soviet air and rocket power must depend on the modern weapons it makes and on how effectively it can operate them. Thus the five chapters on strategic air defence, on long range attack, on jet fighters and fighter bombers, on aircraft and rocket production and on Soviet rocket developments may be the most important ones for those who are making an appraisal of the air and rocket potential of the Soviet Union. The main assessments in these fields of Soviet air and rocket forces are by William Green, Air Chief Marshal Sir Phillip Joubert and Richard Stockwell. These are supplemented of course in other chapters, notably in the introductory chapter to the book and the final chapter pointing to future developments.

The chapter on the 'Air Allies of the Soviet Union' seemed worth writing since the air forces of the Warsaw Treaty Communist powers in Europe are of more than passing importance to NATO, though it is likely that the Kremlin is even more puzzled than the West about their fighting value in time of war and how best to fit them into over-all Soviet plans for air defence and for an air offensive against Western Europe.

What one must regret are the inevitable omissions in a book of little more than a hundred thousand words, which deals with such a vast canvas as forty years of Soviet air and rocket power. There was perhaps need for a chapter on Soviet intelligence. For this the reader is referred to Liddell Hart's book on *The Soviet Army*. Soviet intelligence does not differ in essential methodology from that of other countries. It lays more emphasis on agents and spy-rings, it decodes Western wireless and other communicating traffic, it takes photographs and so forth. But in the final analysis it has to make its judgements of what is false and true, what is important and unimportant, from the massive mixture of truth and fiction which it inevitably deals with.

For the development of naval air forces, the reader is referred to Chapter IX of Commander M. G. Saunders's book *The Soviet Navy*. A short list of post-war publications on Soviet Air Forces will also help fill some of the gaps. Needless to state, all the pertinent material in this brief bibliographical list has been drawn on for the purposes of this book.

London, November 1958.   A.L.

BOOKS ON SOVIET AIR POWER

Soviet Air Power, Richard Stockwell. (Pageant Press, New York).

Russia's Jets, William Green and Derek Wood (Smith & Hallam, Ltd., England).

Military Aircraft of the USSR, Charles Cain and Denys Voaden (Herbert Jenkins, London).

The Soviet Air Force, Asher Lee (Gerald Duckworth & Co., London).

The Red Air Force, John H. Stroud (London).

How Russia Makes War, Raymond L. Garthoff (Allen Unwin).

Soviet Strategy in the Nuclear Age, Raymond L. Garthoff (Praeger).

In addition the *Royal Air Force Flying Review* has in the past few years regularly contained valuable up-to-date information on Soviet air and rocket developments, as has Jane's *All the World's Aircraft.*

PROLOGUE *By Asher Lee*

THE RISE OF the Soviet Union to the position where she has achieved at least strategic air and rocket parity with the Western powers is due to a series of remarkable post-war Soviet developments in jet fighters and bombers, in the various branches of electronics, especially radar, to the developments of guided systems for both defensive and offensive missiles, and finally to the production of modern jet and rocket engines for her long range missiles and for her aircraft and helicopters. Today there is no important branch of modern air and rocket power in which the Soviet Union can be considered to be notably behind the NATO powers and in some fields she is clearly ahead. It is hoped that the chapters that follow do not seriously underrate or overrate the enormous technical progress which Soviet weapons of air fighting have achieved since the end of the Second World War. There is always a danger, when writing of the USSR, of painting a picture either of gloom or of rosy optimism. I will begin with some measured optimism.

The Soviet Union has, it is true, a wide range of all the modern air and rocket weapons adequate to enable her to fight an all-out strategic thermo-nuclear war across the oceans and land masses of the world, or to fight limited local wars of the nuclear or non-nuclear variety. But both in the broad canvas of defence strategy and policy, and in the more detailed back-cloth of her weapon development, the USSR has many problems that need consideration. One might, perhaps, begin with Communist China, her most powerful ally at the moment. In the past five years, Pekin has reiterated that she will liberate Formosa, although Chinese Communist offensive military operations have been virtually limited to moderate bombardment from the air or from coastal batteries of the offshore islands such as Quemoy, Matsu and the Tachen Islands. If Communist China were to drag the Soviet Union into a global war what forces could and should Marshal Biryuzov, head of the Strategic Air Defences of the Soviet Union, allocate to the huge, impossible task of the metropolitan air defence of the Chinese mainland? If this

Soviet support were not adequate, even if the USSR were to win a global struggle, could she contain the subsequent bitterness of her newly industrialised Communist ally? China, if not the Yugoslavia of Asian Communism, has at least already shown signs of independence of utterance even during the present period when she is so largely dependent on Soviet political, economic and military support.

Chapter VII in this book on 'Strategic Air Defence' indicates that the Soviet Union has, at the moment, little prospect of even defending her own home territory from the potential long range thermonuclear assault by the United States and her NATO allies. While it is true that she has developed supersonic jet fighters fitted with air to air guided missiles, as well as hundreds of batteries of ground to air guided missiles for local defence, these are only likely to be effective against high flying jet bombers such as the British *V* bombers or the United States *B 47* and *B 52* strategic bombers. Even against these aircraft the *MIG*, *Yakovlev* and *Sukhoi* fighter machines cannot hope to inflict the rate of loss of fifty per cent or more which is a minimum requirement if the USSR is to be effectively defended against catastrophic damage from Western nuclear and thermo-nuclear attack. But the high-level bomber attack is the least of Marshal Biryuzov's tactical defence headaches. NATO forces are developing the low-level toss bomb techniques which must increase the vulnerability of the air defences of the USSR. Their radar early warning system can only hope to give patchwork warning of low-flying incoming raiders, even if Soviet early warning radar is not subjected to systematic jamming, as it undoubtedly would be. Nor are Soviet defensive guided missiles likely to be effective against Western jet bomber squadrons making effective use of the new stand-off bombs with a range of up to 100 miles, because their own effective range, in many cases, is much less than this. Moreover there is the prospect that the stand-off bomb will double its range in the foreseeable future. Even if the Soviet ground to air guided missiles do the same, they must rely for initial operation on the help of an early warning radar service unadulterated by enemy jamming and other radio counter-measures.

Western intermediate range and intercontinental range rocket missiles may well present Soviet air defences with an insoluble problem. The USSR, like Britain and the United States, is doing all she can to develop an atomic anti-missile missile, but a recent pronouncement on its progress and potential by G. Pokrovsky, a leading Soviet rocket specialist, does not hold out any great hopes in this field at the moment. He began optimistically enough in a Soviet Air Force periodical by writing: 'First of all it must be kept in mind that a missile's warhead moves along a trajectory and cannot manœuvre at all. Therefore if a rocket is pin-pointed in two points in succession by radar, it is possible to determine the rocket's further path, the point of fall and the moment of explosion by means of electric computers in a fraction of a second. This enables anti-missile missiles to be directed automatically into the area through which the missile will pass and to be exploded a little in advance of its path. The rocket, moving with tremendous speed and meeting these fragments in its path, will be seriously damaged. Any damage to its warhead may lead to its burning out like a meteor, or to destruction through premature detonation.'

Pokrovsky ended his statement cautiously, however, with: 'Of course, all such measures demand a complex development of technology and tactics. However, in principle an anti-missile of defence is possible.' Remembering that this article was intended to be optimistic and for consumption by the Soviet armed forces its conclusion seems rather lame. In principle of course anti-missile air defence is possible but not really feasible. It would for instance be interesting to know how Soviet radar is going to pin-point two points in succession from the flight of a series of *Polaris* thermonuclear missiles fired simultaneously from a range of submerged US atomic-engined submarines, when perhaps at the same time the same group of radar early warning stations are asked to monitor and assess the height, speed and direction of incoming low-flying bomber planes, as well as pilotless aircraft and land-based long-ranged rockets with all four types of attack coming in at different speeds and heights. Clearly, when Mr Khrushchev told the world in the autumn of 1957 that the Soviet Union could defend its territory and those of its Communist allies against Western air and rocket attack, he was making a political speech and not a serious military statement.

The development of the *Polaris* and other rockets fired from submarines seems to present an insuperable problem to Soviet air defence just as Soviet rocket-firing submarines do to the defence of the Western hemisphere. At the moment the USSR, like the USA, has no underwater radar or its equivalent which can, from long range, track the movement of hostile submarines, which means that both in peace and war they can in the main take up action stations undetected by the Soviet air defence system. As for tracking incoming rockets, how can mute radar distinguish initially between a rocket flare, a dummy tactical non-atomic rocket and the real thermo-nuclear or atomic missile as they take off from adjacent submarines, or perhaps from the same one? And if two atomic-engined submarines, lying roughly in tandem at a distance of say 500 miles or so, were to fire a long-range rocket simultaneously at Leningrad and Moscow from somewhere in the Baltic it is hard to see how radar could pin-point two points of their paths in succession and so determine the point of explosion.

If, perhaps, I have laboured the point about the weakness of the Soviet air defence system, it is because it may be the crucial factor in today's Soviet foreign policy. People talk of this being based on Machiavellian manœuvring of the Communist allies of the USSR and the so-called uncommitted nations of Asia and Africa with a view to eventual world domination by the Communist bloc. But the Kremlin and the Communist Party of the USSR have a deeper need overriding their desire for power. It is the simple instinct and need to survive. They know how vulnerable and inefficient any radar early warning system can become locally. They know that it is virtually impossible to ring round the USSR with effective air defence in depth, however much it may be necessary to do this to ensure the survival of the regime in a global thermo-nuclear war. If the public utterances of Mr Khrushchev and his colleagues of the last two or three years reveal no fear of such a global struggle, Soviet action, or rather lack of military action, would appear to suggest that Soviet foreign policy is cautious and intends to get its victories by probing, infiltrating and propaganda rather than by direct military action. The action in Hungary in the autumn of 1956 was not a test case. After all, it was on Communist territory and is to be contrasted with Suez where Soviet announcements of Communist volunteers pouring into Egypt from China and elsewhere in support of Nasser and the reported threat to attack London and Paris with long-range rockets, were in fact accompanied by an order to Soviet air technicians and pilots in Egypt to fly away from the danger zone of battle to Syria or the Sudan. In subsequent periods of war threat, for instance on the Turkish-Syrian border, or when the crisis in Jordan and Lebanon produced intervention by British and American troops or in the near war atmosphere of the summer and autumn of 1958 when the offshore islands of China were under air and sea attack, the Soviet Union has taken no military action. The opinion that the British Royal Institute of International Affairs (Chatham House, London) expressed in a publication produced on the eve of the Korean War in 1950 that Soviet policy was 'all mischief short of war' would still seem to be accurate. There is no obvious reason to alter that view, even if Mr Khrushchev sometimes seems to like to emulate Mr Dulles in essays of brinkmanship.

Another defence problem, which must harass the Soviet Union, is the balance of air forces between strategic air defence and the tactical support of the large Red Army. The Ministry of Defence continued to make the tactical air forces the strongest arm of the Soviet Air Force in the early post-war period despite the obviously growing importance of strategic air defence and strategic air attack. Some two thirds of all Soviet air regiments between 1945 and 1947 were fighters, fighter-bombers or medium tactical support planes. But from 1946 onwards it was recognised that only a strong jet interceptor force could provide the basis of active air defensive. By 1955 the Fighter Air Armies under the command of General of Aviation Klimov, Commander-in-Chief of the strategic air defence fighter units, had absorbed most of the *élite* fighter pilots and fighter planes the bulk of which had been previously allocated to the tactical air forces or what is now termed 'Frontal Aviation'. Klimov's pilots and aircraft are part of a greatly expanding PVO[1] strategic air defence command under Marshal of the Soviet Union S. S. Biryuzov. Biryuzov holds a position of great military importance in Soviet defence councils roughly on a par with the Commander-in-Chief of Soviet ground or naval forces.

Marshal Biryuzov's radar warning system and defensive fighters and ground to air guided missiles may be incapable of providing practical defence against either missile or bomber attack in the nuclear and thermo-nuclear age. Soviet political and military interests which have spread to the Arab world and to China, may, later, involve the USSR in even more air aid to other territories of Asia and Africa. This air aid would, in the first instance, require the

[1] The initials PVO stand for anti-aircraft defence.

provision of large numbers of Soviet jet fighters and light bombers. It must be a nearly insoluble problem of current aircraft production planning in Moscow to know what weight to give in the next five or ten years to the production of fighter and fighter bombers. Some of the queries which Soviet air planners can scarcely avoid or answer are: (i) What will be the output of the Chinese jet aircraft industry in the 1960s and, perhaps less important, the industries of Poland, Czechoslovakia, Hungary, Roumania and Bulgaria? (ii) What will the jet fighter and fighter bomber requirements of the Arab world be in 1965? (iii) To what extent will they have to be met from Soviet or other Communist aircraft factories? It is reasonably clear that, for the next five years or so, it will be difficult for the Soviet air and rocket planners to know if they are striking the right production balance between the requirements of jet fighters and fighter bomber output, to meet the triple needs of air defence, tactical air support and their numerous allied commitments both inside and outside the Warsaw Treaty framework, and at the same time balance these needs with the output of defensive guided missiles and tactical atomic artillery and rockets. Should they concentrate on the anti-missile missile and the expansion of their present 50–100 mile range defensive guided missile batteries until they give fairly complete coverage of the USSR? Should they concentrate on the more flexible 2,000–2,500 hp jet- and rocket-engined fighters of the next few years because the defensive guided ground to air missile is a less flexible weapon?

These air planning problems are of course not confined to the USSR but in a period in which there is a tendency to trumpet Soviet technical achievements in aircraft and rockets it is sometimes useful to remind oneself that the aeronautical headaches of Washington and London are to some extent shared by the Kremlin.

What, for instance, is to be the future Soviet air policy on strategic long range air attack? In a paper issued to Soviet Air Force Staff Officers in 1955, Air Chief Marshal Zhigarev, then Commander-in-Chief of the Soviet Air Force, gave the strategic appreciation that intercontinental rocket missiles would replace long range bombers. He gave this explanation of the change over: strategic long range bombers are expensive to build, man and maintain and they need to be housed in large airfields where they are vulnerable to air attack, they tie up large numbers of maintenance personnel and need great supplies of fuel. Missiles, he pointed out, can be built more easily and cheaply, do not need such a complicated supply and servicing organisation, can and are easily concealable and so are less vulnerable. His successor as Commander-in-Chief of the Soviet Air Force, Air Marshal Vershinin, repeated this view of Soviet air policy in an interview with *Pravda* in September 1957. This was the great period of long range rocket pronouncements by Soviet leaders. Khrushchev said in an interview with the *New York Times* that he doubted if the bomber or the fighter had a future. But within the last year or so there are signs that Soviet military and political leaders are changing their view. Both Vershinin and Khrushchev have said that in a future war there would be bomber attacks on enemy cities. The development by Soviet bomber designer Myasishchev of a more powerful four-jet bomber than the Bison in the 1957–8 period is confirmation that, as Pokrovsky, himself a leading Soviet rocket specialist, has said: 'In war the long range intercontinental missile cannot completely replace aircraft piloted by men. Soviet military science teaches that only a purposeful combination of various forms of military equipment can ensure the successful achievement of victory.' The dichotomy of bombers or missiles is as much a problem in Moscow as in Washington. The advent of US atomic submarines and the imminence of the *Polaris* will impose a rethinking of Soviet strategy: equally, Soviet rocket-firing submarines must influence US policy. How many Soviet air regiments of long range jet anti-submarine aircraft will the Kremlin have trained in the next five years or so to meet the new long range rocket threat from US submarines? Should they rather concentrate on submarine hunters of submarines to meet the *Polaris* threat? That is indeed the sixty-four dollar question in Russia, which must cause one or two brows to wrinkle in Soviet defence meetings.

If there are inevitable Soviet problems, it is hardly surprising. Never before in military history have weapons changed their emphasis so often or with such speed as in the last decade. In this period, Soviet air and rocket power has risen from being well behind that of the West to a position of over-all strategic parity, with the possibility of gaining over-all strategic superiority in the next five years or so.

Amongst the many fields of progress, Soviet jet fighters, bombers, rocket missiles and earth satellites have been most publicised. But

the transformation in the field of transport aircraft and helicopters
is in some ways the most impressive. Up to 1950 post-war Soviet
transport planes were well behind those of the West. US Douglas-
C 47s of the Second World War and the Soviet version of the pre-
war US *DC 3* the *LI 2* (or *PS 84*) were the principal types in use.
Many of these were still in use in the middle 1950s. The only
important transport aircraft product of the fourth Five Year Plan
(1946–50) was the twin-engined non-jet *Ilyushin 12*. The great
changes achieved by 1958 can be seen in the June 1958 report of the
International Civil Aviation Authority. The Soviet Union had only
two types of non-jet four-engined transport planes in the early
1950s, the *TU 70* and *IL 18* and these only in very small quantities.
Now it is engaged in large scale production of several medium and
long range four-jet transport planes for military and civil purposes.
Describing the new Soviet turbine powered transport aircraft, the
report says: 'The technical development of air transport in Russia
is more or less parallel to that in Europe and North America.' It
compares the twin-engined *TU 104* and the four-jet *TU 110* with
the British *Comet* and the US *Convair 880*, the two Soviet four-jet
turbo-prop transport planes are compared with the US Lockheed
Electra and the British Vickers *Vanguard* and the giant four-jet turbo-
prop *Rossiya*, the *TU 114*, is compared with the US Boeing *707* and
Douglas *DC 8*. The report adds: 'If these Soviet planes are ever
offered for sale in quantity and at attractive prices, and particularly
if their operating costs are as low as they have been claimed to be,
they could have a profound effect on the economics of world air
transport.' Certainly the sixth Five Year Plan, begun in 1956, has
laid more stress on civil and military transport machines than any of
its quinquennial predecessors. It may well set *AEROFLOT*, the Soviet
civil airline, on the road to being the world's largest airline and
certainly one of the best equipped.

   Soviet helicopters have also made great progress in the 1950s and
are now certainly ahead of those of the West in some respects. The
YAK 24 for instance has been in large scale production since 1955 at
Leningrad and Saratov and can carry about 5 tons of equipment
such as field artillery or up to forty troops. The *MI 6*, a twin-engined
jet helicopter which can carry over 12 tons of equipment or more
than seventy troops, is far the largest and most powerful helicopter
in use at the moment. The military implications of these develop-

ments in Soviet air transport in the last two or three years are clear. Compared with the air regiments of the Second World War, the Soviet Air Force of today is more flexible, mobile and resilient. In supplying their atomic air forces, either bomber or rocket bases; in switching fighter units from strategic defence to tactical support in local or global wars; in carrying on in the 'broken-back' stage of a thermo-nuclear war, if ever it comes, the Soviet defence authorities can make greater use of air transport than ever before. The days when the USSR lacked a force of long ranged four-engined air transport machines, or indeed twin-engined machines, to make the best use of her airborne forces of paratroopers and *élite* infantry are now over. If only because of these major developments in the Soviet air transport arm, the past operational record of airborne troops dealt with by J. M. Mackintosh in a later chapter is probably not typical of future potential fighting value. The Soviet airborne forces of the future will be better trained and better equipped than those of the past. But the biggest difference will be that they will have enough modern long range transport machines to carry them: machines fitted with the latest radio and radar navigational aids. The new generation of Soviet jet transports will also compete with the West for the future new international aircraft markets in Asia, Africa, Latin America and the Arab world. On the whole the USSR is, for the first time, as well equipped as the West in the field of air transport and could gain the lead in the coming age of supersonic air transport in the 1960s.

Perhaps because people have a nodding newspaper acquaintance with the *MIG 15* since the Korean War, they tend to be less impressed with the recent developments in Soviet jet- and rocket-engined fighters. William Green's chapter on the post-war developments in this field is a sharp reminder of its continuing importance to the Soviet defence authorities, despite the continued development of defensive guided missiles and tactical atomic weapons for ground warfare. The period in the late 1940s, when the Soviet aero-engine designers relied to some extent on British or German centrifugal or co-axial engine prototypes to boost the power and performance of the first post-war generation of jet engines, is over. In the last few years the USSR has installed her own native designed *Klimov* jet engines of 6,000–7,000 lb static thrust for her *MIG 17* fighters, while designer A. M. Lyulka has produced a range of more powerful jet engines of 8,000–15,000 lb static thrust to power the supersonic jet fighters of the middle and late 1950s, the *MIG 19*, the *MIG 21* and the more recent *Sukhoi* delta wing 1,200–1,500 mph fighters now coming into service. In an interview with TASS on the occasion of Soviet Aviation Day in July 1958, General of Aviation Andre Rytov said that Soviet aero-engine designers were working on the problem of raising the speed of their fighters to 2,000–2,500 mph, that is about three to four times the speed of sound. Since they already probably have engines of about 20,000 lb thrust fitted in their latest jet bombers and have developed rocket engines to boost the performance of their jet-engined fighters at heights of 40,000 feet or more, the power units are not likely to be a limiting factor in the next few years. Reports suggest that Soviet chemists, metal-lurgists and aircraft engineers are working to use new heat resisting alloys from metals such as magnesium, titanium, gallium, indium, germanium, tantalum, etc. as well as using plastic and ceramic materials; they are also working on special cooling systems for the wings, fuselage and electronic equipment in order to ensure that the heat barrier does not impose speed limits on the Soviet fighter aircraft of the next few years.

After a visit to the USSR in the summer of 1956, during which he visited Soviet air bases and aircraft factories, General Twining, then Chief of Staff of the United States Air Force, was quoted as saying: 'The Soviet Air Force is very good, with good equipment and organisation. The Russians have either overtaken us or can overtake us in all categories of warplanes except that of the medium jet bomber.' Since General Twining made this speech two or three years ago, nothing important has happened to shift the broad balance of fighter planes either for the West or for Communist air power. Both sides have planes fitted with radar gunsights and air to air missiles guided by radar or with infra-red detection equipment. The air defence potential of both sets of fighters against long range rockets is virtually nil and against manned bombers they may not be very effective against low-level attacks on coastal targets. In the next few years what surely will be more important is the strength of supersonic fighters and fighter-bombers to support limited land and sea battles of a local kind. One can scarcely write too often that the Soviet Air Force is better equipped than the West for such air combat because it has larger tactical air forces with atomic bomb

capabilities and with a much larger number of supersonic and subsonic fighters of a technical performance roughly equal to its prospec-
tive Western opponents. The question no one can answer either in
the Kremlin or elsewhere is the relative quality of air crews, especially
pilots. In the air war over Korea, in the Suez campaign of 1956 and
in the air operations between 1955 and 1958 carried out by the
Sino-Communist Air Force we have seen that the *MIG 15, 17* and *19*,
though broadly speaking equal technically to the US *Sabre* and
Super Sabre, have not been able to assert themselves and gain local air
superiority, though they have enjoyed local numerical superiority.
To the uncertain and varying quality of pilots, one must add the
uncertainties of the local help given in combat tactics by efficient
radar which can give height advantage in combat and efficient radio
telephone instruction and warning which can help air leaders direct
the fortunes of air battle. Because even in the atomic age, fighters by
maintaining local air superiority can sometimes alone ensure the
successful landing and re-supply of parachute and airborne troops,
the bringing up of regular air supplies and the protection of atomic
artillery from enemy bombing attack, they are likely to remain a
major arm of the Soviet Air Force in the foreseeable future. While
Soviet official statements in 1957 emphasised rockets at the expense
of manned bombers and fighters, the 1958 view, which is likely to
persist for many years, is rather that the armed forces of the USSR
will possess a range of atomic and thermo-nuclear weapons including
tactical and intermediate long range rockets, but also a series of
first-rate jet air regiments of both fighters and bombers in which a
place for several thousand supersonic jet aircraft is likely to be found
in the next five to ten years. To quote an illustrative phrase from a
1958 speech by a senior air staff officer: 'Along with manned aircraft, the Soviet Air Forces are beginning to lay emphasis on pilotless
weapons.' At the moment of writing the bulk of Soviet defensive and
offensive air power is manned: no doubt at some time in the 1960s
the bulk of its offensive and perhaps defensive power will be unmanned guided rockets. But as long as the Kremlin has plans to
fight local wars and equip other countries' air forces, both Communist and non-Communist, the USSR will have to produce large
numbers of modern fighter planes.

In a 1958 article, Alastair Buchan, the London *Observer*'s defence
correspondent, remarked that the atomic-engined submarine with

the ability to fire a dozen or more 1,500-mile atomic or thermo-nuclear rockets has revolutionised defence strategy the world over. It is clear that Soviet submarines present a formidable threat to US air defences and may well call for a major re-emphasis in US defence policy in favour of greater emphasis on the anti-submarine arm. Marshal of Aviation Vershinin's statement published in *Pravda* and *Isvestia* in September 1957 made it clear that part of the Soviet submarine fleet was, even then, equipped with rockets carrying nuclear warheads which could fire several hundred miles at least. As is usual with Soviet leaders' speeches, especially in the days of the early *Sputnik* exultation in the autumn of 1957, the basic facts are larded over with layers of expectancy rather than accomplishment. Vershinin claimed that every air base of NATO was subject to nuclear attack by Soviet rockets fired from the ground, from the air or from submarines. Even allowing the Russians a wide margin of technical superiority in the development of long range rockets it is difficult to see how Soviet *Komet* or *Golem* rockets, with a nuclear warhead, fired from a submerged submarine can be accurately aimed at an air base. The fact is that the detection, hunting and destruction of US submarines must now pre-occupy Kremlin defence strategists as much as any other contemporary defence problem. As Air Chief Marshal Sir Phillip Joubert says in Chapter VI, while one looks overhead at raiding bombers and long range stratospheric rockets and finally at earth satellites either *Sputniks* or USA *Discoveries*, the real long-term weapon of strategic air attack is lurking beneath Polar ice or the waters of any of the five continents with no present means even of detecting its progress. When the Soviet Air Force Commander-in-Chief said towards the end of 1957 that he had powerful means of defence against an all-out air attack from NATO powers that was in a sense true, for the PVO strategic air defences commanded by Marshal Biryuzov were then as now the strongest the Soviet Union has ever had. But by some irony they are also the weakest, for they cannot stop the West from imposing crippling damage on the USSR any more than Western air defences can stop an all-out Soviet long range attack. And as the forces of ocean-going submarines armed with the respective rocket weapons grow—that is the *Polaris* potential of NATO and the *Komet* and *Golem* rocket potential of the USSR—so the chances of successful air defence become more remote.

But at the moment and for the next few years, it is land-based rockets and aircraft which will be the chief source of long range air attacks. At the moment of writing (end of 1958) it is certain that the long range jet bombers are still the chief weapon in any all-out attack by the USSR in a global nuclear and thermo-nuclear struggle. One is always in danger of exaggerating rather than underestimating the present strategic capabilities of Soviet long range rockets. It is less than eighteen months since the USSR test-fired successfully her first intercontinental ballistic missile able to carry a thermo-nuclear warhead for a distance of 5,000 miles or more. The comment then published even in the reliable newspapers of the West put the East-West military position rather out of focus. 'The mere fact that the USSR had such a rocket puts her in a terrifyingly strong position,' wrote one correspondent. Another wrote: 'The great deterrent is deleted from the vocabulary of Western diplomacy.' But until 1960 and perhaps much later, it is the 750–1,000 twin-jet *TU 16* Soviet bombers and its supersonic successor, comparable with the United States *Convair B 58 Hustler*, which will be the main weapon of long range attack in Europe and against NATO bases in North Africa and the Middle East. The further force of perhaps some 350–500 turbo-driven four-engined jet bombers will bear the main burden of any attack on North American targets. This does not mean that there will not be more than 1,000 intermediate ranged nuclear and thermo-nuclear rockets which can be fired from bases in Europe or elsewhere, but they would not constitute the main armoury of weapons in a European or other local war. The atomic bomb-carrying *MIG* fighter-bombers, the atomic artillery and the medium-jet *Tupolev 16* bombers and the *TU 14* and *IL 28* twin-jet light bombers are together both more powerful and more flexible weapons which can be used with greater discrimination and more reliability. They are certainly more numerous than Soviet inter-mediate-ranged rockets and are likely to remain so well into the 1960s and perhaps beyond.

In any intercontinental struggle in the next few years involving the United States, it is the Soviet jet strategic bomber arm which will probably be the main weapon of attack. This arm of the Soviet Air Force has had a chequered career. Prior to the wars in Spain and Manchuria it had the largest force of four-engined bombers in the world. Despite the bombing failures in the Finnish War and the lack

of suitable modern Soviet long range bombers in any quantity, the
Soviet strategic air arm was reconstituted in 1942, under General
(later Marshal) Golovanov. By the end of the Second World War,
it was designated the 18th Army and, ill-equipped, it had a poor
long range bombing record. In that war the main operations of the
Soviet strategic air command had consisted of tactical or air transport sorties. In the post-war period under a new Commander-in-
Chief, Marshal of Aviation Vladimir Alexander Sudets, it has grown
in strength and efficiency to the point where it is almost as potentially effective as, though no doubt less experienced than, the US
Strategic Air Command. By 1953 it had expanded to three Air
Armies, with a combined strength, according to a statement made
by General Twining, of 1,000 four-engined *TU 4* bombers. A man
of Sudets calibre (he had been Chief of Staff of the Soviet Air Force
under Marshal Vershinin) was clearly not to be satisfied with what
was then an obsolescent bomber force without radar aids or fast
turbine powered bombers. In the 1953–8 period the gap between
US jet bombers and the Soviet strategic bomber air force was closed
to the point where their capabilities were not vastly different. In the
same period the Soviet lead in developing intercontinental ballistic
missiles was worth about a year or perhaps two of development and
production. By 1954 the *TU 16* medium jet bomber was entering
service in the Soviet DA, the Strategic Air Command. While its
range of some 4,250 miles does not apparently make it a great threat
to the United States, the development of in-flight refuelling and the
possible Soviet seizure of Iceland (perhaps by airborne attack) in the
early stages of a future global struggle make the *Badger*, as it is called,
a real threat to part of the North American continent. Its top speed
of 560 mph would make it vulnerable to the latest US supersonic
jet fighters, but its ability to drop nuclear and thermo-nuclear
weapons means that the defending fighters would have to inflict a
higher loss rate on this and other Soviet jet bombers than anyone
could reasonably expect if they were to save the US mainland from
devastating and even crippling damage. The heavier Soviet *TU 20*
turbo-prop bomber would suffer from the same speed disability as
the *TU 16* but with a range of some 7,000 miles, which could be
increased to over 8,000 and perhaps 9,000 by flight-refuelling, it can
reach any target in North America from present Soviet Arctic DA[1]

---

[1] DA stands for long-range aviation.

bases. Myasishchev's four-jet turbo bomber, in its latest version, may be faster, but still subsonic, and probably has less range. Nor should one forget that there are currently several hundred obsolescent *TU 4s* in the total long range and medium bomber force of some 1,500 planes which the USSR has at its disposal according to available estimates. The crews have been trained to a high standard in the past few years. Radar bomb sights and navigational aids are being fitted at the moment to all Soviet jet bombers of this command, standards of navigation and blind flying are better than ever before and there is operational training by day and night in all kinds of weather either from the advanced Arctic bases or from base airfields near Moscow, Kiev and in the Carpathian and Far Eastern areas.

The Soviet bomber force has been stock-piling atomic and thermo-nuclear weapons from the size of the Hiroshima and Nagasaki bombs to those of the multi-megaton category for more than five years and probably has more than enough of them to carry out any destructive task to which it is assigned. To assess its future long range capabilities in details and to estimate its importance compared with Soviet *Komet* and *Golem* missiles launched from submarines, and cruiser-borne missiles or land-based intercontinental missiles, is a task which cannot be achieved without more knowledge than is currently available. In *The Soviet Navy* (page 170) it is estimated that the USSR has 250 long range submarines, but no one knows what proportion of them are really fitted with long range nuclear weapons. Soviet cruisers currently able to fire intermediate range nuclear missiles up to 1,000 miles are likely to be few at present and the number of batteries of Soviet long range intercontinental ballistic missiles is not likely to exceed half a dozen at the time of writing. One wonders what proportion of them would misfire just as the simpler and easier to handle and service *V2* rockets did in 1944.

It is for these reasons that the perhaps 1,000 jet bombers of Marshal Sudets' air regiments will constitute the chief weapon of Soviet air attack in the 1959–60 period. The Soviet long range rockets, dealt with in detail in a later chapter, are not yet weapons to neutralise the American capacity for retaliation with manned bombers operating from such a widely dispersed network of air bases, nor can they in the longer run be very effective against US rocket-firing submarines. At present both East and West can inflict crippling damage on each other and neither side has achieved a decisive break through in modern weapons. In the next five years or so by producing the *Titan* or *Atlas* in large numbers, and by making a successful anti-missile missile and by expanding her submarine arm, the United States could perhaps regain the ascendancy of the late 1940s and early 1950s which she has now lost. But there is no fore-seeable reason why the Soviet Union should not be able to keep pace with any American technical development in modern air and rocket weapons or in long range radar, atomic aircraft or rocket engines, radio counter-measures or any other aspect of weapon development likely to affect the present strategic stalemate.

This strategic stalemate, if it has not abolished global war, has made both sides pause before they are over the brink on a number of occasions in the last ten years. Because rocket and bomber weapons are unlikely to be able to deal with the retaliatory power of long range submarines the elements of caution and stability in the present world situation are likely to increase and the prospects of mutual inspection and some form of disarmament may gradually improve.

The unpleasant fact is that Soviet air and rocket power develop-ments of the last five years have brought the Kremlin to the state of military preparedness in which it might reasonably gamble on a victory over the West. Because of its predominance in armed man-power, armour and tactical air power, it can always hope to fight more effective local wars than the West. But despite much discussion and writing there are no real practical plans for the limitation of modern war once it is declared. The spate of propaganda, counter-intelligence and mis-information which modern war brings with it is scarcely conducive to carrying out a clear cut arrangement to limit the use of weapons to specific purposes and specific areas. Neither are air crews or the weapons themselves reliable vehicles of strict limitation in combat.

CHAPTER I

THE CIVIL WAR TO THE
SECOND WORLD WAR

George Schatunowski

THE FIRST SOVIET government decree setting up aircraft and airship formations was promulgated on 20th December 1917. It was a time of chaos and revolutionary disorder during which aircraft and other factories were being pillaged and technicians were running away, either to the country in search of food or to other countries, particularly France and the United States, in search of peace and security. Although the air heritage left by the Tsarist government was meagre, it included a high tradition of flying skill and bravery particularly amongst Russian naval air pilots: also the legacy of the successful construction of one of the first four-engined bombers in aviation history, the *Ilya Muromets*. At first powered by four French 600 hp engines, this plane was later re-engined with a Russian-built product and did useful work in Russian naval air squadrons from 1916–17, flying on the Baltic front against German naval and army targets.

The new Soviet government was soon to become air-minded, but its 1917 air assets were confined to a stock of about 300 assorted aircraft, mainly obsolescent French *Caudron* planes, British *Napier* machines, Italian *Ansaldos*, the Russian-built *M5 Grigorovich* seaplane and the *Ilya Muromets* bombers. Despite the shortage of spares, aircraft maintenance facilities, fuel, technicians and engineers, it staged an air display as early as 1st May 1918, in Moscow. Hunger and civil disorders never prevented the Soviet Union from holding air displays in the forty years that followed, or from using the occasion for denouncing capitalism in virulent terms, however irrelevant the denunciation might be to the general pattern of the air commentary which accompanies the annual flying exhibition.

The Civil War 1917-1921

When the Civil War broke out in the autumn of 1917, the Soviet authorities attached all their airship and aircraft units to the Central Military Revolutionary Council and so established the general tradition that Soviet Air Forces of all kinds were, and would be, subordinate to the needs of the Red Army. This major air tenet dominated Soviet air policy until the end of the Second World War, when the primary needs of strategic defence and strategic long range attack in the new jet, rocket and atomic age became of overriding importance. The Soviet Air Force set up a 'Field Administration of Aviation and Airships' in 1917 which, for the next three or four years, was to be responsible under Red Army aegis for all air operations against the White Russian armies and the various groups of foreign interventionists. With typical Bolshevik vigour the early handicaps and problems were dealt with. Within a year or so, a front-line strength of about 350 aircraft was reached. The squadrons were small, usually consisting of about half a dozen planes. They included about twenty float-plane squadrons and a so-called air division of *Muromets* four-engined bombers which, however, never exceeded a serviceable strength of more than about twenty-five machines. There were also five airship divisions. Two naval air bases and ten flying training schools, all ill-equipped, were soon established as well as about half a dozen supply depots and maintenance and repair centres.

At the beginning, naturally, there was a shortage of flying personnel, for so many of the Tsar's best pilots had come from the suspect bourgeois or upper classes. Many of those who were not shot made their escape, but some remained to fly with the new Communist Air Force of the USSR. The pilot shortage was partly overcome simply by ordering handpicked young Communists to learn to fly. No figures for training crash rates during this formative period are available but they must have been formidable, for the standard of aircraft servicing was low and a lash-up repair with wire and string by an unskilled aerodrome worker was a frequent phenomenon between 1917 and 1920, when about half the pilots were Communist Party members.

The small air squadrons and divisions were usually attached to infantry divisions of the Red Army. In view of the limitations of the

Soviet aircraft industry during the Civil War, it is not surprising that the scale of operations by the new Soviet Air Force was limited and it was frequently heavily outnumbered in the air. On the Archangel front for instance the Soviet air units mustered about a dozen obsolescent planes, while the White Army opposed to them had about a hundred. On the Astrakhan front in the summer of 1919, the Red Army had one squadron to support it (No 47) with a strength of four or five aircraft of which, usually, only one or two were serviceable. Stern representation by Kirov, then the local representative on the Military Revolutionary Council, eventually boosted the squadron strength to less than ten at its peak. Even Budenny's crack 1st Cavalry Army had only a couple of squadrons with a strength of about fifteen planes—but there were less than a dozen pilots available to fly them.

One interesting facet of Soviet air policy in the Civil War after 1921 re-emerged in the major air battles of the Second World War. The Central Military Revolutionary Council kept a largish number of aircraft in reserve to throw into the crisis of a last ditch stand or a final assault by the Red Army. In the Second World War, whole air armies were kept in reserve, fully operational, to be thrown in at the last minute when a serious situation occurred. This, for instance, explains the heavy Soviet local air superiority at Stalingrad at the end of 1942, though the Soviet reserve regiments of the VVS[1] had been available to stem the German advance on Stalingrad as early as September of that year.

On the whole, however, the new Soviet Air Force was unimpressive in the first two years of the Civil War in Russia—1917–19. Most of its limited, obsolescent resources were dissipated in penny packets all over the vast country. Then came a change. The revolutionary military commanders gathered at the end of 1919 and issued a directive on 'the deployment of the Air Force in a mobile war'. This denied air support of any kind to secondary or unimportant sectors of the front. It was a reminder that the Soviet general staff is ready to revise its doctrine radically if common sense dictates. Following this directive, a greater concentration of air effort was possible and the threat to Petrograd at the end of 1919 was relieved, partly because as many as fifty aircraft were thrown in to support the land and Baltic naval forces protecting this key Communist town.

[1] VVS stands for military air force.

Fifty aircraft using 25 kilogramme fragmentation bombs were, of course, puny by Second World War standards, but for 1919 it was quite a respectable concentration of air power.

A further example of concentrated Soviet air action was the employment of twenty-five planes to stem the advance of General Mamontov's Cavalry Corps which had penetrated Red Army positions on the Southern Front and threatened to outflank, if not encircle, them. In this air action a modernised re-engined version of the four-engined bomber the *Ilya Muromets* was used. It was inevitably called the *Red* (*Krassny*) *Muromets*. On this front the technique of low-level assault on enemy ground forces was tried out for the first time and later in greater force against General Wrangel's cavalry. As a result of the success achieved in these two tactical air operations the first *Sturmovik* air unit with a strength of about forty aircraft was formed, and fighter escort was provided by about ten aircraft. This was a first step to the general Soviet recognition of the importance of securing local air superiority to make their bomber attacks effective. Even though they could not always do this, they recognised the need. As a result, the last half of the 12,000 sorties carried out by the Soviet Air Force in the Civil War period were much more effective than the operations of the first half.

It was realised early on that strong government backing for air-craft research was a major requirement if the new Soviet Air Force was to keep pace with its rivals in Western and Asian countries. As early as 1918, Professor Zhukovsky and his technical colleagues established the Central Institute of aerodynamics and hydro-dynamics (TsAGI), an organisation which to this day controls the experimental development and testing of Soviet aircraft of all kinds. When Zhukovsky died in 1921 he had already collected at the Institute a group of gifted aeronauticians whose names are fairly familiar to serious students of Soviet air power. They included Tupolev, Mikulin and Klimov, both subsequently leading Soviet jet engine designers, Chaplygin, Ryabushinsky, Kalinin, the latter an early designer of swept-wing aircraft, and Grigorovich. These, like their engineering colleagues Alexandrov, Yuriev and Vetchinkin were not members of the Communist Party at this time, though no doubt they toed the political line. Zhukovsky was the moving spirit behind much of the pioneering work which gave the Soviet Air Force reasonably good technical standards in the face of all the

handicaps of the early years. He organised the founding of the first
Soviet Air Technical College at Moscow which in 1919 was named
the 'Institute of Red Air Fleet Engineers'. This subsequently became
the Zhukovsky Military Air Academy and amongst its graduates
who are currently leading figures in Soviet jet aircraft design were
Sergei Ilyushin, Artem Mikoyan and Alexander Yakovlev. Most
senior technical Soviet Air Force officers have passed through its
portals.

Although charged with the task of promoting research and aircraft production and the technical training of air and ground
personnel, both TsAGI and the new Moscow Technical Air College
got off to a slow start. In November 1919, because of this, the Soviet
Council of Labour and Defence issued a decree calling up all
engineers and technicians who had had any experience in the aircraft industry. By 1920 a Soviet-built 200 hp aero-engine was
coming out of an aero-engine factory at Moscow and by 1922
Tupolev had designed the *ANT 1* aircraft under TsAGI auspices.
These were modest but important beginnings.

After the Civil War

TsAGI was of course only a small specialised group of technicians.
Once the Civil War was over in 1921, there was the general problem
of making a backward and peasant population air-minded and
technically inclined. By the summer of 1923 the Central Administration of the new Soviet Air Force had been established, supervised
fairly strictly by the OGPU secret police. It was responsible for
personnel, equipment, aircraft training and the medical services. It
worked hand in hand with TsAGI to plan and supervise aircraft
production in the USSR. But to have enough skilled personnel both
in the factories and on the airfields, much indoctrination, publicity
and genuine training and education were necessary. Technical and
general air training in the USSR is dealt with in a later chapter.

The publicity needed to make peasant Russia air-minded was
carried out mainly by the Friends of the Air Fleet Association
(called the ODVF) which was also established in 1923. Within the
space of two or three years, the ODVF, a voluntary organisation
doing promotional and propaganda work for the Soviet Air Force,
working through Communist Party and Komsomol channels,
recruited nearly a million young Soviet air enthusiasts and launched

B

a nation-wide savings campaign much as was done in Britain in the Second World War when individual aircraft and squadrons were named after people and places who had paid contributions. The rouble value of the results of the first savings drive was enough to build about a hundred planes. In those early days public buildings and factories were plastered with posters inviting Soviet youth to join one of about 5,000 branches of the ODVF. Political slogans like: 'Our Reply to Churchill' abounded. Workers were persuaded to sacrifice a day's pay to swell the funds of the 'Friends of the Air Fleet Association'. In time, the ODVF underwent changes and became a para-military organisation and eventually merged into OSOAVIAKHIM, the 'Association for the Promotion of Defence, Aviation and Chemical Warfare'. Despite the menace in the tail of the title, its activities are not known to have included preparation for chemical warfare. But it did co-ordinate the defence training of the civil population, train air-raid wardens, machine-gunners, parachutists and technical specialists as well as provide flying and glider club facilities. Apart from OSOAVIAKHIM, senior pupils of secondary schools were encouraged to make tethered parachute jumps from the jumping towers which sprang up in the parks of Rest and Culture in all the main and secondary Soviet cities.

As with strongly promoted government drives in other countries, the Kremlin's attempts to create a nation-wide appetite for aviation had varying results. There were Komsomol enthusiasts who modelled planes, jumped and studied hard in their spare time: there were other Soviet youths who jeered and watched idly, rejoicing in mishaps and conceiving no ambition at all to join the Soviet Air Force.

During the first decade of its existence, that is roughly up to the period of the first Five Year Plan, the Soviet Union, despite the best efforts of TsAGI, relied heavily on foreign planes, foreign aircraft designs and blueprints to equip the air units of the USSR. Tupolev did, however, design one or two original Soviet machines such as the *ANT 1, 2* and *3* which were two- or three-seater machines intended for short and medium ranged civil and military trainer flights. In the two-seater *ANT 3* Gromov (who achieved international repute in the 1930s as a pioneer Arctic flier) made a propaganda flight tour of Europe's capitals in 1926. In the next year Tupolev produced a four-engined plane given the design bureau number of *TsAGI 5*.

In 1928 a twin-engined transport of his, the *ANT 7*, went into limited production. While Tupolev concentrated on bomber and transport aircraft design, as he did for the next thirty years right into the jet and rocket age, the soft-voiced Ukrainian Grigorovich, who had been designing aircraft since 1914, bent his efforts to fighter machines in the 1920s and produced the first Soviet machine in this category, the *I 2*.[1] Previous fighter aircraft in Soviet air units had been mainly of French and German design. Another prominent designer of this period was Polikarpov who like Petlyakov (co-designer of the Second World War *PE 8* four-engined bomber) was killed in an air crash during the German-Soviet war. Polikarpov specialised in both float-plane and land-based reconnaissance machines and designed the *MR 1* float-plane and the *R 1* land reconnaissance machine.[2] His greatest aircraft success during this period was the *U 2* general purpose biplane which remained in service for over twenty years.

The First Five Year Plan 1928–1932

At the end of 1928, when the details of the Soviet government's first Five Year Plan were formulated, the Soviet Air Force had in its units a weird range of Italian *Ansaldo* and *Savoya* aircraft, German *Junker* and *Heinkel* machines and a number of British de Havilland aircraft with a sprinkling of the Soviet planes mentioned above. The Soviet aircraft industry was set the task of ridding itself finally of foreign dependence. This was an absurd objective for no major aircraft industry in the world can afford to be independent of foreign design, inspiration and technical information of all kinds. TsAGI, however, worked enthusiastically to reduce the Soviet dependence on foreign-made planes. In the fighter category four machines were designed and put into production. There was the single-seater biplane *I 3* designed by Polikarpov, a similar machine designed by Tupolev (the *I 4* was one of his rare essays in the fighter field), the more advanced *I 5*, designed jointly by Polikarpov and Grigorovich, and finally, a Grigorovich product which was one of the first planes in military aviation to be fitted with a cannon, a pointer to the general use of cannon in Soviet fighter planes in the Second World War. In the two-seater single-engined fighter category, used also for

[1] *I* stands for *Istrebitel*, meaning fighter.
[2] *R* stands for *Razvedchik*, meaning reconnaissance.

ground attack *Sturmovik* operations, there were three Polikarpov designs, the *DI 2, 3* and *4*.[1]

The reconnaissance aircraft specialisation, a major weakness in Soviet aircraft production up to the end of the Second World War, had a promising start in the first Five Year aircraft production plan. The *R 3* was designed, based on Tupolev's *ANT 2 bis* single-engined biplane and also Polikarpov's *R 5* biplane. The latter was used later in the Spanish Civil War. Finally, Tupolev's twin-engined monoplane bomber was made in a reconnaissance version designated *R 6*.

Perhaps the most advanced work was done in the heavy and medium bomber category. The *Ilya Muromets* four-engined bomber had pioneered in long range operations in the First World War and the Civil War that followed it. It set the tradition of heavy and medium bomber construction and design in the USSR, a tradition which, however, did not produce very effective medium and long range bomber operations either in the Spanish and Finnish air wars or indeed in the Second World War. Interestingly enough, Tupolev's initial bomber products of the first Five Year Plan were the twin-engined *TB 1* and *TB 2*.[2] Although dubbed 'heavy bombers', these Soviet planes were in fact only medium bombers. They were, however, an interesting pointer to the fact that, at TsAGI at any rate, Tupolev and his design colleagues believed in the future of the long range heavy strategic bomber even though over-all Kremlin military policy was not to encourage large-scale production of this category until the atomic bomb era. Another interesting aspect of Soviet aircraft design and production, which set the seal on one aspect of Kremlin air policy, was the close link between bomber and transport production: closer than in Western countries. Towards the end of the first Five Year Plan, Tupolev developed a four-engined transport machine, the *ANT 6*, and, at the same time, a bomber version of it, the *TB 3*, the first, and indeed only, four-engined long range bomber to go into service in large numbers in any air force between the two World Wars. The simultaneous conception of the *ANT 6* transport and the *TB 3* bomber created a vein of air thinking in the USSR which was later

[1] *D* in Russian stands for two-seater and *I* for fighter.
[2] *T* stands for *Tyazhely*, meaning heavy, and *B* for *Bombardirovshchik*, meaning bomber.

to link long range bomber and air transport units into one long range command, the ADD.[1] The positive aspect of this policy was that in times of crisis when air transport was desperately needed (for instance at Stalingrad) the emergency use of bomber planes for transport work was easier to organise: in this sense the Soviet use of air power was more flexible. There was the danger, however, that through trying to build two planes, a bomber and a transport with one basic design, the bomber would be less modern, less specialised and so less efficient. The close link between bomber and transport aircraft design remains in the jet age. The present Soviet twin-jet airliners, the *Tupolev 104*, and the larger four-jet propeller *Tupolev 114*, both derive from bomber designs of the early 1950s.

One of the least successful aspects of Soviet aircraft design and policy in the period of the first Five Year Plan was the attempt to build a range of transport aircraft for the passenger and freight airlines of AEROFLOT. Thanks to German help and connivance, some kind of commercial flying had started in the USSR in 1921 and on 9th February 1923, the Council of Labour and Defence passed a resolution calling for the creation of a civil air fleet. Despite the obvious importance of civil aviation in a country with poor railway networks, for the first two decades of the new Soviet state the native transport aircraft developed were several years behind those in service in the civil airlines outside the USSR. In the first Five Year Plan (1928–32), TsAGI produced a *Tupolev* three-engined plane, the *ANT 9*, to some extent inspired by a German *Junker* blue-print, a five-engined thirty-four-seater machine and the single-engined long range *ANT 25*. None of these machines was technically capable of meeting the air transport requirements of the 1930s. Indeed it was the Soviet four-engined bomber, the *TB 3*, which was to be used for developing the new air arm of Soviet parachutists. Not surprisingly, Soviet air transport experts including Tupolev and Lusinov were despatched to the Douglas Aircraft Company in the United States to study and later organise the building in the USSR of US transport planes under licence and to gain experience in the production of modern transport planes which could give both long-term and long range service.

The first Five Year Plan for Soviet aircraft production was also marked by the design of a number of float-planes and flying boats

[1] ADD stands for *Aviatsia Dalnego Deistvia*.

intended for fighter and long range reconnaissance operations in the main. In the fighter category was the *MI 4* which was to be short-lived in its flying career. But the two long ranged *MDR 1* and *MDR 2* aircraft were to have long-term employment in naval air units until the end of the Second World War. Grigorovich's *ROM* sea reconnaissance machine had two 500 hp engines and a top speed of 150 mph with a range of about 750 miles which made it quite a respectable naval aircraft for the period.

It was the last two years of the first Five Year Plan which produced the most promising results for the future. Polikarpov produced a blueprint of the *I 15* fighter, a biplane which went into mass production at the end of 1933 but was obsolescent by 1938–9, though it still equipped many Soviet Air Force units. In the same period, 1930 to 1932, the first Soviet designed ground attack *Sturmovik* plane was conceived, the *LS*, powered by a 500 hp engine. This two-seater biplane had both an armoured engine and cockpit. The first Soviet autogyros also belong to this period. Mikhail Mil, nowadays the designer of a range of modern helicopters including the jet-engined *MI 6*, probably the largest in the world, designed and built in 1930–2 two autogyros, with colleagues who were to become national figures in the jet helicopter age which followed the Second World War—designers and engineers such as Kamov, Bratukhin, Kupfer and Kuznetsov.

The two chief aero-engine designers of this period, Mikulin and Shvetsov, were still at work in the jet-atomic epoch. They began modestly during the first Five Year Plan with the five-cylinder 100 hp radial air-cooled *M 11* engine, but by the end of the period had conceived the 600 hp *AM 17*. In 1931 Mikulin designed the liquid-cooled 750 hp *AM 34* which was put into mass production.

Catalogued in this way, the aircraft production achievements of the first Five Year Plan seem quite impressive. But there were failures, inadequacies and disappointments. Bessonov, one of TsAGI's chief engine designers, had three successive checks through poor engine designs which did not go beyond the blueprint stage. Mikulin's *M 13*, a twelve-cylinder engine, never went into large-scale production. In fact the main engine successes of the first Five Year Plan were the French inspired *M 11* and *M 22* and the German inspired *M 17*, originally a BMW design which gave 600 hp from its twelve cylinders.

The biggest disappointment was the failure to achieve anything like the target production figures. In the case of the medium bombers, the *TB 1* and *TB 2*, the intention was to make about 600 a year but only about half this total was in fact made. This production failure was due to three factors: a shortage of skilled workers at, for instance, the airframe assembly factory at Zaporozhye; at the aero-engine plant at Taganrog some of the work was crudely finished and parts had often to be rejected before the assembly stage and at some assembly factories completed planes never got off the ground.

One of the most interesting aspects of Soviet aircraft output during the period 1928–32 was the emphasis on naval aircraft. In 1930, for instance, about 200 float-planes and flying boats came out of Soviet aircraft factories, which was roughly one-sixth of the total annual production at that time. Both the Japanese and the Germans influenced this aspect of Soviet aircraft production policy. It is to the credit of TsAGI and the Soviet air planners that they were quicker to see the limited application of float-planes and flying boats in the coming world struggle than were the *Luftwaffe* and the Japanese Air High Commands.

Looking back historically to the years from 1928 to 1932, it might be considered one of successful initial gestation. The early basis of the Soviet aircraft industry was created in the face of many handicaps; Stalin imposed almost complete isolation from the West; there was a genuine and persistent shortage of skilled factory workers, technicians of all kinds, machine-tools and raw materials. The Communist Party trials of wreckers and saboteurs were ineffective as a means of encouraging the others. The *Stakhanovite* movement stimulated workers to produce more but at the expense of thoroughness and quality. The appointment of aeronautically illiterate Party members to key posts in the Soviet aircraft industry scarcely added to over-all effectiveness of output. In such circumstances it is a testimony to the Soviet authorities and to the dynamism of the Russian worker that the aircraft industry was turning out about 2,000 usable aircraft per annum at the end of the first Five Year Plan. In 1933 Stalin claimed: 'In the past we did not possess our own aircraft industry, now we have got it'; this claim could be largely substantiated. However VIAM (the all Union Institute for Research into aircraft materials) was still conducting extensive research into foreign methods. TsIAM, the Central Institute for Aero-Engine development, was still devoting much of its time to the adaptation of foreign designs to Soviet requirements. But the Soviet Air Force had begun to fly Russian planes in many of the twenty air brigades which made up its front-line strength of between 1,000 and 1,250 aircraft. In 1933, with war clouds on both the European and Asian horizons, the next Five Year Plan was crucial.

The Second Five Year Plan 1933–1937

The period 1933–7 was a crucial one for Soviet aircraft development and Soviet air policy for it involved the Soviet preparations for the approach of the Second World War. It was the period in which a threat matured from both Japan and Germany to the future security of the USSR. It was a period in which the war clouds were gathering and Stalin must have known that his air force was almost inevitably to be blooded in full-scale battle before the third Five Year Plan was completed.

From an aircraft production point of view, one of the most interesting features of the second Five Year Plan was the cut in output of float-planes and flying boats which were reduced to less than half the figures for the first Five Year Plan; indeed, the production of float-plane fighters was dropped altogether. The Kremlin policy-makers are to be congratulated on steering towards this change in aircraft output from float-planes and flying boats to land-based machines and to have done so more quickly than either the German or Japanese High Command.

The main Soviet aircraft effort during the 1933–7 period was directed to the improvement and expansion of the fighter and medium-bomber arm of the Soviet Air Force, as well as to the expansion of the aircraft industry as a whole. It is a measure of Soviet success that by the outbreak of the Second World War the Soviet aircraft industry had as great a production capacity as any of the other major air powers like Japan, Britain, Germany or Italy.

But if there was quantitative output success there was also relative failure, delay and qualitative decline. The large-scale secret police activities encouraged by Stalin and which resulted in loss of talent through arrests, imprisonments and liquidations was partly to blame. Many of the leading Soviet aircraft engineers, scientists and designers were not active supporters of the Communist regime and the Kremlin was determined to stamp out, by coercive methods, passive resistance or even indifference to its brand of Communism.

The Purges

The end of the second Five Year Plan became notorious as the period of the purges. At TsAGI, the head man Chaplygin, one of the ablest of Soviet aeronautical scientists, was replaced by the 'politically reliable' Kharlamov who was a complete nonentity in terms of aircraft design. When Kalinin's experimental $K\ 4$ plane crashed near Kharkov during a test flight, with four Party members on board, the designer was shot for alleged sabotage. Kalinin had been one of the first Soviet air engineers to develop delta-wing aircraft design in the early 1930s. These are but two, if important, examples of the effect of Stalin's repressive police measures. The newly expanded Far Eastern air and ground forces provided many more victims of the new purge. In the early 1930s the training bases of the Soviet Far Eastern Air Army were at airfields near Moscow, Kiev, Smolensk, Rostov and Sevastopol. The Red Army chief political administrator in these air units was the bearded, patriarchal, ascetic-looking Ian Gamarnik. It was he who exercised political control over Lapin, the C-in-C of the Far East Air Army, which in 1934 totalled about a thousand aircraft. On arrival at the operational airfields in Siberia and the Maritime Provinces, an anti-Stalinist plot was hatched which centred around an air division of 100 four-engined $TB\ 3$ planes, commanded by Gorbunov. These machines were to drop leaflets urging the Far Eastern troops to rid the country of Stalin and his henchmen. The plot misfired and the conspirators were arrested in the summer of 1937. Ian Gamarnik, who seems to have been involved, committed suicide in his office at the Kremlin. Some people believe that this Far Eastern Air Force plot against Stalin helped to trigger off the main alleged conspiracy in which Marshal Tuchachevsky was a central figure; this evolved into the great Soviet Army and Air Force purges of 1937–8.

In fact, however, Stalin had already made up his mind to carry out a major purge. In a speech to the Central Committee of the Communist Party on 3rd March 1937, his main theme and title was: 'The shortcomings in Party work and the liquidation of Trotskyites and other tergiversators.' Within a fortnight, two-thirds of the Party's Central Committee were arrested and shot. Amongst the

Soviet Air Force High Command, the Commander-in-Chief, General Alksnis, was executed and so were Lopatin, C-in-C of the Leningrad Air Command, Muklevich, a Tactical Air Force senior general and Khripin, Alksnis's brief successor as C-in-C of the Soviet Air Force; a believer, incidentally, in the value of long range air attack. The purge went on to the end of 1939 and beyond, by which time the Soviet Air Force (VVS) had lost perhaps as many as three-quarters of its senior officers. But Air Force and aircraft industry purges went on until after the beginning of the Second World War. In the first year of the war (1939–40) the chief technical research organisations TsAGI, TsIAM and VIAM were purged of personnel ranging from senior engineering draughtsmen to clerks and typists. The life of a senior Soviet air commander in the 1938–40 period might be compared in length with that of a French Prime Minister of the late 1940s or 1950s. Even the German invasion of June 1941 did not bring the Soviet Air Force purges to a halt. General Pavel Rychagov, made a hero of the Soviet Union for his exploits in the Spanish Civil War and subsequently put in charge of the important 'Baltic Air Command', was shot a few weeks after the German invasion of June 1941 together with Air Generals Pavlov, Klimovsky and Korobkov. General Smushkevich, appointed C-in-C of the Soviet Air Force when his predecessor Khripin was liquidated by an order of Stalin, also became a purge victim when his Air Force was in full retreat before the German advance. It is not surprising that General Walter Schwabedissen, in Chapter II of this book, finds Soviet air leadership unco-ordinated and ineffective in the first year of the German-Soviet war. The surprising thing is that it recovered as soon as it did.

One of the most difficult things to assess is the long-term effect of the great Stalinist purges on Soviet technical progress and air policy in the crucial year or so before the *Wehrmacht*'s 'Barbarossa' attack was set in motion. Most of the senior engine and airframe designers like Yakovlev, Ilyushin, Tupolev, Mikulin, Antonov or Shvetsov survived the purge. Also the worst of the liquidations were over by 1939 and so Stalin had two years in which to repair the ravages he had made in his technical staff. The Napoleonic maxim that stern measures tend to *encourager les autres* may well apply. The stimulus and threat of war itself must have speeded up production and training just as it did in Britain, the United States and other countries.

The Soviet capacity for absorbing punishment and disaster and making up quickly for losses, gaps, destruction and deficiencies has been demonstrated again and again. But one of the factors in the overwhelming air superiority enjoyed by the German Air Force on the Eastern Front in the crucial summer of 1941 was certainly the lack of experienced commanders in Soviet air regiments, divisions and armies. If only a quarter of them had been purged, the effect on operations would have been serious: none of the estimates offered so far has been as low as this.

The Spanish Civil War 1936–1939

Although initially both German and Russian interference in the Civil War in Spain was conducted under cover of camouflage and secrecy, by 1937–8 it was clear that both powers were using the occasion to try out flying personnel and equipment on a large scale under operational conditions. In the spring of 1936, Stalin sent Berzin, then chief of his military intelligence, to Spain to see the nature of the problem of military intervention. Within a few months, the Kremlin began to despatch Soviet pilots, ground technicians and the accompanying complement of aircraft and aircraft equipment, fuel, spares, stores and so on. Between July and September 1936 the first contingents of some 200 pilots and about 1,500–2,000 ground staff sailed from Odessa in the *Rostock*, *Neva* and *Volga*—all three Soviet merchant ships—arriving at the ports of Alicante and Cartagena on the south-east coast of Spain. Some of the aircraft journeyed in crates and there was therefore delay in assembling them and getting them into action. They were mainly biplane *I 15* and *I 16* fighters designed by Polikarpov and built at factories in Gorki and Voronezh. The bomber machines were chiefly *SB 2* twin-engined bombers designed by Tupolev and built at Moscow and Voronezh factories; they were vulnerable to fighter attack by the German *Heinkel 51* and *Arado 68* machines that opposed them. In the first year of the air combats the Soviet Air Contingent was under the command of General Yakov Smushkevich, deputy to General Alksnis, the Soviet Air Force C-in-C in Moscow. The Soviet bombers were commanded by General Andrey Denisov, a very able air officer. Neither of these generals survived the Spanish Civil War by many years. Smushkevich, although he subsequently became Soviet Air Force Commander-in-Chief, was a victim of the Stalinist

purges in 1941. Whatever his political wrongdoings his operational
record in Spain was not impressive. In the first year of the campaign,
for instance, losses in the biplane *I 15* were heavy, due not to him
but to the superior technical performance of the German *Heinkel* and
Arado fighters and the superior training of German air personnel,
both pilots and ground crews.

One interesting feature of the Soviet air contingents which took
part in the Spanish Civil War was the high proportion of relatively
senior air officers. There were over a hundred with the rank of
colonel or higher. One view which has been given for this is that
the Soviet secret police, who vetted each pilot and officer sent to
Spain, adopted such a severe standard of political reliability in the
purge period that ordinary pilots were not considered sufficiently
trustworthy. It is certainly true that those who serve the Kremlin
overseas have to have a spotless record, both they and their families,
according to the curious canons of political acceptability which have
become part and parcel of Soviet folklore.

As for the air operations on the various Spanish Civil War fronts
the Soviet record of achievement was not a very happy one. It
should perhaps be recalled that the Soviet planes were only part of
the Republican Air Forces which also had French, Dutch and
American machines. This lack of standardisation complicated the
problem of spares and servicing in the case of emergency landings.
Moreover, although Stalin sent a force of bomber, fighter and
reconnaissance planes, he sent no air transport units and so the
flexibility and mobility of the Soviet air forces inevitably suffered.
This incidentally was a sign of the times. The second and third Five
Year Plans, which between them spanned the years of the Spanish
Civil War concentrated on output of Russian fighters, fighter
bombers, ground attack (*Sturmovik*) machines and medium 'fast'
bombers (*SB* series) at the expense of long range four-engined
bombers and to some extent multi-engined transport planes.

Although some of the initial Soviet air attacks in Spain were well
executed and achieved good results, for instance those on the
Majorca and Zaragossa area in 1936 and 1937, the losses in aircraft
and the low serviceability of the surviving planes quickly reduced the
fighting value of the Soviet Air contingents. However as assembly
and repair centres were established for the Soviet air contingents at
Barcelona, Valencia, Cartagena, Alicante and Albacete, service-

ability was restored. On 28th December 1937 a formation of
Tupolev SB 2[1] bombers successfully attacked the German cruiser
Deutschland off Zaragossa. The damage caused made newspaper
headlines at the time and the Soviet pilots who took part in the
operation were duly decorated by the Soviet Air Force authorities,
as the Soviet press put it: 'for excellent execution of special services
for the Soviet government.' Following this anti-shipping success,
considerable reinforcements of Soviet fighters and medium bombers
totalling about 250 machines arrived and were thrown into air
battles on the Barcelona and Ebro fronts at the beginning of
1938. The air fighting that year was also notable for a series of
Soviet medium-bomber attacks on the battle fronts at Salamanca,
Cordoba, Toledo, Castellon, Seville and Teruel. But by the end
of the year nearly all the reinforcements had been wiped out in
combat or written off as a result of crashes. Some of the planes had
temporary local successes; the *I 16* low-wing monoplane fighter, for
instance, had a number of victorious air combats on the Madrid
front and the *R 5* reconnaissance bomber was fairly effective in
attacks on the northern fronts. This biplane, known as the *Natasha*,
had a 500 hp engine in the early stages of the Spanish Civil War but
by 1938 had been re-engined with a power unit of 750 hp. But the
arrival of the new German *Messerschmitt 109* single-engined fighter in
the Condor Legion squadrons in Spain presented Soviet pilots with
an opponent they simply could not cope with. By the autumn of
1938, Stalin decided that his air contingents had taken all the
punishment that was good for them and the withdrawal of the Soviet
Air Force began, and was almost completed by the end of the year.

In the Spanish Civil War, a total of some 1,400 Soviet aircraft were engaged. The bulk, about 1,000, were single-engined
fighters, about 500 obsolescent biplane *I 15s* and a similar number
of the more modern low-wing monoplane *I 16s*. About 200 or
250 were twin-engined *SB 2 Tupolev* medium-bombers and the
remainder almost entirely *R 5* biplane reconnaissance planes.
About forty *Sturmovik* type *(RZ)* aircraft also took part. The
remaining Republican air forces totalled only a few hundred
machines from the factories of France, Holland, Britain, the
United States and Czechoslovakia. The chief lesson that the
Kremlin must have learnt in Spain was that the single-engined

[1] *S* stands for fast in Russian. *B* stands for bomber.

fighter was the key to tactical air warfare and that in this category
the Soviet aircraft industry had failed to produce a machine comparable in performance with the *Messerschmitt 109* single-seater
fighter which was in series production at the German factories of
Regensburg and Augsburg. This Soviet air deficiency must have
been a major factor in Stalin's decision to plan a temporary pact of
alliance with Hitler's Third Reich. Like Chamberlain, Stalin had to
play for time. His new fighter-aircraft designers, Yakovlev, Gurevich,
Mikoyan and Lavochkin were hard at work during the Spanish
Civil War trying to close the technical gap between Soviet fighters
and those of Germany, Japan and Britain. But the gap was not in
fact closed even by the end of the Second World War; in the mean-
time, the Soviet Air Force had to face a series of difficult air battles
with a range of single-engined fighters which were often inferior
technically to those in enemy air squadrons.

The Far East

The Spanish Civil War is well known as the pre-war testing ground
of Soviet airmen and aircraft. The air operations over China and
Manchuria have been less frequently chronicled. As far back as 1929
the new Soviet air squadrons had been blooded in minor air combats
in Outer Mongolia, but the chief pre-war combat experience in this
theatre was obtained between 1937 and 1939, during the Sino-
Japanese war, in major operations against the Japanese Air Force.
In 1937, Soviet air interference was limited to equipping and training Chinese air squadrons to fly *I 15* and *I 16* fighters and the
Tupolev SB 2 bombers. But a border clash at Khasan between
Japanese and Soviet air units on the Manchukoan border in 1938
resulted in the despatch of a 'Volunteer' Soviet Air Force of four
fighter and two medium-bomber units, rather on the political
pattern of the intervention in Spain two years previously. These
tactical air units were subordinated to the Soviet Far Eastern 1st and
2nd Red Banner Armies and they fought a series of intensive combats with Japanese army air units in the summer of 1939. These air
combats have been referred to as the Khalkin-gol incident in Soviet
air history and alternatively as the Buir Nuur and Nomonkhan air
battles. They resulted from the Japanese attempt to cross the
Mongolian frontier in May 1939, an attempt which was strenuously
opposed by combined Soviet and Mongolian ground and air forces.

Soviet sources say that in the next two months the Japanese Air Force lost nearly 200 planes while combined Soviet and Mongolian air losses were about a quarter of this figure. The air historian will no doubt be aware that such air claims were probably as wide of the mark as any other subsequent aeronautical mathematics of this kind in the major combat battles of the Second World War or, indeed, the Korean War. For the record the total Soviet claims of Japanese aircraft losses during this Far Eastern air campaign of the summer of 1939 were 600. The figure has not even an academic interest except to indicate a fairly intensive scale of operations. Two interesting new types of air operation were essayed. Three Soviet fighter pilots, Mashnin, Kustov, and Skobarikhin became the first to try head-on ramming tactics, a device which was never seriously pursued on a large scale by pilots in the Second World War, though it was occasionally essayed by 'do or die' squadrons of the Soviet Air Force, the *Luftwaffe* and the RAF. Secondly the Soviet Air Force dropped troops and supplies from four-engined *TB 3* planes to relieve Soviet ground forces temporarily cut off by the Japanese. The result of this Far Eastern campaign became inconclusive when the Japanese Air Force and Army withdrew.

The Finnish Campaign

If only because of its David and Goliath aspect, the Soviet attack on Finland in November 1939 attracted much attention and sympathy for the Finns. It could have developed into a world war against the Soviet Union. The subsequent swift train of events in Europe clouded the fact that, as one Swedish senior officer put it, 'if Sweden had facilitated the passage of British volunteers and interventionists then Britain and France might have had to face the combination of Germany and the Soviet Union in the fateful summer of 1940.'

Perhaps the most striking aspect of the air war between the Soviet Union and Finland was the abysmal failure of the thousands of Soviet parachute troops used. The word parachute is perhaps a misnomer for some of them jumped into the Karelian snow without parachutes. Estimates of the total number deployed range from 5,000 to 10,000. Of these less than one fifth ever went into organised military combat, that is, reached their objectives near the Mannerheim line and completed their tasks. Most of them landed in disorder and disunity and were picked off by crack Finnish marksmen dressed in snow camouflage clothes and who could see without being seen. The supply dropping operations of the Soviet air transport units were equally ineffective. The Finnish troops soon absorbed the Soviet recognition ground signals and often the Russian supplies which were dropped for isolated Red Army units fell into the lap of isolated Finnish units who were signalling appropriately to the Soviet *Tupolev* transport machines.

This Soviet failure in airborne and air supply operations was not surprising. Some five years later at Arnhem British and US transport planes were to decant air supplies into the lap of German troops fighting in Holland and the whole story of parachute operations and air supply in the Second World War is studded with failure whenever local ground opposition was sturdy and well organised. The Finnish Davids were both these things.

The bomber and fighter operations carried out by the equivalent of two Soviet air armies used in the Finnish campaign were only slightly more successful than those of the air transport arm. The modest successes were due to the inevitable local superiority enjoyed by the Soviet Air Force. While individual Finnish pilots, supported by British and other volunteer airmen, fought with heroism and distinction, the Finnish Air Force was obsolescent even by Soviet Air Force standards and pigmy in size. Thus on the second day of the Finnish campaign, formations of four-engined Soviet *TB 3s* and twin-engined *SB 2s* escorted by *I 16s* were able to attack Finnish objectives virtually unopposed from the convenient bombing height of about 1,000 feet at Helsinki, Turku, Lahti, Kotka and Viipuri and to follow up the bombing by machine-gun strafing. But in these and the hundreds of subsequent raids the military effect was moderate. Indeed it was the civilians who suffered most, as happened in so much other bombing in the Second World War. Finnish schools, hospitals and churches were reduced to rubble and ruin as were similar buildings in Britain, France, Germany, and Japan and the Soviet Union in the years to come. President Roosevelt's appeal for mercy to civilians at the time was a curious lack of recognition of the limitations of Soviet (and other) bomb-sights and air navigation in 1939. The Soviet Air Force dropped threatening leaflets, one of which gives an accurate pointer to the scale of bomber attack in the Finnish campaign. It was addressed to the citizens of Helsinki and said: 'If you do not evacuate the capital before

3 pm we shall return with sixty planes and subject your city to a devastating attack from the air.' The Soviet were not innovators in this technique. The Abyssinian inhabitants of Addis Ababa had had similar treatment from the Italian Air Force three years previously.

The Soviet Air Force had a much easier passage in the Finnish campaign than in its two other major combat experiences in Spain and on the Mongolian/Manchurian frontier. There was never any large-scale opposition from Finnish fighters and although Finnish anti-aircraft fire was fairly successful against low-flying Soviet bombers, compelling them to fly at about 3,000 feet in the later stages of this 1939–40 winter campaign, the Soviet air attacks rarely ran into what could be termed stiff local air opposition. The 7,000 to 8,000 tons of bombs dropped by Soviet *Sturmovik*, medium- and heavy-bomber units on Finnish troops, army positions, towns, airfields, and railway communications were decanted in reasonably leisurely conditions, usually in waves of thirty or forty *SB 2s* and sometimes of the new twin-engined longer ranged faster *DB 3* bomber. Despite the lack of serious opposition and some inevitable successes against military targets, Turku, the chief Finnish shipping centre, and the main railway line from Kemi to Tornio were never entirely put out of action though over fifty bombing raids were carried out on each of these objectives. It was in the Finnish campaign that Soviet incendiary bombs achieved notoriety when dubbed 'Molotov Breadbaskets' by the Finns. The hollow iron cylinders each contained about one hundred small thermite magnesium bombs and when the loosely held cylinder fell apart, after being released from the Soviet bomber, the incendiaries would scatter promiscuously over a town area and became the chief cause of damage and distress to the Finnish civilian population. British, German and US incendiaries later achieved much more heavy damage to the civilian populations of Japan, Germany and Britain. The Soviet technical and tactical operating level in the Finnish War did not augur well for the coming large-scale air operations against the battle-tried, technocratic, flexible, well-trained *Luftwaffe* of 1941. The wireless and radio-telephone liaison between ground and air forces left much to be desired. The airborne troops rarely reached and held on to their objectives; the Soviet air attack on Finnish naval communications was poor; liaison between the Air Force and Navy lacked purpose and Soviet torpedo-bombers were undeveloped as were those of other contemporary air forces including the *Luft-waffe*. But the terrain and climate were partly to blame for the ineffectiveness of Soviet air operations. The closely wooded country scarcely lent itself to intensive tactical air operations and in the difficult flying conditions of snowy weather and ice-bound airfields the Soviet flying accident rate was inevitably heavy. It is thought that some 2,000–2,500 Soviet aircraft were committed between November 1939 and the end of February 1940 and that some twenty-five per cent of these were lost. However some of the experience which the Soviet air regiments obtained during the winter campaign and the lessons learnt were to stand them in good stead some two years later when they were supporting last ditch winter stands in ice and snow before Leningrad and Moscow.

Aircraft Developments, 1935–1941

In the five years or so before the Second World War, the expansion of Soviet aircraft production, and therefore of front-line operational strength, was considerably greater than that of any other air force in the world. From a force of about 1,000 aircraft in 1930, disposed in some twenty air brigades, there was an increase to nearly 5,000 operational aircraft in units by the 1937–8 period. By June 1941, when the *Wehrmacht* attack on the USSR was launched, estimates of front-line strength range from 12,000 to 15,000 machines; of these nearly 10,000 were available to oppose the Luftwaffe in the West. These impressive expansions were due to two main factors. First, and perhaps the more important, was the development of a two-front aircraft industry and a two-front air force. To the expanding aero-engine and airframe factories at Moscow, Leningrad, Kiev, Yaroslavl, Saratov, Gorki, Kazan, Voronezh, Ufa and Kamensk were added new factories beyond the Urals, in or near Omsk, Tomsk, Irkutsk (later a centre for atomic bomb production), Novosibirsk, Khabarovsk, Kuznetsk, Komsomolsk, Magnitogorsk and Chita. The second major factor was the concentration on making small single-engined machines.

But the expansion of front-line strength and aircraft production, impressive though it was quantitatively, was not accompanied by the required qualitative increase in the performance of machines and crews in certain vital respects. By the contemporary standards pertaining in the German, Japanese, British and US Air Forces, the

Soviet Air Force was deficient in the combat performance of its single-engined fighters in the crucial 1938–41 period. It had nothing to match the German *ME 109*, the Japanese *Zero* or the British *Spitfire*, though, as William Green points out in Chapter VIII, the new fighter-aircraft design teams of Mikoyan, Yakovlev, Gurevich, Gorbatov and Lavochkin were striving to close the technical gap in this aircraft category. The Soviet Union was also to be particularly backward in the crucial sphere of electronics in preparation for the Second World War. There was to be no Soviet radar equipment to act as early warning which might have prevented some of the early catastrophic losses and damage sustained in the unheralded *Luftwaffe* air attacks in the early weeks of the Barbarossa campaign. There were no radar bomb sights or beam navigation aids which could have made the attacks and other operations of the newly formed ADD long range bomber and transport command more effective, and compensated for the poor standard of blind flying which prevailed even in the crack Guards air regiments.

In the major aircraft categories, it was only the *Sturmovik* ground attack machines and the twin-engined medium-ranged bombers which, roughly speaking, kept pace with development in the West and even here the rate of production of the new anti-tank *Ilyushin 2*, *Sturmovik*, and of the twin-engined *Petlyakov PE 2* and *Ilyushin DB3* twin-engined bombers was not sufficient to meet the deadline of the German High Command—June 1941. The *IL 2 Sturmovik* was not test flown until 1938 and it was not till the end of 1939 that it began to reach the tactical air regiments of the Soviet Air Force from the factories near Voronezh and Moscow.

The *Sukhoi SU 2* close support tactical bomber was not to reach the air regiments until 1940 and was superseded in the next year or so by the new *Ilyushin IL 2* and the successful *PE 2*, an aircraft which had a top speed equivalent to that of the contemporary British *Hurricane* fighter, 330–340 mph. The *PE 2* was, however, equipping the front-line units of the Soviet Air Force in the 1939–40 period in substantial numbers. This twin-engined close support plane was to be one of the most successful Soviet aircraft of the Second World War.

But the weak spot was the single-engined fighter category. These were the aircraft which had to maintain local air superiority over the battle fronts against the attack of the *Luftwaffe*'s bombers

escorted by *ME 109* units, just as jet supersonic fighters would have
to in any so-called limited local war of the atomic age. Although
in the 1939–40 period the Soviet Union was to design and test-fly
and put into production four new single-engined fighters, the
MIG 1, *MIG 3*, *YAK 1* and *LAGG 3*, they were still not the equal
technically of the German *ME 109 E* and *F*. Moreover, very few
fighter regiments were equipped with these new Soviet fighter planes
in June 1941; most of the fighter planes coming out of Soviet factories
in 1940, at a rate, incidentally, of some 400 a month, were *I 16* and
even *I 15* machines which had revealed their combat limitations in
the Spanish Civil War and in the Mongolian/Manchurian air
operations. The new *I 17* fighter, displayed at the Paris Air Exhibition of 1936, had a powerful engine, and, to judge from the Soviet
military press, was full of promise. But like the German *Heinkel 112*
and *113* fighters it flattered to deceive, went only into limited production and played virtually no part in the Second World War.
And it was not only in the speed of fighter aircraft that the Soviet
Air Force was deficient. Its radio-telephone equipment was inadequate and so fighter tactics and successful liaison with ground
control, on which tactics can depend, were not up to the standards
called for in a large-scale air war against the *Luftwaffe*.

But it was in the categories of heavy bomber and multi-engined
transport machines that the Soviet air development was most disappointing in the four or five years prior to the Second World War.
Tupolev's giant *ANT 20*, known as the *Maxim Gorky*, crashed in the
summer of 1935. The *ANT 6* (*TB 3*) four-engined bomber which
was in large-scale use in Soviet air squadrons in 1935 was obsolescent
and under-engined by 1939 and its successors the *TB 7* and *PE 8*,
the latter being a slight revision of the former by designer Petlyakov,
never went into large-scale production, although a large factory near
Novosibirsk was turning out this, the best of the Soviet four-engined
bombers of the Second World War, from 1940 onwards. But the fact
is that when the new long-ranged air command was formed, it had
no force of strategic bombers or long-ranged transport machines
worthy of the name. The *DB 3* so-called long range bomber was in
fact a medium-ranged affair and it was the American medium twin-
engined *B 25 C* planes which were to bolster the strength of this
command to a greater extent than the *PE 8* for the first two years of
the German-Soviet war

It was also to the United States that the Soviet Union turned prior to the Second World War to get experience in making reliable twin-engined transport planes. Tupolev sent designer Lusinov to the Douglas plant in California and later he was to organise the building of the Soviet *PS 84* plane in 1941 under licence from the US patent. This twin-engined transport plane was to be the mainstay of the weak Soviet air transport units for the bulk of the Second World War. Had the Kremlin foreseen the vital factors of mobility of tactical air units supporting modern armoured warfare, both in advance and retreat, and had the USSR built a force of air transport units as the Germans did to meet this eventuality, some of the heavy losses in the retreat of the summer of 1941 might have been avoided. Spares, fuel, servicing, personnel, etc., could have been flown promptly to the advanced air bases in Poland and the Baltic States and also helped to save some of the disasters of the first three months of the German-Soviet war. But in the event, the Soviet Air Force had a transport arm adequate neither to carry its airborne and parachute troops nor to fetch and carry supplies in the 1939–41 period. Nor did it have adequate long range bomber forces to strike at the vulnerable German lines of communication during the first months of the coming Barbarossa campaign, when German fighters and anti-aircraft guns were so heavily committed to the defence of Western Germany and to the close tactical support of the *Wehrmacht* ground divisions.

It is of course easy to criticise Soviet air achievement in the light of the aftermath. Taking all the factors into account, their achievements in the fifteen years that preceded the Second World War were in many ways remarkable. In total aircraft production they were equal or superior to any other air power in the world with a monthly output of some 700 to 750 planes by 1940. The criticism of their slowness to develop modern single-engined fighters with top speeds of 350 mph or more could also be directed at the United States in 1940. The USSR was to the forefront in developing rocket assisted take-off, large cannon and airborne rockets in the pre-war period. No air power in the world had an adequate force of four-engined long range bombers in the 1939–40 period. If the Soviet *SB 2*, a so-called fast bomber (*Skorostnoi Bombadirovchik*), turned out to be slow and obsolescent by 1941, so did its counterpart the German *DO 17* which suffered heavily in the Battle of Britain of 1940.

But the fact is, as Marshal of the Royal Air Force Sir John Slessor has pointed out, that large-scale air operations were full of unknown factors prior to the Second World War and the miracle, as he says, is that all air planners did not make more mistakes than they did. The repressive Communist police system, in particular the purges, must have been a major deterrent on many occasions. But Russian enthusiasm for their country, their ability to work hard and devotedly, and the threat of Germany and Japan must have been important stimulating factors in counterbalance.

Despite the absurd nature of their Communist propaganda which could produce statements even at Soviet 1938–9 staff college lectures that 'accentuation of the bomber arm was characteristic of the offensive aspirations of Fascist bourgeois states', the Kremlin's air policy was, in practice, realistic. Conscious of his country's technical air inferiority, Stalin made secret agreements with Germany just prior to the Second World War to build *Luftwaffe* machines like the *ME 110* and *ME 109* as well as negotiating with US aircraft firms for licences to make American planes. To gain time for his obsolescent air force he concluded a valuable treaty of alliance with Germany in the summer of 1939. It gave him a vital breathing space of two years. Two years in which to repair the breaches caused by the purges and to develop the new second front aircraft industry beyond the Urals and beyond the reach of German bombers and German reconnaissance and spy agencies. In the event, Stalin was surprised by the German attack of 22nd June 1941, though many weather signs and much detailed concrete evidence of preparation for the attack had been available since the autumn of 1940. The Kremlin has at times a genius for refusing to accept the obvious and the concrete. The dogma of Marxism is frequently not an ideal foundation for serious military intelligence.

CHAPTER 2

FROM BARBAROSSA TO STALINGRAD

General Walter Schwabedissen

*A comparison between the German and the Soviet Air Forces
at the beginning of the war*

SOVIET POLITICAL AND military leaders had, for many years and increasingly since 1933, concentrated on building up a strong corps of pilots and planes and had not only used all available psychological and material means but had also drawn upon foreign aid, especially in the technical field. In spite of this, a comparison between the two opposed air forces in the summer of 1941 shows that, at the beginning of the German-Soviet war, nearly all the military factors were in favour of the German Air Force.

The Soviet Air Force, in contrast to the German Air Force, was not an independent military force, but had been developed as an auxiliary arm to the Red Army and the Red Navy. Beginning with this cardinal principle, to which the Soviet leaders held unswervingly throughout the war the organisation and establishment of the Russian Air Force were usually predictable. The anti-aircraft artillery was not a constituent part of the air force; there was little air intelligence designed exclusively for it and, by the autumn of 1941, parachute and airborne troops had been taken out of the hands of the Soviet Air Force. However, at the beginning of the campaign, the Soviet Air Force was far superior in numbers to the German Air Force in the east. On the eastern front the strength of the German Air Force amounted to about 2,800 front line planes, including some 900 bombers, 350 dive-bombers and ground attack planes, 60 twin-engined fighters, 600 single-engined fighters, 700 reconnaissance planes and over 200 transport planes. Against this the High Command of the German Air Force estimated the strength of the Soviet air units in European Russia at about 7,500 planes, including 3,000 fighters, 2,100 bombers and *Sturmovik* (ground attack) planes, 600 reconnaissance planes and 1,800 transport and liaison planes; in addition there were about 3,000 planes in the Far East. This estimate of the German Command proved to be too low; on the basis of later knowledge and established losses, the strength of the Soviet air units in June 1941 might perhaps be put at between 12,000 and 14,000 front line machines, that is about four or five times the *Luftwaffe* strength in the east. However, the effective Soviet operational strength was, for many reasons, vastly less in practice than its actual strength: it was immediately on the retreat and the serviceability of units was soon reduced.

The numerical superiority of the Russians was more than balanced by many factors in favour of the German Air Force. There can be no doubt that the Russian Air Force commanders, lacking the extensive war experience of the Germans, could not be a match for them. The Soviet general staff work was clumsy, lacked flexibility and was occasionally hindered by Communist Party control. In contrast to this, German staff work was energetic and had at its disposal the rich combat experiences of the previous campaigns of the Second World War. The Soviet principle that: 'Air combat forces must be employed in the framework of joint operations with other arms' was certainly followed in the operations of their air force. Soviet reconnaissance planes were used principally to assist the army; the fighters were engaged in support of the ground operations close to the front line of battle and attempted to win air superiority over the front, besides escorting their own bomber and ground attack formations and warding off enemy bombing raids. The *Sturmovik* and bomber units were used in close co-operation with the army, particularly with the tank and motorised units against tactical objectives in the field of battle, such as enemy artillery and tanks. Thus, the main plan of the Russian Air Force was offensive but restricted to a narrow frame of reference.

In battle, the Soviet air units were used according to the instructions of the People's Defence Commissariat and under the direction of the Red Army—and also of the Red Navy. The large number of air divisions, some of which were amalgamated into air corps and a few independent air regiments, were placed under an air commander-in-chief on an army front; he directed the air operations on that front for the army formations. Only one division of the fighter units was employed in home defence and a reserve of air units was held back by the Kremlin's Defence Commissariat.

The organisation of the German air divisions into air fleets, independent of the army, was much more flexible. The *Luftwaffe* could carry out the wishes of the German army in supporting them on the battlefield, but it was also capable of being used operationally as the situation required. Added to this flexibility was the German technical superiority. The great majority of Soviet planes were obsolescent and re-equipment with modern aircraft proceeded slowly. For instance the standard Russian fighter—the *I 16 (Rata)*—was greatly inferior to the *ME 109*, because of its lower speed and climbing and diving ability. This applied to an even greater extent to the older Soviet fighters such as the *I 15* and *I 153*. The newer types *MIG 1*, *MIG 3*, *YAK 1* and *LAGG 3* were equipping air units only to a very limited extent. The same technical inferiority was found in the bomber and ground attack categories. The *TB 3* to *TB 7* four-engined heavy bombers were obsolescent and could be used only on a limited scale at night. The *SB 2* and *SB 3* medium-bombers were weak in defensive armament and so very vulnerable to attack. In this category, only the twin-engined *DB 3* could be rated fairly highly. All the Russian twin-engined bomber planes were inferior in performance to the German *JU 88s* and *HE 111s* in range, carrying capacity and armament. Many of the Soviet ground attack planes at the beginning of the war, especially the *R 10*, *I 4* and *I 15*, were below the performance requirements of modern warfare and could not be compared in performance with the German *JU 87* dive-bombers which had been built specially for this operational work. The Soviet *Sturmovik IL 2*, later so extraordinarily effective, was not in large-scale service by 1941. Soviet reconnaissance and transport planes, like their float-planes and flying boats, were little suited to modern warfare. Some Soviet aircraft equipment (e.g. parachutes) was reported to be good, but the armament of many of the aircraft was weak. In general the VVS (Soviet Air Force) aircraft equipment was decidedly primitive, expecially the radio and navigational equipment, which was decidedly inferior to that of the *Luftwaffe*.

On the other hand, the Russian aircraft industry was in process of catching up the German lead. German knowledge of the conditions in 1941 was scarce because of the inaccessibility of some of the production areas and because Soviet security was good. Even in 1939 total Russian aircraft production had reached that of the Western Powers. Visits by German air force engineers, in April 1941, to various Soviet airframe and engine factories, as well as to air research establishments, revealed the relatively high level of achievement of the Soviet aircraft industry and the good quality of some of the products. But the industry in the Urals and the Far East was regarded as in a weak state of development, though its partial removal to those areas was not fully understood by the German staff at the time.

Although the organisation of airfields and ground servicing had been considerably improved in the years before the war, it was still backward in many respects and had few permanent supply depots. A great part of the airfields were not fully prepared for operations and only serviceable at certain times of the year.

The supply position was not favourable because of the great distances in Russia, the lack of rail communications and the poor condition they were in. There was a shortage of rolling stock and the roads were in bad shape; this was balanced to some extent by the smaller, and indeed modest, requirements of the Soviet Forces' commissariat. The German airfield organisation, with its well-built network of airfields and strong flexible *Luftwaffe* reserve force, held a considerable advantage.

The intelligence section of the Soviet Air Force, which was under the Inspector of Intelligence of the Red Army, was inadequately organised; the information network was so incomplete that versatile Soviet direction of the war in the air was scarcely possible. In contrast the German direction of its air operations, partly because of its independent highly mobile air intelligence service, was more than equal to all the battlefield events of the first few months of the German-Soviet war.

The Soviet parachutists and airborne troops which, at the beginning of the war, were still a constituent part of the Soviet Air Force and worked in the closest co-operation with the army in attack, were a noteworthy body of troops with specially chosen personnel and first-class arms. Their employment in large numbers, however, was improbable owing to the shortage of air transport. In spite of this, Soviet paratroops and airborne troops were a factor to be reckoned with in the ground battles, even if they lacked the combat experience of the German paratroops.

Crew standards had a decisive role to play in the air battles. The relative absence of war experience and the insufficient operational training of the Soviet crews were in themselves a big disadvantage. The German Air Force High Command could assume, from their experiences in the Spanish and Finnish campaigns, that many of the Soviet pilots would be brave but lacking in initiative, and so ineffective in individual combat, because they were trained to develop a sense of dependency on the community and on orders from above. On the other hand, the well-trained German air crews, with their long and tough experience in battle, were inevitably superior.

From this comparison of the German and Soviet Air Forces at the beginning of the Russian campaign in 1941, it emerges that despite the considerable Russian superiority in numbers, the prospects of success in the impending air battles lay with the *Luftwaffe*. The German Air Force High Command was of the opinion that there was a chance of shattering and dislocating the Soviet Air Force within a short space of time, perhaps of bringing it to the point of surrender, by repeated mass surprise attacks, especially on Soviet airfields and supply depots.

From June 1941 to the Winter of 1941-2

The development of the German-Soviet war during the summer months of 1941 seemed to confirm the expectations of the German Air Force High Command. The German army overran Soviet territory in a speedy, unparalleled advance; the German Air Force annihilated the Soviet air units which had been moved up *en masse* to the advanced airfields near the front. The directive to the German Air Force to 'paralyse and cut off the activity of the enemy air force as far as possible and to support the operations of the army at the focal points of the battle', was carried out to the letter.

Within the framework of this task, tactical surprise against the Soviet air units was completely successful. During the early days of the campaign, hundreds of Soviet aircraft were destroyed on the ground or in the air, the ground organisation was seriously incapacitated or engulfed and German air superiority was assured for the next few months. In spite of its numerical strength, the Soviet Air Force was forced on to the defensive for long periods. The losses of Soviet aircraft given by the High Command of the German Air

Force between the 22nd and 28th June 1944 totalled 3,630 planes
of which 700 were in the northern sector, 1,570 on the central front,
and 1,360 on the southern front; the 2nd German Air Fleet claimed
to have destroyed 6,670 planes between 22nd June and 30th
November 1941. In his Reichstag speech of 11th December 1941,
Hitler claimed the destruction of 17,322 planes (!) for the whole
eastern front up to December. Even if these figures are exaggerated,
the total aircraft losses of the Soviet Air Force in the summer months
of 1941 were extraordinarily heavy. The Russians not only had to
bring in aircraft from schools, air transport divisions and from the
civil air fleet to replace bomber and fighter losses at the front, but
also over 1,000 fighters and fighter bombers from the air divisions in
the Far East. The mastery of the air which the Germans gained
early in the campaign was such that they could concentrate on the
support of army operations. The *Luftwaffe* could be employed
almost entirely against local Red Army resistance on the battle
fronts and with the object of delaying or destroying Russian forces
struggling and straggling to and from the front. The co-operation
between army and air force on the German side during this phase
was outstanding, but did not require the air force units to be subordinated to the army formations.

For the first few months, therefore, the role of the Soviet air
regiments was for the most part defensive and confined almost
exclusively to the support of the retreating army. The air leadership was often aimless, rigid in outlook and lacking in effective
co-ordination. Depressed by German successes and the realisation of
their own inferiority, the operational conduct of Soviet flying
personnel suffered. Incomplete training, lack of battle experience,
obsolescent principles of the use of air power, ineffective staff
direction and a certain lack of mental agility had detrimental effects
upon the performance of the Soviet air divisions. Nevertheless, it
must be stated that the Russian flying personnel endeavoured to
carry out their missions with courage, dash and a total contempt for
death. But for the reasons given above the Soviet pilot was not a
foe of equal status to the *Luftwaffe* pilot. At this time the whole
Russian military mentality and education favoured battles *en masse*,
not the individual combatant, although flying operations for the
most part depend on individuals. Thus the Soviet Air Force in the
first months of the war was only of slight military value, was rarely

capable of launching offensive operations on a large scale and enjoyed only moderate success in defence.

By the autumn of 1941, there were signs of recovery in the Soviet Air Force, especially at the focal points of the main ground operations. In the battle of Leningrad, the raids of the crack German 8th Flying Corps could not penetrate as effectively as before; in the tough Kiev battles, strong Russian air formations were directed chiefly against the German tank divisions at the front and they frequently produced a significant effect on the battle. By this time it was clear that, following the defeats of the summer months, the Russian Air Force had been strengthened in the southern sector of the front. The strengthening of the Soviet Air Force, however, was most striking during the German air attacks on Moscow which had begun on the 21st July 1941. Reinforced units of Soviet fighters, combined with anti-aircraft artillery and searchlights, reduced the expected effect of the raids carried out by four German bomber air formations (*Geschwader*) which were too weak.

The reasons for the recovery of the Russian Air Force, in spite of its catastrophic defeats at the beginning of the campaign, were these: the considerable reserves of flying personnel (due to the fact that in the early successes of the *Luftwaffe* more aeroplanes were destroyed in the ground than flying personnel put out of action in the air); the successful removal and expansion of the Soviet aircraft industry in the vast territories of the east (this production was undisturbed by the *Luftwaffe*); the modernisation of the air depots; the supply of planes from Britain and America; the fact that the long, fierce, first winter closed in early; the German Air Force battle strength was reduced to about 2,000 front-line aircraft; moreover wear and tear through continuous employment and lack of replacement planes made their serviceable strength low.

The picture of the development of the position in the air in the east European theatre of war in 1941 was similar for all types of air operation. Soviet air reconnaissance served, almost exclusively, the tactical purposes of the army and was carried out in the general vicinity of the front. The long range reconnaissance planes were not in a position to bring back useful information about the movements of the German army to the Soviet command. Even the Soviet tactical air reconnaissance was defective and unsystematic; its results were seldom translated into air action. Reconnaissance aircraft design and equipment, especially photographic equipment, were obsolescent, so that after a short time, Soviet ground attack and fighter aircraft had to be turned over to reconnaissance work. With the employment of the *PE 2* aircraft a gradual change took place. But the influence of Russian air reconnaissance on German operations at this time was very small. On the other hand the German command got results from air reconnaissance: valuable up-to-date information which helped German battle decisions and made for more effective use of weapons. The Soviet fighter units, at first strong in numbers and in a high state of serviceability were, nevertheless, not aggressive in combat. This was due to the heavy early losses in personnel and equipment; their tactical and technical inferiority to the *Luftwaffe;* the lack of war experience and training and, above all, to caution resulting from lack of confidence. This lack of confidence frequently showed itself in a tendency to open fire when out of range and to break off combat after the first attack. The Chinese Communist fighter pilots in the Korean War often did the same. Though not very flexible as individual pilots and sometimes uncertain of their tactics, Russian fighter pilots, as a whole, were a tough force which had to be reckoned with.

The basic unit of Soviet fighter planes was a regiment of between thirty and forty; the combat formation usually consisted of a tactical flight of two or three planes and later, following the German example, a flight of five or six. In 1941 there was a tendency to avoid battle against German *ME 109* fighter units as much as possible and to avoid the fire of the *Luftwaffe* bomber and dive-bomber units if they were flying in close formation. On escort flights the Soviet fighters were no match for the attacking *Messerschmitt* fighters. Only the arrival in larger numbers of the new Soviet fighters, *MIGs* and *YAKs*, in autumn 1941 and the additional battle experience, paved the way for a slow improvement which was noticeable in the Red Army's defensive battles of Leningrad and Moscow in the autumn of 1941. Considered as a whole, Soviet fighter pilots were inferior to their German enemy; nevertheless their personal courage and toughness prevented the collapse of the Soviet fighter arm and formed the prelude to a remarkable recovery of fighting value in air combat.

The development of the Soviet *Sturmovik* ground attack units nto a strong air arm began to show itself with the appearance of the

Ilyushin IL 2 aircraft in August 1941. The *Sturmovik* aircrews were bold and determined in action; the usual Soviet defects were less noticeable in the divisions of these newly-arrived *Ilyushin* formations and they were used chiefly over the battlefield in support of the army. Although their success was comparatively slight and they had high losses, they brought increasing moral support to the hard pressed Soviet army. The raids, made mostly from heights of 1,000 to 300 feet, after diving from a much greater approach height, were often carried out unskilfully through lack of experience and so led to heavier losses. In spite of this, the Soviet *Sturmovik* regiments of 1941, after overcoming the early setbacks, laid the foundations for the successes of the later years of the German-Soviet war.

The Soviet medium and long range bomber units were neglected by the Russian General Staff. They suffered specially heavy losses at the beginning of the war from which they did not recover until the end of 1941. They were used for the support of the Soviet army near the front, i.e. on tactical raids. The Russian bomber regiments had only minor success, mainly on the southern sector of the front. The raids consisted of concentrated formations by day, and isolated aircraft by night; they showed no ability to penetrate to difficult objectives; bomb aiming was uncertain and co-operation with escort fighters was often poor. The military effect of such raids was slight and bomber planes were mainly obsolete. However the harassing raids at night and the partisan supply operations were fairly successful.

In 1941 Soviet transport planes were employed mainly to supply industry by air to maintain production. The air transport allocation for the parachute and airborne formations was not maintained and this explains partly why these troops were not used in their normal role. This excellent body of men was used substantially in the ground battle as infantry, and to a small extent in the partisan struggle. The placing of these forces immediately under the People's Commissariat for Defence occurred in the autumn of 1941.

The Soviet Air Force ground organisation, despite its relative primitiveness, was equal to the modest demands of the flying units. Airfields were mainly grass and so runways developed deep ruts which were often not filled in; there were few maintenance or other buildings and often no road link with the railway. But the ground organisation was flexible and adaptable and was constantly being extended and improved. It had a remarkable faculty for improvisation both in overcoming the first heavy German air raids on the airfields and in clearing important equipment at the right moment when in retreat.

In 1941 the Soviet Air Signals organisation was not up to combat requirements. The radio network was badly organised; training in the use of radio and the repairing of equipment was defective. In this field the gap between the Soviet and the German air forces was considerable.

Despite the transfer to the east, destruction and losses, the Soviet aircraft industry succeeded in keeping up production and in avoiding collapse. It was helped by the fact that German Air Force bombers could not reach and attack the production areas on the Volga, in the Urals or in Siberia. Nevertheless it is questionable whether without Anglo-American aid the Russian aircraft industry would have been in the position it was early in 1942 of providing enough planes to supply the Soviet Air Force adequately.

To sum up, the *Luftwaffe* definitely had air superiority in 1941. The Soviet Air Force was brought almost to the point of collapse by its losses in personnel and equipment. The effective measures taken by the Soviet Air Force Command; the tough determination of aircrews; German inability to destroy the productive sources of strength of the Soviet Air Force, together with the onslaught of a severe winter, led to a gradual recovery.

From the Winter of 1941 to Stalingrad

1942 was a year of growing strength for the Soviet Air Force and of weakening for the German Air Force. This weakening was caused by the pressure from other theatres of war which involved the transfer of German air formations from the east and by considerable losses. These affected bombers and transport planes especially, as well as irreplaceable flying personnel and occurred, mostly, during the fighting at Stalingrad. The unusually hard winter of 1941–2, for which the German Air Force was less well prepared than the Soviet Air Force, meant that the German direction of its air force, which up to then had been systematic, became disorganised. The enforced winter air lull at the front was the prelude to the reorganisation of the Soviet Air Force.

The main events of the year 1942 were the Soviet winter offensive on the eastern front which lasted from January to March, the German summer offensive in the southern sector, which lasted from May to September, and the battles near Stalingrad which lasted until the beginning of February 1943. In these battles, the air forces on both sides were used to support the army and the most intensive air operations were on the southern sector of the front.

In reorganising the air force, the Soviet planners concentrated on fighter and ground-attack planes at the expense of bomber and reconnaissance units. The production of single-engined planes for fighter or ground attack is, of course, simpler and quicker than that of multi-engined bomber planes. The modernisation of aircraft designs was satisfactory and so led to a standardisation of air weapons and equipment. It was this that, in 1942, enabled Soviet fighter aircraft to reach an output total of about 9,300 aircraft—excluding 2,200 fighter aircraft from allied sources. These included many *Hurricanes* and *Tomahawks*. Germany produced about 4,600 fighter planes in the same period. The new *MIG, YAK* and *LAGG* aircraft designs were only a little behind the German *BF 109 F* and *BF 109 G* in performance. The *LAGG 3, LA 5* and *YAK 9* became the standard Soviet fighter planes, equipped with better machine-guns (mostly 12·7 mm calibre) and with cannon (mainly of about 20 mm calibre). The *IL 2*, at first a single-seater, was produced in a two-seater version which, with its armament and weapons—consisting of two fixed and one movable machine-gun, two fixed cannons (20 or 23 mm), apparatus for firing rockets, its general technical flying performance, its bomb-carrying capacity and its radio equipment, fully met the combat requirements of the front. The *IL 2* embodied the Soviet policy of strong fire-power and armour at the expense of speed: German policy was to stress speed rather than protective fire-power. The Soviet policy was much more effective. On the other hand the construction of Soviet bomber and reconnaissance planes was poor. The existing twin-engined types, the *DB 3, DB 3 F* and *PE 2*, were only slightly further developed in 1942. Of these aircraft designs, the best was the *PE 2*, a dual-purpose bomber and reconnaissance plane with a crew of two and able to carry extra tanks.

A change in the principles of the employment of the Soviet Air Force also took place in 1942. It is true that it held fast to its

C

major maxim, the use of the air force in support of ground operations, but the units achieved greater adaptability and mobility
through more concentrated and stronger formations. A more
sensible management of air resources was noticeable. The Soviet
fighter units concentrated over the front and the areas near the front
and tried to accomplish their principal task of sustaining an offensive
against the German Air Force and its air bases, while at the same
time acting as escort to Soviet attacking formations. With the increase in material and numerical strength, there was a growth of
self-confidence and battle experience so that Soviet air successes
gradually mounted. The *Sturmovik* units, concentrating on objectives on or near the battlefield, had a steadily increasing effect upon
the prosecution of the ground operations. Though determined and
enthusiastic in battle against ground objectives, they still fought shy
of German fighters and tried to avoid combat in the air. The long
range bomber units of the ADD, which usually played a tactical
role, remained unsatisfactory because of the lack of suitable planes,
experience of battle, low morale and poor training. While the night
harassing raids increased, tactical night raids in force were comparatively few and most raids were carried out by solitary aircraft.
This was mainly because blind flying training was inadequate. In
1942 Soviet air reconnaissance was still limited and used practically exclusively for army purposes. However there was progress in the quality
of the tactical and battlefield air reconnaissance, which made itself
unpleasantly noticeable to the German army. Soviet long range
reconnaissance, on the other hand, was not very successful; here the
lack of well-trained aircraft observers was evident.

Few changes were made in staff organisation in 1942. The Soviet
ADD long range air units were released from their subordination to
the army and, like the parachutists and airborne troops, were placed
under the People's Commissariat for Defence. They were concentrated on airfields in the Moscow area and were transferred to
other sectors of the front as the need arose.

The Soviet air supply and replacement organisation, with its
shorter lines of communication, could now meet all the demands
made on it: the *Luftwaffe* organisation could no longer do so. The
Soviet signals organisation, despite certain advances in radio equipment, still left room for much all-round improvement.

These general trends in the 1942 air situation on the eastern front found their full expression in the battle of Stalingrad. During the German advance in the autumn of 1942, the Luftwaffe still showed itself to be superior. German bomber formations, with fighter escort, raided the town day and night almost ceaselessly. It is true that they suffered losses, but neither Soviet fighters nor anti-aircraft guns could check these operations. Later in the year, however, with the Russian air raids on the Don objectives and the surrounding of German ground forces, the picture changed. Air supplies to the encircled German 6th Army became of primary importance and a number of *Heinkel* bomber units had to be transferred to this duty. At the beginning of December there were eleven transport groups of *JU 52s*, two transport groups of *JU 86s* and six groups of *HE 111s* (of these, four were bomber units) with a total of 320 aircraft engaged in supplying the 6th Army. These figures decreased steadily and the required daily air-lift of 300 tons was never reached. Up to the beginning of the Russian attacks on the encircled 6th Army, it amounted on an average to only about 105 tons: later it decreased even further. In the final air evacuation, about 25,000 German wounded were saved. As long as the German transport aircraft flew with fighter protection air supply was to some extent assured, but as German front line air bases withdrew under Soviet pressure, German escort fighters could no longer be used. The *JU 52* transport formations, the chief carriers of supplies, were withdrawn in the middle of December 1942 because Soviet fighter opposition had become too strong. After this air supplies were mostly carried by solitary aircraft flying at night. The hard winter was also difficult to contend with; very low temperatures, icing, fog and drifting snow created technical and personnel difficulties. From 28th December 1942 to 4th January 1943, *Luftwaffe* casualties caused by the weather amounted to 50 per cent of the total loss of aircraft. The actual strength of the German transport units in the last weeks fluctuated between 10 per cent and 25 per cent of the statutory number of aircraft.

This situation, caused both by the development of the position on the ground and by the weather, was used to the full by the Soviet Air Force. Soviet fighter interception stopped the use of the *JU 52* transport flights by day and added to the considerable losses of other transport aircraft taking off and landing in the area of encirclement. Soviet *Sturmovik* and bomber units had considerable success in their large-scale raids against the German operational and supply airfields and put out of action up to 50 per cent of the German personnel and equipment material. Non-stop night harassing attacks often made the loading and unloading of German transport aircraft impossible. With the narrowing of the area and the final Soviet ground assault on the surrounded German 6th Army on 10th January 1943 the support of the Red Army by Soviet attack planes was stepped up. Soviet air supply and Army support increased, virtually unhindered by the *Luftwaffe*, while German Air Force support for the German Army practically stopped. At the end of the struggle for Stalingrad, the German Air Force had been significantly weakened by the loss of about 1,000 of its best flying personnel and 500 aeroplanes. Air superiority was, for the first time, clearly on the Soviet side.

Comparison of the German and Soviet Air Forces after the Fall of Stalingrad

At the turn of the year 1942–3 a comparison between the Soviet and German Air Forces revealed the following differences:

The German Air Force was weakened by inroads on its strength; the transfer of fighters to Western Germany and the Mediterranean, the wear and tear of non-stop operations, lack of replacements, and by the losses sustained at Stalingrad. The Soviet Air Forces grew in strength continuously both in personnel and equipment and broke away from the defensive attitude often adopted till then. Only the superior training, the greater experience of combat and higher performance of the German aircrews enabled the *Luftwaffe* to prevent the steadily growing Russian superiority from being generally effective. Nevertheless a fundamental change in the position in the air had begun to show itself in the 1942 battles in the Caucasus and at Stalingrad.

CHAPTER 3

FROM STALINGRAD TO BERLIN

Peter Williams

THE DEFEATS OF the German and Italian ground forces at Stalingrad and Alamein have been regarded by most military commentators as turning points in the history of the European War of 1939–45. But Stalingrad was more significant still, for it also marked the turning of the tide in terms of air power.

It was at this period (in January 1943) that the United States 8th Air Force began its daylight attacks on Germany. The damage inflicted by these raids, together with that caused by the continual pounding by the Royal Air Force at night, was serious enough for the Germans; but the most devastating long-term effect was that they were forced to build up strong daylight fighter defences in the west at the expense of those supporting the *Wehrmacht* divisions on the eastern front. *FW 190* and *ME 109* squadrons which might have been employed against the Russians were, in fact, heavily committed against the Western Allies.

The story was the same at night. By its heavy attacks at the heart of German industry, the RAF attracted to the west both the bulk and the *élite* of German twin-engine fighter units: *ME 110s* and *JU 88s*.

By the beginning of 1943, these day and night strategic long range attacks had created a vitally important air front which was to absorb over half of Germany's total air resources for the rest of the war. While the Russian leaders were condemning Britain and America for their delay in starting a second front on the ground, nearly three-quarters of all Germany's fighter squadrons were pinned down in permanent defence of the Third Reich to meet the endless threat of the Anglo-American bomber assault. And, more important than numbers alone, the crews who manned these German fighters in the west were the most experienced to be found in the German Air Force.

61

Little wonder, then, that the Russians found themselves with a local air superiority at Stalingrad which was to develop into continual air superiority in nearly all the subsequent battles from Stalingrad to Budapest and Vienna, from Orel-Kursk to Berlin via Warsaw, and from Leningrad to Koenigsberg.

Consider the Soviet air situation in contrast to the major strategic commitments of the *Luftwaffe*. The Soviet Air Force had no important diversion from its major task of supporting the advancing Red Army and driving the *Wehrmacht* back to Germany. There was no air threat to the USSR from the east: the Japanese Air Force was far too busy protecting its new and temporarily won territory in south-east Asia and the Pacific for that. There was little or no threat to Soviet cities, industries and communications from German bomber attack and only a mere handful of Soviet fighter squadrons were needed to provide the local air defence in western Russia. In fact, the supply of fighter planes from the USA to Russia could be regarded as sufficient to cover and thus cancel out this modest requirement of Soviet air defence.

So, by 1943, the entire balance of air power in the Soviet-German conflict had shifted in favour of the Soviet Union.

This, indeed, had been the plan devised by the Allies at Casablanca at the end of 1942. The Anglo-American long range bombing was deliberately devised to support the Red Air Force and to ensure that it could maintain superiority on the eastern air front. Stalin could now count on the help afforded by a series of major bombing assaults on Germany's cities, industries and communications which freed his own bomber squadrons to support his infantry and armoured divisions.

In this sense, perhaps it would be correct to regard Casablanca as the real turning point in Soviet air fortunes in the Second World War; certainly it was as significant a milestone as Stalingrad itself. Moreover, the defeat of Rommel at Alamein, and the landing of Anglo-American forces in North Africa behind him, was to denude the *Luftwaffe* of part of its limited tactical air forces. These had to be brought back from the central front in the east to help defend the 'soft underbelly' of the Axis in Sicily, Italy and Greece.

For all these reasons, the Soviet Air Force from 1943 to 1945 was in the happy position of being able to concentrate on one simple objective: to support the Red Army all along the line. It is true there were to be one or two minor local diversions, but most of these were the concern of the Soviet naval air forces. In 1943 and 1944, for instance, Soviet air units of Admiral Kutnezov's command attacked German convoys in the Baltic and the Black Sea. But on the mainland fronts from Leningrad to the Crimea the Soviet Air Force was able to build up, with very little opposition, a modernised air armada which totalled some 12,000 to 15,000 aircraft. The total number of Russian air armies at this time was eighteen, and it is probably a fair estimate that between twelve and fifteen of them were committed in the west.

The German air strength that opposed this formidable array consisted basically of two air fleets with a strength of 2,000 to 3,000 machines. And this numerical disparity was not all. Whereas the Soviet Air Force was modernising its squadrons with every month that passed, the *Luftwaffe* (especially after the air débâcle on the Kursk-Orel front in the summer of 1943) was compelled to use many obsolescent aircraft from training schools, including *Gotha*, *Heinkel* and *Arado* machines, to bolster its waning strength. Because of the major commitments in the west, the new German rocket and jet planes such as the *ME 163* and *ME 262* could not be spared for use against the Soviet Air Force except on one or two sorties.

In making this appraisal, however, one must bear in mind, and give full credit to the Soviet air authorities for, the extraordinary revival of their aircraft industry following the chaos and disorder created by a long series of hasty abandonments and retreats. Aircraft and aero-engine factories at Kharkov, Leningrad, Taganrog, Voronezh and Zaparozhe were destroyed or abandoned, and new production facilities were established at Kuibishev, Saratov, Kazan, Sverdlovsk, Novosibirsk and Komsomolsk. In this great renaissance and modernisation of air equipment the Russians showed their talent for what the psychologists have called: 'the ability to switch over religious energy to non-religious objectives', a quality which has remained with them in the age of atomic weapons and long range rockets.

As a result of this almost fanatical energy and determination, they produced, in the midst of devastating setbacks on the front, a series of fighter planes which very nearly closed the performance gap between the East and West. Stalingrad had marked the appearance in numbers of the *Lavochkin LA 5* and *YAK 9* fighters with engines of over 1,500 hp and top speeds in excess of 350 mph. And within the next two years before the end of the war the Soviet aero-engine industry had, in the words of Gordon Dean, Chairman of the US Atomic Energy Commission, compressed into two years the jump from 1,500 hp to 2,200 hp: an achievement which took the United States four and a half years.[1] The major technological developments which were to stagger the Western world in the 1950s had, in fact, begun in the 1940s. Before the end of the Second World War, Soviet *YAK* fighters with 1,500 hp engines had reached maximum speeds of 375–380 mph and *Lavochkin* fighters a speed of 400 mph.

In the fighter-bomber, close support and ground attack (*Sturmovik*) categories, the Soviet Air Force's native-designed planes of the 1943–5 period compared quite favourably with those of their German opponents or their British and American counterparts. Of these, the *Ilyushin IL 2* is the best known and was most used up to the Stalingrad battle, but by 1944 an improved version, the *IL 10*, was beginning to equip Soviet air regiments, fitted with a 2,000 hp (*AM 42*) in-line engine giving a top speed of 335 mph, a useful bomb load of about a ton, and both forward- and rear-firing cannon of 23 mm or 37 mm calibre. Both the *IL 2* and *IL 10* were rocket-firing: indeed, the Soviet Air Force can rightfully claim to have pioneered air-rockets in the tactical air role of attacks on armoured forces.

But the plane that formed the backbone of the tactical air forces of the 1943–4 period was the *Petlyakov PE 2* twin-engined attack bomber, a sturdy, compact and reliable machine. This low-winged monoplane with engines of over 1,100 hp each had a genuine top speed of 340 mph. Royal Air Force *Hurricane* pilots who had escorted these Soviet planes on the Murmansk front in 1942 reported that they were so fast that even the *Hurricanes* found it a difficult task to escort them. Another first-rate Soviet tactical bomber was Tupolev's *TU 2*, a twin-engined machine fitted with Shvetzov's radial motors. With a top speed of over 350 mph, a normal range of over 800 miles and a bomb load of 2 tons, the *TU 2* compared favourably with most of its contemporary tactical bombers.

To these technical developments in aircraft must be added improvements in the ground and supply organisation of the Soviet Air Force. The disaster of 1941–2 against the *Luftwaffe* galvanised

---

[1] *Report on the Atom*, US Atomic Energy Commission, 1954.

the Soviet Air Force into desperate action; it brought out the traditional Russian capacity for hard work, hard drinking and the ability to produce concrete and far-reaching achievements in a fantastically short time. A flexible organisation was set up to meet the needs of each Army Air Command with its own local stock of aircraft spares, bombs, guns, fuel, ammunition and airfield construction materials. There were now more transport planes available to move these air store depots westwards with the Russian advance; airfield engineers and signal units and repair shops were now becoming mobile, as they had been in the *Luftwaffe* in the previous three or four years.

The Soviet Air Force was not only recovering and expanding. Its qualitative standards were also developing, especially its mobility, thanks in no small measure to US transport aircraft and the American generosity in providing about a quarter of a million motor trucks. When the remnants of Von Paulus's army surrendered at Stalingrad in February 1943, the Soviet Air Force was ready to support the new ground offensives of that year with reinforced and reinvigorated air armies.

Thus in the early spring of 1943 the Russians were able to bring the strength of their 13th and 15th Air Armies up to about 1,000 aircraft each to help the Red Army's assault on Rzev and Vyasma. The German Air Force on this front was less than a quarter of this strength and especially weak in tactical reconnaissance machines; the Russians could therefore achieve local surprise with almost certainty and impunity.

Further south, on the Don/Donetz front, Goering's special concentration of air forces, totalling some 1,000 aircraft, had been of no avail. The Red Army, advancing across the steppes, had recaptured Kharkov and Bielgorod in February; and the Soviet Air Forces under General Novikov, later C-in-C of the Soviet Air Force, could dispose as many as four air armies with a combined strength of over 6,000 planes. Their crews, moreover, were rested and refreshed.

Opposing them, the *Luftwaffe* units under General Richthofen had less than a sixth of the Russian total, and they were manned by tired aircrews who knew the bitterness of defeat and retreat, and who were led by squadron commanders who realised how much they were suffering from low serviceability of planes, shortage of supplies and difficult aerodrome conditions. Goering had to admit the loss of his air superiority to the Russians: in some sectors of the front he could only provide a small token air force of reconnaissance aircraft, some obsolescent biplane fighter-bomber units and a few inexperienced fighter squadrons to preserve the semblance and illusion of an opposition.

Only one thing saved him from a complete débâcle. But for the unexpectedly early spring thaw of 1943, which hampered Soviet supplies and communications, the story of German air disaster during this period might have been even more harrowing.

Here and there, it is true, the Soviet Air Force and Army did lose the local initiative. Richthofen's 8th Air Corps and Von Manstein's ground forces falling back on main rear supply bases at Nikolaev and Poltawa were able to help the *Wehrmacht* to re-occupy part of the Donetz line. But in the main, as for instance at Chuveyev and Issum, Russian *YAK*, *Lavochkin* and *MIG* fighters patrolling over Red Army bridgeheads were able to neutralise German air power and at the same time effectively escort *IL 2s* and *PE 2* light bombers in successful attacks which caused havoc and dislocation amongst the German armoured forces on this front.

Still further south, on the Kuban and Crimean fronts, the tale of Russian air success continued. Here, air forces under Vershinin (later to be twice Commander-in-Chief of the Soviet Air Forces) and his senior colleagues, Generals Krukov, Tupikov and Dzusov, had a special run of triumph in April 1943. In the previous months the *Luftwaffe* had transferred 500 fresh planes from its limited resources on to Crimean airfields, and their object was to support both the German Army and Navy. But Soviet long range reconnaissance machines (*PE 2s* and *IL 4s*) had spotted the concentration well in advance and a mass assault on the German-occupied airfields was made by Vershinin's air army. He had over 1,000 fighters and bombers, mainly *LA 5s*, *YAK 9s*, *IL 2s* and *PE 2s*, at his disposal, and they proved as effective as in the Soviet Air Force attacks on German shipping operating from the Crimea across the Kerch Straits into the Kuban.

Just as Germany was losing her bridgehead in Tunisia because of the air domination of Anglo-American forces at this time, so she lost her Kuban bridgehead to Soviet air superiority. By desperately straining her failing resources, the *Luftwaffe* in each case put up an ineffectual effort of a few hundred sorties a day, against more than a thousand sorties put up by the Soviet Air Force which dominated the sea communications. The only result was to weaken the German Air Force for the major effort it was asked to produce in the summer of 1943 on the Russian front, in the defence of Sicily and, most important of all, the air defence of the Reich itself.

Now with local air superiority assured, the quality of Soviet air operations increased. Airfield and shipping attacks could be well planned, preceded by thorough reconnaissance and pressed home in the face of only light opposition. The Soviet Naval air forces had no great trouble in defending the Black Sea ports: Russian torpedo-bombers hit hard and often at the ill-protected German-Roumanian convoys in the Black Sea which suffered as much from lack of air cover as had the German-Italian convoys in the Mediterranean in 1942 or as would the Japanese convoys in the Pacific in the year to come.

But in spite of the overwhelming defeats of the *Luftwaffe* and the German Army at Stalingrad, in the Kuban, the Crimea, Moscow and Leningrad fronts, in spite of the obvious Russian air superiority, Hitler would not concede defeat. Stubbornly and fanatically he laid down the theory that attack, even with inadequate resources, was the best method of defence. And so the *Luftwaffe* indulged in the absurd luxury of a major air offensive on the central eastern front in the summer of 1943. They gathered together the remnants of the Roumanian air formations, which they had re-equipped with modern *Junkers JU 88*, *ME 109* and *Henschel 129* units, and also a few Hungarian bomber formations recently trained in France. With these went all the *JU 87* dive-bomber and *Messerschmitt* single- and twin-engined fighter units that Goering could muster. In all, on the German side, there was a grand total of 2,000 planes.

Opposed to them on this Kursk-Orel front, the Soviet Air Forces had concentrated over 10,000 planes, including the 1st, 4th and 16th air armies and the French squadrons of the Normandie air regiment which was to render them such valuable service in the air battles of the next two years.

The German High Command did nothing to hide the approximate timing and direction of the new offensive, and it was a comparatively easy job for Soviet intelligence, aided by the intelligence resources of Britain, to anticipate the offensive and build up major air and land forces to oppose it during the two months before the attack began.

Despite the strain on its slender pool of bombers, the *Luftwaffe* opened up with a series of night bomber attacks in June 1943, on industrial targets in the Soviet rear. Why, at this stage, they directed their limited tally of *Heinkel HE 111* and *Junkers JU 88* bomber units to attack targets like the tank works at Gorki, the rubber plant at Jaroslav and the fuel depots at Astrakhan remains a mystery— like so much other desultory bombing in the Second World War. Soviet *PE 2* and *PE 3* night fighters reacted to these raids but were somewhat ineffective.

Offensively, the Soviet Air Force showed that its High Command had anticipated the *Wehrmacht*'s offensive by carrying out large-scale attacks, using up to 200 planes per raid, on German-held Orel and on railway junctions near the front at Briansk, Roslav and Gomel. German air units staged retaliatory attacks on Soviet air-fields behind the front, and the combat reports of the French air regiment operating in this sector clearly indicate the intensity of the air fighting. At this stage there were heavy losses on both sides, losses which the *Luftwaffe* could ill afford, but which the Soviet Air Force could take in its stride.

On 5th July the German Army at last went over to the offensive in the much-postponed 'Citadel' operation, the last major German offensive in the east. For a few days it prospered in a limited way: the German 9th Army penetrated about nine miles in the first two days and, according to German records, the Russians lost 24,000 men in prisoners in little more than a week. The German offensive had tactical air support to the tune of about 3,000 sorties a day, as against the Soviet reply of some 4,000 to 5,000 sorties.

But within ten days the German air effort began to peter out; the news of the Allied landing in Sicily caused Hitler to order the discontinuance of the 'Citadel' operation, and all the fruits of the initial advance were thrown away. With this decision, Hitler finally passed the initiative in the eastern theatre of war to the Russians and, on 15th July, the Soviet Army launched a counter-attack on Orel and an assault on the lower Donetz front; the Soviet Air Force supported them with one of its biggest efforts of the war so far.

According to documentary sources, it achieved a total of over 10,000 sorties on some days on these fronts and averaged over 5,000 a day during the crucial third week in July. The German air effort, by contrast, dipped ominously to less than 2,000 sorties a day.

On 23rd July Stalin announced with more than justice that the German attack had collapsed. The revitalised Soviet Air Force had shown that it could dominate the air on the eastern front against the best opposition the *Luftwaffe* could provide at that time. Above all, Soviet air reconnaissance and intelligence had been really effective: mobile front-line equipment developed the evidence of Soviet air cameras to show the damage caused by the *IL 2* and *PE 2* attacks; the radio intercept service monitoring German conversation and wireless messages had provided the Soviet Air Staff with up-to-date information on the combats over the battle zone and the movements of German air units. Soviet women pilots flying the ever-faithful *PO 2* biplane harassed the battle-weary German troops in a series of night attacks on front-line positions. (This technique of using obsolescent biplanes to harass troops at night was an example of Soviet flexibility in the use of its air power, a flexibility which the German Air Force flattered by using the same technique against the Red Army in 1944.)

The air battle on the Kursk-Orel front in the summer of 1943 was the last big concentration of *Luftwaffe* air resources with which the Soviet Air Force had to contend. One measure of its air domination was the extent to which it was able to divert bomber and transport planes in the next year or so to give support to Tito's partisan forces in Yugoslavia: many thousands of missions of this type were flown with *PS 84* and *IL 4* aircraft.

The *Luftwaffe* now began to split its resources into weak air groups to cover regional fronts. Thus the 4th Air Fleet in the south split its meagre strength, partly to cover the Stalino-Taganrog front and partly to stem the tide of the Soviet advance to the Dnieper via Kharkov and Poltava. Kharkov and Taganrog fell in August. On the central front, the Soviets occupied Briansk and Smolensk in September and, further north, the capture of Nevel in October opened the gateway to the Baltic.

In November, Kiev fell to the Red Army, and German-Roumanian forces in the Crimea were virtually cut off.

In this Soviet advance of the last half of 1943, twelve of the best Soviet air armies were deployed, totalling over 100 divisions or over 350 air regiments totalling more than 10,000 planes. On the Briansk-Smolensk front the Soviet 4th Air Army had a complete field day with virtually no German opposition, and this was to become a typical air situation on so many of the fronts for the rest of the war. The operational records of Soviet air regiments were now often to record such phrases as: 'attack on German airfield at. . . . no opposition', or 'light flak'.

The published accounts of French pilots under the command of Colonel (later General) Pouyade show how German air opposition declined after the hectic air battles of the summer of 1943. They show also the determination of Soviet aircrews in pressing home their attacks, maintaining formation and flying their aircraft skilfully.

It is interesting to note that just as Soviet bombers on the Murmansk front preferred to be escorted by British-flown *Hurricanes* in 1942, so on the central and Baltic fronts French-flown fighter escort was specially employed. It seems that Soviet fighter pilots, in their anxiety and keenness to get at the enemy, would often leave their close-escort job; the type of operation that they preferred was the offensive freelance patrols over the front which they called *Svobodnaya Okhota*, or 'free hunt'.

But occasional lack of escort discipline was not important when air superiority, and indeed supremacy, had been won.

The machinery of close support for the ground forces was being perfected. General Katakov of the Soviet Armoured Forces claimed that in the last year or so of the war he could obtain air support within half an hour of the request for it, and this estimate is broadly confirmed by German eye-witness sources. There were, of course, the inevitable accidents in which the Soviet Air Force attacked its own troops and artillery, but these were rare cases. And such occurrences were regrettably common to all air forces in the Second World War.

By the beginning of 1944, the Soviet Air Force was in a position to engage in large-scale offensive action all along the eastern front from Leningrad to the Black Sea. And while the *YAK*, *MIG* and *LA* fighters rode the skies as they wished, German *Junkers 87* bombers had to be directed to night operations for lack of fighter cover during the day. By the spring of 1944, the Red Army had pushed into southern Poland and was threatening the Roumanian oilfields. And, further south in the Crimea, Soviet air squadrons were showing the same resilience and flexibility in support of combined land-sea forces as Anglo-American air arms were to show in western Europe a few months later.

General Tolbukhin was given the job of recapturing the Crimea with support from General Vershinin's air armies. Under him were the air divisions of Generals Tupikov and Ermochenkov. Their reconnaissance forces successfully located some hundreds of German coastal guns, and this was no doubt due to the Russians' continuous reconnaissance experience on this front. It was Soviet air policy to confine such units to regional tasks on one front so that they would get increased knowledge of their target areas and spot any changes in terrain or unusual movements more quickly. This policy certainly paid dividends, not only in the German campaign of the spring of 1944, but elsewhere too. Strong fighter patrols were maintained over the Kerch Straits, and non-stop attacks were made on *Luftwaffe* airfields. The Crimea was captured and the road to Roumania was wide open.

For the great summer and autumn offensives of 1944, the Soviet Air Force had substantial reinforcements of more modern *Lavochkin LA 7* and *YAK 3* fighters included in its great strength. French pilots have particularly praised the *YAK 3*. Although it had a top speed of over 400 mph thanks to its modest all-up weight of about 5,000 lbs, it was well-armed with a 20 mm and two 13 mm guns and was easy to handle and very manœuvrable. Soviet and French pilots reported that it could deal effectively with German *ME 109* and *FW 190* machines.

The real gap between the Soviet Air Force and the *Luftwaffe*, however, was in the number and experience of pilots. German air units were now being manned by inexperienced and ill-trained crews, and so the Soviet Air Force in all the air battles of the last year of the war from June 1944 to May 1945 operated at will under the most favourable conditions.

Vitebsk, Mogilev, Orscha and Bobruisk fell quickly under the first impact of the Soviet summer offensive. In July, Vilna, Lublin, Polotsk and Minsk were added to the list of Soviet victories, and the Air Force tactical units followed up the advance. Fighter units were based generally between ten and thirty miles behind the battle-front, with the *Sturmovik* and light bomber units anything from twenty to sixty miles behind.

In August, there was a pause for regrouping of both Soviet army and air units. Radio Moscow in Polish called on the Poles to rise up against their German oppressors in Warsaw, and 50,000 men in the

Polish capital responded to the call. But they had acted too soon.
Expecting the Russians to liberate the city within a few days, the
Poles were ready to hold on, but Stalin ordered his armies to remain
where they were. He not only refused air support for the martyred
Polish patriots, but until it was practically too late he also refused
to allow British and American air forces the use of Soviet air bases
for their missions of mercy to the Polish capital. The cynical Soviets
even went on to accuse the Poles of 'rising' without orders with the
intention of sabotaging the operations of the victorious Red
Army.

It was left to aircraft of the Mediterranean Allied Air Forces,
many of them with Polish pilots, to bring such aid as they could to
the patriots in Warsaw. For five consecutive nights from 12th to 17th
August, and again later in August and September, their parachutes
dropped over the Polish capital. Of the 181 machines involved,
thirty-one did not return.

Not till the Poles had been fighting against tremendous odds for
well over a month did the Russians make a face-saving gesture and
allow 100 Allied aircraft to refuel at Russian bases for one last supply
mission to Warsaw. But by then it was too late. The Poles, starved
of supplies and ammunition alike, and having suffered grievous
losses, could fight no more, and, on 2nd October, Warsaw surrendered to the Germans.

The precedent of using Soviet airfields for RAF and USAAF
refuelling had, however, been well established before then. As early
as June, the bases at Poltava, Mirgorod and Pirjatin had been
allocated for this purpose by the Russians, and by August a two-way
shuttle service was in operation. A typical operation was that on
7th August when US 8th Air Force bombers from Britain attacked
an aircraft factory in east Germany and then flew on to Russia. At
the same time, other American bombers flew from Russia to Britain
and bombed a synthetic oil plant near Cracow on the way.

But by now the German defences on the southern part of the
eastern front were beginning to crack. Between Russia and Roumania,
from Cernowitz to the Black Sea, the *Wehrmacht* was giving way
under the sledgehammer Russian attacks. Soviet bombers provided
tactical support for the advancing Red Army but, by and large, they
never did more than this. It was almost as if the Russians were
content to devote all their air strength to the immediate task of

supporting the ground forces. They did their work well, against practically non-existent opposition. And now the places which had originally been targets for Anglo-American strategic bombers came into the range of Russia's tactical air forces. Ploesti, once an almost entirely American target, was bombed in August by the Russians and was captured by their ground troops on the 30th of that month. The same pattern was noticeable in the speedy campaign that followed all along the line from Riga in Latvia, through Roumania, Yugoslavia, Bulgaria and, a few weeks later, East Prussia.

A notable exception to the Russians' 'bomb-and-capture' technique was the long-term assault on Budapest which opened with a raid by Soviet bombers in September, over three months before the first elements of the Red Army were to begin their seven-weeks' battle for the Hungarian capital.

In Roumania and Yugoslavia, however, Russian advances were so rapid that the Germans in Greece were almost cut off. Recognising the danger of an uncontrolled and uncoordinated Soviet advance, Winston Churchill hurried to Moscow on 9th October for urgent talks with Stalin. The all-important Yalta conference was four months away, but before Churchill, Stalin and Roosevelt met there for the last time, the Russians had begun their victorious march through Poland which was to lead swiftly through Czechoslovakia, Austria and Germany itself. Warsaw, Cracow, Poznan, Danzig, Bratislava, Koenigsberg, Vienna: the names came and went in Russian communiqués during the first months of 1945.

Then, on 16th April, the Soviet Army launched its great offensive across the Oder and reached points only about thirty miles east of Berlin. The end was obviously in sight. Ten days later the Russians had encircled the heart of the Third Reich and Adolf Hitler was preparing his suicide plans in the Chancellery.

In these later stages of the war, the Russian Air Force was not called upon to play an important part. Obviously, with three great air forces coming daily more and more into each other's orbits, a careful demarcation of targets was essential. The Russians were careful to keep out of the way of the RAF and USAAF who, during the final Soviet march on Berlin, had been left to hammer home their attacks on the German capital. During the period from 2nd to 20th April, the RAF alone were operating over Berlin on each of thirteen nights. Then, as the Red Army began moving through the outskirts of the capital, the British and American attacks ceased. The co-operation was as good as that.

Looking back on the activities of the Soviet Air Force in the Second World War, we can see the trend towards the great achievements of the present time; the *trend*, but nothing more than that. Its operational efficiency was proved, but the Air Force was never fully tested or demonstrated.

Technically, the Soviet Air Force ended the war four or five years behind the German, British and American Air Forces in jet fighters, bombers and transport planes, modern radar equipment, long range rockets and helicopters. Yet it was able to close the gap in all four fields in the following decade.

As for the actual achievements in battle, Soviet sources are, of course, notoriously unreliable as a basis of military history. General Rudienko claimed, after the war, that the chief credit for defeating the *Luftwaffe* must be given to the Soviet Air Force, 'which destroyed 75,000 of the 80,000 planes produced by Germany from June 1941 to May 1945.' Even allowing for propaganda and military pride, this is surely one of the most absurd claims in a war in which overclaiming was endemic. The Russians have claimed, too, that most of the German fighter planes were lost on the Soviet-German fronts. But the captured records of the *Luftwaffe* are there to correct this gross mis-statement.

The plain fact is that, from Stalingrad to Berlin, the bulk of German single- and twin-engined fighter units were not even engaged against the Soviet Air Force. This, more than any other single factor, was the underlying reason for the non-stop air superiority which the Russians enjoyed.

CHAPTER 4

SOVIET AIR STRATEGY IN THE SECOND WORLD WAR

Hanson Baldwin

STRATEGY CAN BE described as the science of planning, arranging and managing military forces to achieve victory; in a broader sense it is the mobilisation and application in war of the power of a nation.

But strategy like diplomacy is also the art of the possible.

Judged by the first definition of strategy, the title of this chapter represents a contradiction in terms, for history would find it difficult to prove that Russia had, in a classical sense, a defined and systematic air strategy at least in the first part of the Second World War. But against the yardstick of the latter definition (the art of the possible) one can discern through the improvisation and desperate makeshifts of Soviet air operations some prevailing patterns.

Russia, confronted with the German onslaught of 1941 and conditioned by centuries of experience to key her strategy to land battle, was forced during the Second World War to define air strategy: first, as the art of survival; then, later, as a function of ground strategy, that is to say, to give maximum support to Russia's land armies.

During the first two years of the great battles on the eastern front, Soviet strategy, though improvised and opportunistic, rather than precisely planned and managed, in general, traded space for time. Later, on the offensive, Moscow utilised essentially a meat-axe strategy of mass assault against German forces bogged down in vast spaces and numerically far outnumbered by the Soviet hordes. The Russian conception of the Second World War represented a campaign of attrition; the German blitzkrieg technique faltered and failed in front of Moscow. From then on there followed the slow triumph of numbers, of mass arms, guns and planes. There was nothing novel about either the strategy or the tactics of Soviet

75

victory; German mistakes, Hitler's paranoid management and the great weight of unequal numbers, more than skilful Russian general-ship—these led to catastrophe for the Third Reich. Germany fought a war of unlimited objectives, with limited means. This megalo-maniac strategy, which has led conquerors through the ages of history to ultimate destruction, contained within it the certain seeds of defeat.

But when all this is said, there were certain influences which, after the first improvisations, tended to shape and pattern Soviet air operations.

Three of these were of paramount importance: geography, the concept of mass, and the dominating influence of land power.

To Soviet Russia, the great heartland of Eurasia, the lessons of Napoleon's defeat were still vivid in the Second World War, despite the new pseudo 'strategic principles' of Marxism and Leninism. Space, depth and climate were Moscow's great allies. These same factors complicated and shaped the development of Soviet air power.

Air power, prior to the Second World War, did not have the global mobility it has today; aircraft ranges were limited; navi-gational aids, particularly in Russia, were relatively simple and few. Russia was a vast almost roadless area, with few railroads and widely separated urban and industrial centres. Soviet Siberia (particularly the maritime provinces and the disputed border area adjacent to Manchuria) and western Russia, history showed, were both vulner-able to land invasion, and the Black Sea-Caucasus area was another danger point.

Consequently, Soviet military organisation has always stressed, since the Revolution, the development of more or less self-contained military districts, each grouped around a natural industrial and/or geographic area, each with its own supporting arms, and each, as Soviet air power grew, with its own air army (in pre-war years, 'air brigades').

The Far East, linked to European Russia only by the tenuous link of the Trans-Siberian railroad (then single-tracked throughout much of its length), was necessarily a region where military autonomy was more pronounced than elsewhere. The Special Red Banner Far Eastern Armies of the USSR, supported by the Far Eastern Air Armies, tested the strength of Soviet military power against the

Japanese in repeated border skirmishes (some of divisional and corps size) during the 1930s. These battles, virtually unknown to the outside world, became part of the Soviet military tradition; in 1937, for instance, this writer saw many show-cases in the Red Army Museum in Moscow filled with trophies and accounts of this unknown war. Air power apparently played a strictly subordinate and unimportant role in these Russo-Japanese border struggles, but the Soviet Air Force and Soviet pilots were first 'blooded' in Siberia, and the experience they gained, particularly in reconnaissance, was of some importance in the great struggle of the Second World War.

Russian pilots also gained experience in China from 1937 to 1939. Moscow sent four fighter and two bomber squadrons (rotated every six months) to help the Chinese fight the Japanese. According to Major-General C. L. Chennault, United States Army Air Force, in his book *Way of a Fighter*, the Russians learned ramming interceptor tactics in China (later used occasionally in the Second World War) and, as a result of their combat experience, they modified their gunsights, machine-guns and gun barrels.

The Civil War in Spain was similarly used as a proving ground, just as Korea was a few years ago.

Despite these experiences in combat and liberal borrowing from other nations, the quality of Soviet aircraft, particularly fighter aircraft, was inferior to the planes of Germany, England and the United States in the first years of the Second World War.

Geography and the vulnerability of far-flung frontiers forced, therefore, some physical decentralisation of military air power in Russia, though it is important to remember that Moscow held (and still holds) tight political reins over all her military forces. This decentralisation, particularly influenced by the pre-war five-year plans of the Soviet Union, which witnessed the beginning of construction of complementing and to some extent self-supporting factory complexes in each of the more important military areas, was to be of major importance during the great war, when Russia's traditional industrial districts in the west were overrun.

Geography and climate had a direct influence upon the design of Soviet aircraft. There were few airfields in Soviet Russia prior to the Second World War, and many of them were unprepared sod fields, or strips laid out on the *tundra* or ice or snow. Soviet planes, particularly their landing gears, had to be relatively rugged to with-stand the abuse of repeated bumpy landings. A report of 1942, until recently classified, by Major-General Follett Bradley, US Army Air Force,[1] on a mission to Russia, commented on what seemed to American pilots the hazardous nature of take-offs and landings of *PE 2* twin-engined bombers from a natural sod field. General Bradley reported that the 'roughness of the field combined with the short travel of the shock struts made each take-off appear haz-ardous. . . .

'A run of about 2,500 feet was used before a plane got into the air and when it did get off it appeared to be in a stall and did not fly normally or gain any altitude in another 2,500 feet. . . .'

The bone-chilling cold of Russia also forced the development of winterisation techniques long before these were familiar to most of the rest of the world. The problem of starting an engine after all night out at thirty below was 'old hat' to the Russians, and they were experienced hands in Arctic flying and in the use of snow and icefields. (Soviet aircraft scouted and helped to pioneer the Northern Sea route long before the Second World War.)

Despite the skill of many individual Soviet pilots in bad flying conditions, Soviet meteorology and weather forecasting ranged from poor and primitive to modern and excellent. General Bradley noted that in some fields instrumentation and methodology were advanced, in others, years behind the West.

Aircraft communications were primitive but effective. The radio compass was used extensively on homing stations; there were no voice communications at the time of General Bradley's mission, and 'Soviet radio construction (was) generally primitive'.

Finally, the almost flat terrain of western Russia, scarred by the great watercourses of the Volga, the Don, the Dnieper and their tributaries was a contributing factor in the development of that form of low-altitude flying which has so often alarmed foreigners travelling aboard Soviet aircraft.

In 1956 I flew to Stalingrad and back in Soviet military aircraft and from Moscow to Helsinki in an *IL 14* of AEROFLOT. In two of the flights, the pilots stayed just 'off the deck', ducking under clouds,

---

[1] Report of Major-General Follett Bradley, United States Army Air Force, 17 Sept. 1942, to Commanding General, Army Air Forces, on *Observations of Russian Equipment and Operations.*

and flying through them only when the planes could go no lower. This terrain flying, about the only kind of flying that many of the Soviet pilots of the 1920s and 1930s knew, is adapted to much of Russia; there are no mountains in the clouds or rain squalls to provoke disaster.

Terrain flying today, hedge-hopping over terrain contours and navigating visually by following a railroad track or the course of a river, is still intensively practised in Soviet Russia, but scarcely anywhere else in the world's military forces, except by the light plane and helicopter pilots of the United States Army, and to a lesser extent by the pilots of the US Navy's low-flying attack planes. In Russia nearly every pilot knows the art of hedge-hopping; many of them prefer to fly this way, and today their proficiency has an important military advantage, for the low-flying attack plane can often escape radar's groping beams.

Geography also had a complementary influence upon another major factor of importance in Soviet air development: mass. The sheer size of the country dictated numbers for defence. The Russians always have believed in the big battalions, and they applied their emphasis upon mass numbers, not only on the ground, but also in the air in the Second World War in the form of massed air fleets over their ground armies and mass production in their aircraft factories.

But land power was the most important influence upon the pre-war, and war-time, development of Soviet air strategy. It is still a key factor today. The Red Army is the heart of the modern Soviet military concept; Red Army artillerymen serve and maintain the giant missiles which are air power's most modern manifestation. Russia's strategic concept prior to (and during) the Second World War was a land concept, and air support was under the operational control of ground commanders. Deep invasion and serious danger always had come to Russia by land; it was on land that she must be strong. The fringe peripheral conflicts, the Crimean War and the Russo-Japanese War, that had touched her borders had never threatened Moscow, the mother city, or her great sprawling land body. Therefore, the Russian Navy was regarded purely as an extension of the army's land flank, a coast guard, a sentinel for Russia's land-locked seas.

Similarly, air power existed to aid the army, to support it, to protect its air flank, to extend its tactical eyes. There was no concept

of long range (strategic) reconnaissance or of independent air operations. Even the parachute troops, trained in large numbers in Soviet
Russia prior to the Second World War long before Germany made
them famous, had a para-political and army-support role.

Guerrilla operations behind the enemy's lines, always an important Marxist-Leninist concept (deriving from the concept that
war is a class struggle with the international proletariat everywhere
the allies of communism), had played a role in Napoleon's defeat a
generation before. The plane was a modern means of dropping
guerrilla leaders, weapons and supplies behind enemy lines; the
concept of mass drops of men, though rarely practised by the
Russians in the Second World War, probably derived from this.

Still another factor of importance at the start of the Second World
War was the (relatively) primitive nature of Soviet industrial
development. Russia in 1941 was fundamentally an agrarian economy and relatively few of her peasants were accustomed to machines.
This affected maintenance and dependability. General Bradley
found that 'the maintenance of Soviet aircraft in general can be said
to be adequate,' but servicing was slow.

'Maintenance,' he wrote, 'cannot compare with US Army
maintenance. This is caused by a lack of trained personnel and in
some cases lack of proper facilities. Engines are generally dependable
but miss and splutter at times and are still kept in service. Warming
up of engines . . . is unknown . . . .' (Rapid take-offs without warm-
ups still provide thrills for the Soviet air traveller today, though in
this respect, as in nearly all aspects of Soviet operations, there
appears to be no uniformity: some planes use seat-belts; some do
not; some pilots hedge-hop; others do not, and so on.)

These indigenous influences upon the development of a Soviet air
strategy were complemented and reinforced by the strong German
influence of the 1920s.

Soviet air power may be said, in fact, to have been born with the
aid of a German midwife in the period between 1922 and the rise
of Hitler to supreme power. German aircraft and armament design
served as a basic pattern for many Soviet developments during that
period of military *rapprochement* between a Germany defeated in
the First World War and the political system of Soviet Russia.

More important, perhaps, was the influence of the German concept of air power which fitted neatly into the Soviet concepts of land power as the principal arm. Russian military theorists had, of course, read Douhet and were familiar with the arguments and controversies about air power's strategic role that marked the development of military power in both the United States and the United Kingdom. But Soviet history, tradition, geography and climate all tended to undermine the theories of Douhet and to reinforce the arguments of those German thinkers who regarded aircraft as the air part of a combined arms team, the objective of which was to defeat the enemy's military forces rather than to blast his cities or destroy his nation's will to fight.

In 1948, Colonel-General Sudets declared: 'In Stalinist military theory it is considered that victory in contemporary war is attained only by the combined efforts of all types of forces, and therefore the training of air force units is planned so that they can first of all provide direct assistance to the ground forces in all types of operations. The development of all branches of the Soviet air forces is carried out in accordance with this fundamental principle. The course of the war [the Second World War] confirmed the soundness of this policy regarding problems of development and deployment of the air forces.'[1]

Dr Raymond Garthoff in an article, *Soviet Attitudes Toward Modern Air Power*, in *Military Affairs* (Volume XII, Number 2, Summer, 1955) points out that Douhet was read, though criticised, in the Soviet Union, and 'from about 1933 to 1937 particular attention was given to heavy bombers capable of "independent missions of strategic significance"'. This digression, however, was never a dominant policy, and ended as the Second World War approached and many of its adherents were liquidated in the great purge.

Garthoff, like all other students of Soviet military policy, stresses that: 'One basic tenet of Soviet military doctrine, adopted in the 1930s and dogmatised in the Second World War, required that air power be integrated into a mutually supporting ground-air force combined-arms team. Another basic doctrinal tenet, complementing the first, was the emphatic rejection of reliance upon any single weapon or strategy as capable of gaining victory.'

In part, perhaps, this concept was strengthened by two other factors. One was the lack, in 1941 and throughout the war, of any

[1] Quoted from *Soviet Military Doctrine*, by Raymond L. Garthoff.

Soviet aircraft really suitable for long range bombing. The failure to develop such an aircraft was partly deliberate, the result of the Soviet concepts of air power; partly enforced, since the Soviet pre-war and war-time aircraft industry, despite its considerable size, had a very limited capacity for multi-engined bomber production.

Another factor may have had a political tinge. The Communist concept of war always has been keyed to the class struggle; an important part of Russia's strategic concept was the belief, justified in part by the mutinies and uprisings in Germany at the end of the First World War, that the working class of an enemy state repre-sented an ally of Communist Russia. The bombing of industrial areas and of cities thickly settled by this working class would represent, therefore, a negative strategy: one which might rob Russia of the aid of a subversive Fifth Column in the heart of an enemy country.

All these diverse influences produced, therefore, at the start of the Second World War, Soviet air power that was keyed to the concept of surface support. There were no Soviet aircraft carriers (as there are none today); in fact, Soviet naval concepts never contemplated blue-water or high-seas operations but simply envisaged the seas as extensions of the land flanks. Soviet naval operations in the Second World War, if they can be dignified by this phrase, which implies an organised strategy, never extended beyond easy range of land-based air power, and even today (despite an immense Russian submarine fleet) a great part of the Russian Navy seems geared to coast defence, dominance of Russia's narrow seas and extension of the land flank seawards.

Russia, when invaded by Hitler's legions in 1941, had no radar and virtually no night fighters. But she had developed to an advanced degree fighter-bombers and light bombers well armoured against ground fire, and equipped with rockets, fragmentation and light bombs, as well as heavy machine-guns and light cannon. General Follett Bradley noted 'the development of rockets as an offensive air weapon' at a time long before the United States or Great Britain had become really interested in this field.

From the Soviet point of view this ground support concept of air power made sense, and, with some exceptions, the course of the Second World War seemed to verify this concept.

In 1941 Soviet air power had only one advantage *vis-à-vis* the

Germans, a great numerical superiority (at least two to one in over-all numbers in the first summer of the campaign; as high as ten to fifteen to one in the last two years of the war when the German Air Force was worn down and heavily engaged in the west). In quality of aircraft, doctrine, technique, training and personnel, the Germans were far superior. Only one plane, the Soviet *IL 2 Sturmovik*, heavily armoured ground attack type, was superior in speed, armour and armament to its German opposite number, the *Junkers 87*.

Like the Soviet Army, the Soviet Air Force suffered tremendous losses in the first year of the war; some authorities estimate that 5,000 Russian planes were lost in the first two months.

These losses, coupled with the millions of Soviet casualties inflicted by the Germans in the summer and autumn of 1941, demonstrate not only the ruggedness and resilience of the Russians, but, even more important, the fact that German mistakes, as much as or more than Soviet achievements, led to Hitler's ultimate defeat. The Russians hastily transferred all available aircraft from the Far East and elsewhere to the western front; they traded space for time. 'General Winter' came to their aid, and Berlin, prepared for blitzkrieg but not for attrition, had few reserves when victory did not come quickly. The sheer size of the Russian front also revealed a German weakness in numbers; the *Luftwaffe* simply did not have enough aircraft to go around.

During 1941 and 1942 Soviet air strategy, as well as Soviet ground strategy, was mainly a strategy of desperation, of recuperation, of makeshift opportunism, of 'plugging the gap'. But gradually Russian factories, many of them beyond the Urals, started to turn out more and more planes; American and British aid contributed, and the German Air Force became dispersed and weakened by its three-front war, against Russia over the vast plans of the east; against Allied ground-sea-air forces in North Africa, the Mediterranean and Italy; against Anglo-American air forces in the west. Operational Soviet aircraft increased in the last years of the war to 15,000 or 20,000 planes and in some periods were opposed by no more than between 500 and 2,000 German planes. German ground troops early became accustomed, as they later had to do in the west, to fighting without German air support, and the *Luftwaffe* itself came to reckon twelve to one odds on the eastern front as acceptable.

In 1943–5 Soviet air strategy became less inchoate and more organised, rational and controlled. The Russians were on the offensive, the Germans on the defensive and the sheer weight of mass, in the air and on the ground, wore down the dispersed and overcommitted German forces. The Soviet Air Forces had one major job and one only, the mass support of the Red Army. There was no bombing threat to Soviet cities or industries from the *Luftwaffe*. Even in the first two years of the war the German long-range bombing attacks in Russia (upon Moscow and elsewhere) had been of small importance; the major power of the German bomber forces had been concentrated upon London and other British targets. The best fighter planes and pilots of the German Air Force were, moreover, concentrated in the west in the defence of Germany. Consequently, the Reich's early technical superiority was markedly reduced on the eastern front in the last years of the war. The *LAGG*, *MIG* and *YAK* fighters of 1943 and 1944 were superior to the American *P 39 Airacobras* and the early British *Hurricanes*, and they were probably a stand-off for the earlier models of the German *ME 109*.

It is all the more remarkable, therefore, that the Germans were able, until almost the close of the war, to muster occasionally on the eastern front local and temporary air superiority. The German Navy evacuated hundreds of thousands of troops and civilians from the Baltic States and East Prussia in the face of the advancing Red Army, and Soviet air power interfered scarcely at all. At the same time the Soviet submarine fleet (then as now the largest in the world) which should have had good pickings in the Baltic and Black Seas as the Germans retreated, had inconsequential successes, partially because there appeared to be virtually no co-operation between Soviet naval patrol aircraft and the submarines. Soviet long range bombers (most were really, by Anglo-American standards, medium bombers) in the last part of the war attacked Berlin and other cities at night, utilising the four-engined *PE 8*. But these were flea bites; the participating bombers were usually numbered in two figures, and Soviet navigation and bombing techniques left much to be desired.

These and other contradictions and anomalies can be explained by two factors. One was the concept of Soviet air strategy. Over-simplified, this strategy was simply ground strategy transferred to the air: the concentration of an overwhelming mass of aircraft in one or several areas of the front to support the attacks of the Red Army. The Soviet Air Forces were used as flying artillery with fighter cover and little more. The second factor was the spotty organisation of Soviet air power, indeed, of Soviet military strength. British and US technical and material aid and Russia's own indigenous resources helped to effect major improvements in air tactics, maintenance, supply, weather forecasting, aircraft design, arms and training during the four years of fighting. But until almost the end there were great and glaring contrasts (as, indeed, there still are today) between units of the Soviet Air Force; some were equal to the best in the West in proficiency; others were poorly trained 'air fodder'. Supply, a particularly weak point, was often haphazard or makeshift; the late General of the Air Force, H. H. Arnold, described their 'system of logistics' as 'terrible'. Maintenance was in no way equal to that of the West, and there were many other organisational deficiencies. Germany's level of experience and skill in all branches was, on the other hand, more uniform, less spotty and higher than that of the Russians until just before the final collapse.

There is an old axiom that everything one says about Russia is true. The USSR was a land of startling contrasts in the Second World War, and even today its society and its military system embody at one and the same time the most advanced and the most backward.

Soviet air strategy in the Second World War was at first extemporised, opportunistic, a fill-the-gap strategy; later, it represented, essentially, simply the utilisation of massed 'flying artillery' to support its ground armies.

The instruments it used were a product of, and were defined by, the environment in which they fought. Russia was right, in its context, in subordinating long range independent air operations to ground support. The means available and the pre-atomic bombs at hand could not have achieved a decision in the war against Germany. Moreover, there was no Soviet background of experience to induce the development of long range bombing; German air attacks upon Soviet cities and industries had been unimpressive, and it was not until Stalin and his generals saw photographs of bombed German cities and talked to the United States Army Air Force officers about strategic bombardment that Russia developed any real interest in this concept. In April 1944, Stalin asked the United States for more than 500 four-engined *Liberators* and *B 17s*, but even then, as Major-General John R. Deane, head of the US Military Mission to Moscow from 1943 to 1945, explains in his book *The Strange Alliance*: 'it was plainly evident that neither he [Stalin] nor any of his military advisers had any conception of the specialised technique required to ensure target coverage, formation control, or defence against hostile fighters.'

But the interest then aroused, far too late to have any influence upon the Second World War, continued after the peace, and with American *B 29s* forced down in Siberia and pre-empted by the Russians as models, the Soviet Government started the development of what has now become in the age of A-bombs a significant strategic factor in the world power balance: the Soviet long range air armies.

The other manifestations of the somewhat haphazard Soviet air strategy were similarly understandable in the light of Moscow's concentration upon ground power and the dispersion of the German air effort. The emphasis upon close support for sea-borne forces to the neglect of long range patrol aircraft and maritime attack planes was logical in view of the then Soviet concept of sea power as a water-borne extension of the land army. The training of large numbers of airborne troops, as many as 100,000 at a time, and their subsequent use largely in a ground (not an airborne) role, though wasteful in a nation like the United States where manpower is more carefully handled and such training is far more expensive, was understandable in Russia where the first requirement was for mass manpower on the ground, and where training of paratroopers is nowhere near as organised, detailed or expensive. To Russia, too, civil and military air transport, always (and still) indistinguishable, represented identical halves, both to be used for the political purpose to be achieved, whether in peace or war. Similarly night fighters represented, in the Second World War, when the distant cities and industries of Soviet Russia were not exposed to serious bombardment, an unnecessary luxury, as did anti-aircraft artillery. Soviet troops in the latter part of the war were rarely exposed for long to German air attack; they needed, and got, masses of field artillery rather than anti-aircraft support.

One can say with some assurance that there was little that was basically new that was contributed by Soviet air power in the

Second World War. Even the large-scale use of airborne troops was pioneered by other countries including Britain, Italy, Germany and the United States; Russia, however, developed this tactic of vertical envelopment and trained mass numbers of parachutists well before any other nation (though, ironically, she rarely used mass airborne attack in the war). Russia also showed that mass in the air, as on the ground, is important to victory. Her development of the armour-plated *Sturmovik* and of heavy machine-guns and cannon and her early use of rockets pioneered in these fields.

But these are tactics and techniques rather than strategic concepts. And Russia's 'air strategy' (if, indeed, it can be so called) was never really tested in the last two years of the Second World War: the only period during which Moscow actually had what might be called an air strategy. The German Air Force was too weakened and too dispersed; Russian air power fought this phase of the war against only intermittent and local opposition.

These and similar lessons drawn from the campaigns on the eastern front, valid then, must today be re-appraised in the light of the technological revolution in weapons, and the tremendous development of Soviet industrial and military strength since the Second World War.

It is clear that Russia still believes in the principle of mass numbers; she operates, and her vast space undoubtedly requires, large numbers of fighters and fighter-bombers and light bombers. She has built long range air forces with strategic capabilities: far more formidable, now armed with the A-bomb and H-bomb, than their numbers and experience indicate. She still has an air force of widely unequal potentialities. Soviet fighters and pilots used against American and Allied air forces in Korea, despite their advantages of an un-bombable 'sanctuary', their proximity to the area defended, greatly superior numbers and (for a time) superior flying machines, were no match whatsoever for the Western air forces. Soviet *MIGs* had good flying characteristics at high altitudes (as the Jap *ZERO* did at the start of the Second World War) but as combat machines or weapons systems they had grave deficiencies: in gun-sights, armour, strength, range, etc. Soviet pilots were nothing like as well-trained as their American counterparts.

Time has passed since Korea and all available data indicate that the latest Soviet aircraft are about on a par, as aircraft, at least with the best in the West. Certainly the qualitative advantage, once so enormously enjoyed by the West, a factor that explained German ability to resist the Soviet hordes in the Second World War, has been reduced if not eliminated by time. Russia today is no longer an agrarian economy; she is a modern, technically advanced industrial power, though many elements of her strength still lag far behind the West. Her strategic concepts, too, have undoubtedly changed.

The dreams of Douhet, always overstated and unrealistic in the age of bombs employing conventional explosives, have become possibilities in the age of the atom. And Soviet submarines and long range maritime attack and patrol aircraft and minelayers make possible the extension of the Soviet land flank very far from her coasts into blue water.

Russia is still the 'heartland', still the greatest land power in the world, and the bulk of her air power today is still earmarked for close support of her surface forces and (in contrast with 1941) for air defence of her land spaces. Khrushchev and his peers undoubtedly understand Douhet, and worry about John Foster Dulles and the politico-strategic concept of 'massive retaliation' as a deterrent to war. But they have not gone all the way. Russia has broadened her air horizons but she has not forsaken the concepts that served her well in the Second World War: the concepts of mass, of flying fire-power, of aerial artillery.

CHAPTER 5

POST-WAR STRATEGY

Dr Kenneth Whiting

AT THE END of the Second World War the power positions of the United States and the Soviet Union rested upon very dissimilar strategic concepts. The Soviet Union contributed to Germany's defeat by sacrificing huge land areas until it could adequately organise and deploy a local superiority in manpower, artillery and armour. As a logical consequence the Soviet Union, at the end of the war, seized the traditional 'platforms of invasion' in the Baltic, eastern Europe, and the Balkans, consolidated its position on the Pacific littoral and in central Asia, and maintained much of its huge ground force. On the other hand, the United States acted to acquire control of the seas and to use strategic air power. Also, the United States emerged from the war with a monopoly in nuclear weapons. In short, the United States fought on a world-wide scale and developed the weapons and strategic concepts for such a war; the Soviet Union, to all intents and purposes, fought a local war using battering-ram tactics and did not develop the weapons and strategy that would enable her to reach the United States. It is not surprising that post-war Soviet spokesmen stressed Stalin's military science with its glorification of the infantry and artillery, and avoided mentioning the nuclear threat, or did so only in a derogatory manner. But in spite of this obeisance to artillery as the god of war, with air power as only one of the handmaidens, there must have been agonising re-appraisals under way in the Kremlin. The Russians were sitting under the United States Strategic Air Command's bomb-sights, and they were not happy.

From 1945 until 1949 the Soviet Union had no real answer to the strategic striking force of the United States. During this period the public utterances of Soviet military leaders and politicians were restricted to belittling the effectiveness of nuclear weapons and to the apotheosis of Stalin as the architect of a military 'science' based on the tactics and strategy of the USSR in her struggle with Germany. A mighty chorus, led by Voroshilov and Bulganin, praised Stalin as the greatest military thinker of the ages. Stalin, superbly using the tools of Marxian analysis, had developed the Stalinist 'science of war', had established the 'permanently operating factors', and had brought the counter-offensive to the point of a personal creation. In short, Soviet military doctrine, at least that given public expression, was synonymous with the Stalinist 'science of war'.

The Stalinist doctrine can be easily summarised. Its simplicity, or rather triteness, is appalling. According to Bulganin, Voroshilov, Taranchuk and others who sang its praises, its great advantage was in its being 'military science' as opposed to bourgeois 'military art'. This science enables one to appraise correctly the economic and moral capabilities of one's own country and the enemy's. The Germans in the Second World War, so the Soviets argued, relied on military plans that were unsuited to their own economic and moral capabilities and completely disregarded those of the Soviet Union. Having ascertained the over-all picture, Stalin formulated the 'permanently operating factors' developed by him between 1918 and 1945: the stability of the rear, the morale of the army, the quantity and quality of divisions, the equipment of the army, and the organising ability of the command personnel. A sixth factor is sometimes added: the importance of reserves. What is baffling is that these factors have no deep, hidden meaning; they mean just what they say and are hardly the sole possession of Soviet military thinkers. To complete this picture of the deification of the trite, the adulators praised Stalin's 'invention' of the counter-offensive.

The dependence of the new 'military science' upon Soviet experience in the Second World War is more vividly revealed by the list of so-called 'temporary or fortuitous factors' that cannot bring victory in a war. These are usually listed as surprise attack, outstripping the opponent in speed of mobilisation, experience in warfare, and the transformation of the national economy to war production in peacetime. The Germans had the advantage in all these 'temporary' factors in 1941, according to the Soviet theorists, and still they went down to defeat. Thus they are not vital factors in winning a war.

The main puzzle during this first post-war period was the contradiction between the apotheosis of this Stalinist formula for victory and the suspicion that competent military leaders would not confine their planning within the framework of such a theoretical hodge-podge while facing the task of utilising a radically new weapon system in a completely changed strategic situation. But while Stalin lived, his doctrine was constantly reiterated; at least publicly. The new weapons of mass destruction were derided or ignored, and the analogy of the failure of the Nazi blitzkrieg was applied whenever the strategic bomber was mentioned. As late as January 1955 Lieutenant-General N. F. Grichin of the Soviet General Staff proclaimed that Western reliance on an atomic blitzkrieg was reminiscent of Goering's posturings before the Second World War and would fail just as dismally if tried on the Soviet Union.

If the Soviets believe this doctrine, then there is some hope that if they should achieve technological superiority in the future they may be hesitant to risk total war. As aerial blitzkriegs are supposed to be ineffective and wars are long, drawn-out affairs involving all types of forces, the Soviets should be very cautious in attacking the West in the expectation of a quick victory.

So much for the public façade. What was actually taking place in Soviet military thinking? How sincere were the derogatory remarks about the extremely limited effectiveness of the nuclear weapons possessed by the West? To some extent Soviet thinkers, military and political, were probably victims of their intellectual setting; propaganda is bound to stain indelibly those who manufacture it, as well as those who are passive recipients. But the tremendous advantage conferred by hindsight now enables us to see that the top echelon of the Kremlin was well aware, between 1945 and 1949, of the better cards held by the West. The denials of the power of the new atomic weapon system began to soften with the first Soviet chain-reaction device in 1947, became softer still with their atomic explosion in 1949, and died out entirely when they got a thermo-nuclear bomb in 1953.

Soviet Nuclear Development

Soviet scientists began to work in the nuclear field in the 1920s, and a number of them went abroad at that time to study in the laboratories of Lord Rutherford at Cambridge and the Curie Radium Institute in Paris. Peter Kapitsa's sojourn at Cambridge has received the most publicity, but probably more important for Soviet nuclear studies was V. I. Vernadsky's lengthy stay at the Curie Radium Institute, and the latest edition of the *Great Soviet Encyclopedia* points out that he publicly stated as early as 1922 that atomic energy would revolutionise human life in the near future and hinted at the enormous responsibilities such power would bring. V. I. Vernadsky also founded the State Radium Institute in Leningrad in 1922. In 1930 A. F. Ioffe began to develop nuclear research, especially at his Physical-Technical Institute in Leningrad. Centres for nuclear research also existed in Moscow and Kharkov. The line-up of Soviet atomic scientists working in these institutes is impressive: L. D. Landau, K. D. Sinnelnikov, Ya. I. Frankel, and I. V. Kurchatov are a few examples of high calibre of Soviet scientists in the field. In 1940 a Special Committee on the Uranium Problem was established to further the work in nuclear research and the personnel of this committee included the outstanding Soviet nuclear scientists.

The Soviet nuclear physicists had the backing of large government funds, and the Radium Institute in Leningrad had a cyclotron by 1937, the first one in Europe. Two larger ones were scheduled, but their completion was held up by the war. The commitment, however, of state funds for such expensive equipment is good evidence of Soviet interest in nuclear research before 1939.

On the eve of the German attack in June 1941, Soviet nuclear research was probably on a par with that of the West in the quality of its scientists and was rapidly catching up in equipment. Nuclear research in the Soviet Union, however, was abandoned during the war, and the leading physicists, such as Kapitsa and Kurchatov, were assigned to more pressing tasks in the war effort. Thus, while the war acted as a stimulant to nuclear research in the United States and Great Britain, the Soviet Union was temporarily eclipsed in that field. The touch-and-go situation from June 1941 until the German set-back at Stalingrad made an effort such as the US Manhattan Project out of the question in the Soviet Union: the latter had neither the manpower nor the resources for such a calculated gamble at that time. Furthermore, it is doubtful whether the Kremlin leaders were aware of the implications of nuclear energy in the military field during the early period of the war. It is true that Kapitsa, in the autumn of 1941, spoke of the awful power that could result from atomic bombs, but his was a lone voice. Furthermore, the Soviet military strategy of enormous masses of ground troops backed by artillery and close air support was not conducive to a whole-hearted search for weapons useful to strategic aircraft.

After the atomic bombing of Hiroshima on 6th August 1945, there could have been no ignorance in the Kremlin concerning the fact that it now faced a weapon of a new magnitude. But a week later, when General Eisenhower was in Moscow for military discussions with Stalin and the Soviet High Command, the Russians made no mention of the bomb. The *use* of the new weapon may have surprised the Soviet leaders, but certainly knowledge of its development was no shock to them: the espionage trials of May, Fuchs and others demonstrate that the Kremlin had been well informed during the war of the progress of the joint American-British atomic work. The official policy from then until a Soviet atomic weapon could be produced was to talk down the whole subject of nuclear weapons.

Early in 1944 Soviet scientists once more began to work in their own laboratories under more normal conditions and there was a resumption of nuclear research. According to Igor V. Kurchatov, in a speech before the Supreme Soviet in 1958, Soviet physicists began working on nuclear weapons during the latter part of the Second World War. But, unlike the pre-war period, there was now a blackout on all information concerning nuclear research. This blackout lasted until the International Conference on the Peaceful Uses of Atomic Energy held in Geneva in 1955. Some time in 1947, probably late in the year, the Soviets put into operation their first reactor, and it was almost a replica of the early American reactor, *Hanford 305*, which began operation in April 1944. There were probably several reasons for this seemingly leisurely approach to catching up with the West. Funds, equipment, and skilled manpower were in short supply in the Soviet Union at the end of the war. Even with the information they had on the American-British experience, their own scientists had to have some time to digest and evaluate it. Producing enough uranium and graphite of the requisite purity was a formidable task at the end of the war. Furthermore, the 'cold war' was in its infancy and haste was not yet the watchword. Finally, the Soviets did not have an adequate bomber or rocket vehicle to carry the bombs even if their scientists could have produced them immediately.

Once the reactor was in operation, the biggest hurdle had been taken: from now on they were confident of their ability to catch up with the West, and by 1949 they exploded their first nuclear device. Just how rapidly the Soviets developed atomic weapons after 1949 is a moot point, but the speed was probably very much greater than that of the United States in the early days of the development of atomic weapons: the usual advantages that accrue to the late-comer in any industrialisation process applied in this case also.

The Soviet scientists moved from the relatively primitive atomic weapons into the field of thermo-nuclear bombs in a very short time. The United States exploded a thermo-nuclear device in November 1952, but the Soviets countered in August of 1953 with a thermo-nuclear *bomb*. Academician Igor V. Kurchatov, probably the best of the Soviet nuclear physicists, made a speech to the Supreme Soviet at the end of March 1958, and he outlined the whole business of priorities, at least the Soviet version of it. He asserted that the American 1952 detonation was of a device so large and clumsy that it could not be delivered, thus it was not a weapon. On the other hand, the Soviet detonation of 1953 was of a relatively small bomb that could be delivered, or even used in a ballistic missile. The first usable American thermo-nuclear weapon was not exploded until March 1954. Regardless of the pros and cons of the debate, the fact remains that the Soviet scientists made the transition from an atomic device in 1949 to a thermo-nuclear bomb in 1953: a tempo that is really amazing and can only be explained on the basis of brilliant scientists and all-out government support.

Just how the nuclear-armament race stands today is hard to say since neither side is prepared to publish any figures on its stock-piles. But a rough appreciation can be made from the number of tests of each power to date. By the time the United States finishes its 1958 series of tests in August the American total should come to about 120 tests since the first one during the Second World War. Since 1949 the Soviets have probably detonated something like fifty or sixty devices and weapons. The Atomic Energy Commission has announced thirty-nine, Prime Minister Macmillan put the figure at fifty, and Hanson Baldwin guessed it to be nearer sixty. The magnitude is not too different in spite of various figures given. Most informed guessers feel that the US has far more weapons and a greater assortment, but the Soviets probably have enough seriously to damage both the United States and Europe.

Once the Soviets had entered the nuclear race and had their first weapons, the problem of delivery vehicles became acute. This also was solved in rapid order: by 1955 they had long range and medium jet bombers such as the *Bear*, *Bison*, *Badger*, and *Beagle*; their long range bombers, especially if they used the Polar route and flight refuelling, were capable of two-way missions against the United States, and their numerous medium bombers could be used effectively against the NATO bases in Europe. But the world was relatively relaxed as the United States Strategic Air Command still had the upper hand in numbers and the geographical location of its bases. The gap was narrowing, however, and strategists were becoming ever more puzzled by something they vaguely referred to as 'mutual deterrence', a 'nuclear stalemate', and the heretics were likely to call 'mutual suicide'.

Missiles

In August 1957 the Soviets announced that they had successfully fired an intercontinental ballistic missile. The almost instinctive Western doubts at any Soviet boast were somewhat tempered by a growing respect for Soviet technical achievements. Then on 4th October 1957, the Soviets put their first *Sputnik* into orbit and the world was stunned. This was proof positive that the Soviets had a rocket with enormous thrust; to lift the 185 pound *Sputnik* into orbit must have taken a rocket with a thrust in the range of 200,000 pounds or more. On 3rd November the Soviets put a second satellite, with a dog in it, into orbit. This one weighed 1,120 pounds, and must have used a rocket with a thrust of around 400,000 pounds. There was no avoiding the fact that the Russians had developed powerful rockets, or as *Pravda* put it recently: 'Only after the development in the Soviet Union of the intercontinental ballistic rocket was it possible to launch an artificial earth satellite.'

Academician Blagonravov, in April 1958, discussed a single-stage rocket that lifted one and a half tons of instruments and animals some 473 kilometres; it was recovered undamaged, according to Blagonravov. He also discussed the success of a new stabiliser which made telemetering more accurate. The launching of *Sputnik III* with a 2,940 pound payload lent credence to Blagonravov's statements, at least in the magnitude of the propulsion needed.

Missiles had played a dramatic, if ineffectual, role in the closing months of the Second World War, and the armed forces of both the Soviet Union and the West have been developing them ever since the end of the war; but to the general public, and to many military people, they were still mysterious devices which would probably supplement bombers some time in the future. Then came the 'bleep-bleep' of the Soviet *Sputnik*: the knowledge that any rocket that could push that much weight into orbit could also span oceans brought about an almost hysterical reaction, especially in the United States. There were 'agonising reappraisals' of the US missile programme, the American educational system, especially in the field of science, and even the over-all military structure was closely examined. The fact that the missile was still far from being perfected and would still be only supplementary to the strategic bomber in the immediate future had little effect on the uproar. Only when the United States finally got a satellite into orbit did the situation return to normal. It was obvious to everyone, however, that missiles with nuclear warheads were about to become a leading element in the arsenals of both camps.

The strategical concepts developed in the Second World War and during the years when the United States had an atomic monopoly had already been badly shaken by the Soviet achievement of technological parity in nuclear weapons and the aircraft to deliver them. Ballistic missiles made the problem much more complex. But before looking at some of the strategical problems that the Soviet missiles have foisted upon Western strategists, a brief listing of the peculiar strategical characteristics of the ballistic missile would seem desirable.

The main asset of the ballistic missile is its hypersonic speed. At present this speed makes effective penetration of any defence not only probable, but absolutely certain. A major limitation on the missile's effectiveness is the accuracy of its guidance system: something the defenders have nothing to do with. Warning time is now a matter of minutes, not hours, and the evacuation of the population from cities is well nigh impossible at such short notice.

Ballistic missiles, especially the 'second generation' vehicles of the near future, can be more easily camouflaged and located in hidden launching sites. They will be much less vulnerable to counter-attack than are the large air bases of the present time with their 10,000 foot runways and complicated equipment. A ballistic missile counter-attack must be fool-proof. Most commentators stress the fast reaction time necessary in the missile counter-attack, and admit that making the decision to launch a counter-attack in the fifteen or thirty minute warning period is an awful responsibility. If the reaction is immediate, then it must be in response to a real attack and not a 'spoof' or a mistake. There is no safe system of dealing with ballistic missiles, at least without destroying them while in flight: a rather risky business when even the longest range missile should be on the target in less than a half-hour. This means that the command system from the radar-warning screens to the top commander must be perfect. Intercontinental ballistic missiles with nuclear warheads are the weapons of total war. They do not fit in well with such concepts as gradual deterrence and tacit bomb lines, and an order to launch them would be a serious, even desperate, act, which could be ordered by only the highest authority.

The use of ballistic missiles requires complete and detailed planning before hostilities. The targets, as well as the synchronisation of the respective missions of the missiles and bombers, must be preplanned down to the finest details as there will be no time to study these problems once hostilities are under way.

A system of ballistic missiles, if it is going to keep one of its prime advantages, invulnerability, must be widely dispersed in hardened camouflaged launching sites. This means that an elaborate logistics system must be superimposed on the already complex one taking care of aircraft. This applies to the present first-generation, liquid-fuelled ballistic missiles; the solid-fuel missiles, when they are operational, will require far less in the way of logistic support and can be set up in almost perfectly hardened launching sites, or even in submarines beneath the Polar ice.

Effective defence against the ballistic missile may be possible. Offensive capability far outweighs the defensive, and it would be a hardy soul who would state with absolute certainty that a ballistic missile careering along at 18,000 miles an hour is capable of being intercepted. It is believed, however, that the fixed trajectory and the hypersonic speed of the ballistic missile may be its undoing. Once the missile is committed to its course, its path is predictable. Therefore, given a reasonable warning time and an accurate fix on the trajectory, it may be possible to intercept it. Another scheme being discussed is the use of billions of sand-like particles laid in rather dense clouds over hundreds of miles of the missile's path. The extremely high velocity of the missile would make their impact completely out of proportion to that normally expected. But all these schemes are in the future, how far in the future is impossible to predict with certainty. Until such defences are attained, the offensive capacity of the ballistic missile is limited solely by the accuracy of its guidance system and the geodetic knowledge of those launching it.

Faced with a weapon system endowed with the above characteristics, what is to be done? First, every effort must be made to keep pace with the Soviets in the development of missiles in order to insure deterrence. Second, the present vulnerable base structures must be dispersed. Third, the planners must carefully evaluate the capabilities of aircraft versus missiles, especially as the missiles become more numerous and more accurate. Finally, the United States in addition to the tools for a total war must have weapon systems to fight limited wars successfully.

The United States in the face of the growing Soviet might in nuclear weapons, long range aircraft, and ballistic missiles must keep reasonably close to parity with the Soviet Union in these tools of total war. Absolute equality or superiority is not necessary as one of the characteristics of the new weapon systems is their enormous destructiveness. Once a power has *enough* bombs, aircraft, and missiles to demolish the enemy, then stock-piling beyond that point brings rapidly diminishing returns. President Eisenhower stated several years ago that the United States did not have to maintain parity in long range aircraft with the Soviet Union, and the same argument would seem to apply to long range missiles once an adequate supply has been attained. But until that stage is reached, every effort must be made to match the Soviets in that field.

Of immediate concern is the problem of dispersal. Even before the advent of the operational ballistic missile, the vulnerability of the large base bothered strategists. Considerable doubt was expressed in many quarters concerning the ability of United States overseas bases to live if attacked by Soviet medium range bombers. Many felt it highly unlikely that any air defence could ensure an absolutely impregnable cover for these bases, and anything short of that in this age of thermo-nuclear bombs in the megaton range would be as useless as no air defence. The ballistic missile complicates the problem. Inasmuch as there is no defence as yet against the ballistic missile, there is no defence of bases within its range. The answer to the problem lies in dispersal. Many small bases widely scattered make harder targets to hit and require many more weapons to do the job. But long range bombers cannot operate from cow pastures and the logistics problem would become almost impossible.

The ballistic missile, especially the solid-fuel missile, would seem to be the answer to the dispersionists' prayers. The Air Force Minute-Man concept of solid-fuel missiles set in concrete underground shelters seems made to order for widely dispersed missiles in well-hardened sites. The Navy's nuclear submarine firing the *Polaris* solid-fuel missiles is dispersal *par excellence*.

The fundamental core of deterrence lies in the threat it poses to the population centres and industries of both powers. No matter how much destruction the enemy can wreak upon the cities and industries of the opponent, he cannot do this in any comfort as long as the opponent has his reprisal force intact. To get down to the concrete case, as long as the United States SAC is still capable of launching a reprisal attack on the Soviet Union it would be suicidal for the Soviets to attack other targets. Barring a new technological break-through which would give the Soviets a 90 to 100 per cent effective air defence against bombers, the only chance of eliminating the reprisal threat would be to destroy an overwhelming proportion of SAC's striking power while it was still on the ground. It is true that accurate long range and intermediate range ballistic missiles make this more feasible than it would be with aircraft that could be picked up some distance out by radar. But for the time being the effectiveness of SAC operating from advanced bases more or less balances out any advantage the Soviets may have in missiles.

An equally hard task faces the planners in evaluating the capabilities of their aircraft versus the effectiveness of new missile systems. The old complaint that soldiers plan the next war with the concepts of the war before the last one is certainly not true of all military planners today. Ever since Douhet's doctrine of victory by air power alone, a doctrine proposed at the time when the aeroplane was hardly capable of destroying the tents of a command headquarters on a bright and sunny day, there has always been a group of devoted 'futurists' who 'often evaluate future expected capabilities of a new weapon system within the present-day framework, with everything except their new weapon system remaining at today's state of development'.[1] The problems facing the strategist since the long range ballistic missile emerged from the realm of science fiction into an actual piece of military hardware are therefore doubly complex:

[1] Colonel Alexander Sheridan, *Impact of the Ballistic Missile on Warfare*, Air University Quarterly Review, Summer, 1957, p. 121.

the capabilities of the new weapon system must not be overestimated as the 'futurists' tend to do, and at the same time the chant of the old soldiers that there will always be a man in the foxhole must not lead to a complacent view that the new weapon is just a new-fangled piece of artillery. When a missile can do a job more efficiently at a cost not out of reason, then the planner must make the substitution. But the planner must be sure that the missile can actually do the job, and not be swayed by a group of enthusiasts who are talking about its future potentialities.

One of the dilemmas of today for the West is the subject of limited wars. Much has been written on this topic and it is beyond the scope of this chapter to go into any detail on such a controversial matter. Furthermore, the advent of the operational long range ballistic missile will not greatly change the strategic problems involved. The main problem is whether the West is to be committed solely to a strategy of massive retaliation, that is, nuclear weapons delivered by bomber and missile, or to a major nuclear deterrent force supplemented by more flexible forces armed with both conventional and 'miniaturised' nuclear tactical weapons. The utilisation of strategic bombers in limited wars often may be impracticable and inadvisable. But ICBM ballistic missiles may be even more difficult to utilise in limited wars although this may not be true with shorter range missiles. Therefore, if the West relies more and more on ballistic missiles, costly armaments that they are, there may be a tendency to cut even further into the type of flexible forces that would be most useful in conflicts of a limited nature. Massive retaliation, which has never been a very convincing threat against limited wars, will become even less convincing if undertaken against a power that has large quantities of ICBMs zeroed in on the retaliating power's own cities. At this point of mutual deterrence, surface forces, perhaps armed with small nuclear weapons and supported by tactical air forces and short range missiles, could, conceivably, engage in limited local wars of considerable duration. Bluff and counter-bluff in a cosmic poker game of this type would require that statesmen have iron nerves and that military forces possess weapon systems which allow the strategists the greatest freedom of action. What may rob strategists and statesmen alike of freedom of action is the sober realisation that organised war in the face of the large-scale use of atomic weapons, either long or short range, cannot last for long.

CHAPTER 6

LONG RANGE AIR ATTACK

Air Chief Marshal Sir Phillip Joubert

WESTERN MILITARY AUTHORITIES have always had to speculate substantially about Russia's power in the air from the Kaiser's war, in which many Russian fliers became very good pilots, right up to the present day. The establishment of the Soviet Communist state has prevented complete documentation of the subject, for many who might have written on Soviet air affairs have been liquidated and the most enthusiastic authors who have survived have been scarcely encouraged to write a straightforward account.

It is, however, very safe to make the guess that in the First World War the Russian Air Forces were subordinated to the Army and its requirements almost throughout the fighting. Strategically and geographically the Tsar's government and its successor, the Soviet Union, were bound to put the emphasis on tactical air power. Though from the days of Peter the Great, Russia had flirted with the idea of becoming a great sea-power, her preoccupations with the strategy and tactics of the land campaigns that faced her imposed this policy. It was also unlikely that the naval air arm would make much progress. Russia's clash in the early twentieth century with an island power, Japan, had brought her maritime pretensions to nothing.

After the First World War, with the new air developments taking place in other countries, it would have been natural for the more advanced military thinkers of the Soviet Union to stray from the narrow path of close co-operation with the army and the navy. It has been suggested that the great purge of 1937–8, when over half the officer corps died, led to the promotion of a number of officers with more advanced views. But the only new air doctrine that seems to have emerged was related to the support of artillery and tanks. An article in a British technical magazine written in 1948, with all the appearance of the authority of a Soviet staff officer, confirms that in the Hitler war the Russian Air Forces were little more than a form of medium range artillery used to promote the advance and add to the protection of the land forces. Inevitably the Russian Air Forces played an ancillary role to the huge armies which the available manpower, stupid but tough, put at the disposal of the Soviet High Command. Douhet's theories of the employment of long range, strategic, independent air power, though they found a faint echo in the minds of some of the more intelligent of Russia's aircraft designers and thinkers, could hardly survive against the weight of Red Army military opinion.

Beaten to the ground in the first months of the German attack in 1941, Russian military aviation slowly recovered. Factories were moved into the depths of Russian territory and the national toughness and patriotism did the rest. But no effective long range air bombardment of German cities was launched from the eastern front, and none of the advanced techniques of air navigation that were the foundation of success in the west touched more than the fringe of Russian military interest.

During the Second World War the Russian Air Force had little real conception of the problems of air defence of vital targets and of radio counter-measures. But the Russians are not fools. They are, these days, experts in radio jamming and it is more than probable that they have already developed an effective system of radio counter-measures. If war presents these problems in an acute form the same sort of surprise that the *Sputnik* sprang on the West might well occur. The present situation with which the West is faced gives every reason for thinking that this may be so.

The German angle on air fighting during operation 'Barbarossa' is interesting. A few comments appear in the books that have been written by the leaders of the *Luftwaffe*, and in the diaries of some of their junior pilots. Arrogantly, the complete defeat of the Russian Air Force is announced and afterwards the entire interest is concentrated on the battle in the west. And yet it was the bleeding to death of the German Air Force in Russia which gave Britain a vital respite from 1941 onwards. Those of us who were concerned with the air defence of our country were heartened when, after Fighter Command had fought a very successful air battle over London in the spring of 1941, the attacks against our homeland diminished. We were deceived however. It was not so much our defensive counter-measures as the fact that Hitler dared to adventure where Napoleon had failed. Not only did we get immediate relief when the attack on Russia was launched in June 1941, but never again was the *Luftwaffe* to dispose of the forces necessary to carry the air war effectively to Britain.

One of the most profound remarks made by an uneducated American general of the Civil War was to the effect that he 'who got the mostest and the soonest' to the decisive point would win the battle. Hitler thought he could achieve this against Russia. But he had not enough aircraft and his objectives were too many and too widely scattered. His aircraft were relatively short ranged and they lost themselves in the immensity of the Russian steppes. So he never achieved the necessary concentration in the air. Without complete air superiority, without the possibility of knocking out the sources of supply to the Russian armies in the field, he had no hope of success. Geography, numbers and the Russian winter were bound to defeat him.

For the reasons already stated the Soviet record of long range bomber attack from 1941 to 1945 was poor. The form of war that faced Russia was primarily a matter of land operations against Germany and the Japanese forces in Manchuria: no other power threatened her seriously. The secret understanding of 1922 between the Soviet Army and the *Reichswehr*, one of the sad results of the Treaty of Versailles, carried German facilities for the production of aircraft and pilots to the USSR. In return Soviet staff officers came to Germany. Thus German views on tactical air power, embattled in the experiences of 1914 to 1918, largely influenced Russian air policy until, in the early 1930s, Hitler's seizure of power put an end to this most unnatural honeymoon.

With the decline of German influence and the Soviet decision in 1930 to develop airborne divisions, Russian air thinking underwent a complete change. The conception of a force of long range heavy bomber-cum-transport aircraft began to emerge. Three distinct categories of bomber came into being in the Soviet Air Force; the *Sturmovik* ground attack light bomber; the *SB* medium bomber; and the *TB* heavy bomber. The latter category at first had twin-engine machines (the *TB 1*) designed by Tupolev, who has been working on Soviet heavy bomber and transport planes for about thirty years. By 1935 the Soviet Union had built a force of 300 to 400 four-engined *TB 3* planes, had formed a number of long range bomber regiments, and was pioneering long range Arctic flights from Kamchatka and northern Kolimsk over the Pole to California.

Thus five or six years before the 1939–45 war, the USSR was the only country in the world with a substantial force of four-engined bomber-type aircraft. This situation was to undergo a rapid change, due to new facts and factors.

The first and perhaps the most important of these was the desire of the Red Army to develop transport aircraft for the expanding airborne and parachute divisions. But the Soviet aircraft industry failed to produce any successful long range transport aircraft in the middle and late 1930s. It is of interest that although the Soviet Union from 1936 to 1939 despatched large numbers of fighters and medium bombers to help the Spanish Socialist Government in the Civil War, no transport planes were sent because there were none to spare. Clearly the Red Army, which had the greatest influence in Soviet defence councils, could not allow long range bomber production to flourish while transport production languished. The development of heavy bombers was further cramped by the disappointing results obtained from medium range bombers in the Spanish Civil War. Those were the days when much was hoped of the strategic heavy bomber though it was still untried in war on a large scale. In Spain the scale of air bombardment was far too small to have a decisive effect.

There were problems of engine production as well. The four-engined bomber needed a great deal of power and this was not yet available in the Soviet Union. Finally, Marshal Tuchachevski and his air chief General Alksnis, two of the major Soviet protagonists of the importance of strategic air power, were purged in the 1937–8 large-scale liquidation of military leaders and Tupolev, the doyen of Soviet heavy-bomber designers, was sent as a suspect to Siberia.

So when Germany attacked the USSR on 22nd June 1941 the Soviet Air Force had no modern long range bomber arm. There was no general tradition of air training in long range navigation and blind flying, without which (saving beam navigation and radar bombing which the USSR did not have until the early 1950s) no modern heavy bomber force can be effective in night operations. Daylight operations were not possible since the USSR had no force of long range fighters to act as escorts. The early night operations of the obsolescent *TB 3* air regiments were disastrous. General Ionov who commanded some of them was disturbed at the failure of their operations against Koenigsberg and other targets in East Prussia in the summer of 1941. One of his generals, Lieutenant-General Kopets, is reported to have committed suicide because of these failures.

In spite of these early disasters, in the spring of 1942 Stalin re-created the ADD, the long range flying command, under General Golovanov. This organisation was renamed the DA in 1946.[1] Its influence on the general war situation was trifling. It should be emphasised that, like the *Luftwaffe*, the Soviet Air Force was and is ready to use its bomber planes for large-scale emergency transport work. Indeed, the *Luftwaffe* and Soviet Air Forces can claim to have been more flexible in this dual use of bombers than British or American Air Forces.

The new ADD command of General Golavanov had a strength of about fifty regiments of some thirty planes each. But this force had only a few regiments of four-engined bombers, some of them the obsolescent *TB 3*. Some others were equipped (from 1943 onwards) with the more modern *PE 8*. This four-engined bomber designed by Petlyakov and Tupolev (the former was killed in an air crash in 1944) was similar to the *TB 7* four-engined plane which flew Molotov to Britain and the USA in 1942. It had a bomb load of about five tons for a radius action of 600–700 miles. But the bulk of the ADD bombers were twin-engined Soviet *DB 3 Fs* which, though nominally long ranged, had a poor radius of action and twin-engined American Lend-Lease Mitchell (*B 25s*). The Soviet tried to get Lend-Lease long range *B 17s*, *Flying Fortresses*, without success. The transport aircraft in the Soviet ADD were mainly twin-engined *PS 84s*, a plane similar to the *Dakota*, or perhaps the *DC 2*.

There were three good reasons why Stalin reformed the ADD in 1942. In the previous nine months the *TB 3s*, *DB 3s*, and *PS 84s* had suffered heavy losses in a futile and expensive attempt to stem the German advances on Leningrad, Moscow and Rostov. Used in this tactical role and often unescorted in daylight, these Soviet planes were bound to suffer at the hands of the *ME 109* formations. Secondly, there was the natural desire to hit back at Germany, if possible at targets on German territory. A long range bomber command was the only early prospect at the beginning of 1942. Finally, Stalin wanted an air force directly subordinated to him as Defence

[1] D stands for long range and A for aviation.

Minister, to act as a general strategic reserve, a fundamental conception of Soviet military policy. This policy endeavours to keep
divisions and aircraft in reserve under the direct control of the
Defence Ministry, and hence the Central Committee of the Communist Party. Today this is the position of Soviet long range rockets.
They are part of what is called the Commander-in-Chief's, or
General Staff, Strategic Reserve.

The Second World War long range bomber operations of the
ADD were modest enough. In the heaviest attacks they carried out
on Berlin, Bucharest, Warsaw and Koenigsberg, less than 200
bombers were used. An average bomber raid of the 1943–5 period
when the ADD was at its best used 75–100 bombers. Normally less
than 50 per cent reached the target and sometimes only 20 or
30 per cent. Although picked crews were selected for these
night operations they lacked the help of navigational radar aids.
Even in crack Guards long range bomber regiments only about
50 per cent of crews were trained and ready for night and blind
flying.

Most of the ADD resources from 1942 to 1945 were used on
tactical work in the battle zone. They ferried troops to reinforce
Stalingrad. They carried equipment and specialists to Tito's
partisan forces. They attacked targets behind the battlefront. When
these needs were met, secondary forces were available for night
attacks on Tilsit, Ploesti, Danzig, Budapest, Constanza or the targets
mentioned above.

It would be wrong to write these operations off as completely
ineffective. The *Luftwaffe* reacted sufficiently to set up a night
fighter organisation in East Prussia, Poland, Roumania and Hungary,
and so further weakened their air position on the western front.

At the end of the Second World War Stalin and his staff were
quick to realise the implications of the atomic bomb, of the heavy
damage caused by Anglo-American strategic bombing in Germany
and Japan and of the emergence of the *V2* long range rocket as a
practical weapon of war. In all the post-war fields of long range
air attack, from submarines, land-based rockets and aircraft, the
USSR has put out a maximum research and production effort in the
last decade. It is possible to forget that Stalin threatened to attack
New York with long range rockets in 1945. This he did in private
conference with his air staff. In 1957 Marshal Vershinin, Chief of

the Soviet Air Force, and Khrushchev said the same thing in public, but added the names of other US cities and NATO bases.

It is now necessary to consider the development of the main lines of Soviet strategic air attack in the twelve or thirteen years from the time of the muttered threat to the United States and the serious reality of today. The first five years from 1945 to 1950 were spent in developing and creating a force of non-jet four-engined bombers, in getting an improved *V2* rocket into series production, and in trying it out as a weapon from ocean-going submarines.[1] The standard long range bomber of the early post-war period was the four-engined *Tupolev*, copied in the main from the US *B 29 Super-fortress*. In 1944 three USAF *B 29s* force-landed at an airfield near Vladivostok and were retained by the Soviets as a priceless acquisition. Lieutenant-General Tupolev (Soviet aircraft designers have military rank) reconstructed a design from the *B 29s*, using the US planes as prototype models, except for wireless equipment and armament. By early 1946 this long-ranged four-engined bomber was in large-scale production near Moscow, Kazan, Kiev, Novosibirsk and Tashkent. The Soviet-built engines were virtual copies of the US Wright *Cyclone* 2,200 hp radial engines. Soviet 12·7 mm guns replaced the USAAF half-inch Brownings and the Soviets preferred their own design of four-bladed air-screws. But it was the legacy of the *B 29* which enabled the ADD to have a force of several hundred of these machines by the outbreak of the Korean War.

But the Soviet *TU 4*, as it was called, was only a medium bomber in terms of global strategy and the atomic age. It had a maximum radius of action of less than 1,500 miles, although more powerful 3,000 hp *Svetsov* radial engines were fitted later, which increased the range and the bomb load. But in the summer of 1950 when the Korean war began the Soviet Union had no long range bomber worthy of its atomic bomb. The USSR had acquired the blue-prints and one prototype of a *Luftwaffe Junkers* four-jet bomber, but Ilyushin's attempt to build long range jet bombers in the first five years after the war had been a failure. No doubt this is one of the reasons there was great emphasis on the long range rockets. Intensive Soviet firing trials were reported in the Baltic in 1950 in which *V2*

---

[1] It was during this time that the Soviets really began to consider the implications of strategic sea power. They had seen sea power help to win two wars and thus were much impressed.

type improved rockets were also being fired from submarines. Despite the priority for building heavy strategic bombers, the development of Arctic bases and flight refuelling, the Soviet ADD constituted no threat to the USA in 1950, and because of its non-jet obsolescent bomber force, only a secondary long range threat to Europe. The vulnerability of the American *B 29s* in Korea to resolute fighter attack was a measure of what would happen to Soviet *TU 4s* in any air conflict with the West.

The chief reason why the USSR failed to develop a heavy jet bomber force by 1950 and in the year or so that followed was the lack of a suitably powerful jet engine to fit in the new aircraft. When the *MIG 15* fighter was first flown in 1947 and the design plans called for a jet engine with some 4,000–5,000 lb static thrust, the Soviet Union had to turn to the Rolls Royce *Nenes* which they purchased from Britain to give them the thrust that was called for. It was a Soviet version of this British engine which powered the first *MIG 15* Chinese-flown air regiments on the Korean front. But to engine the *Ilyushin* and *Tupolev* heavier jet planes which they were planning to make at the outbreak of the Korean War called for jets of 10,000–15,000 lb static thrust, and the Soviet aero-engine industry was incapable of meeting this requirement at that time. And so up to the end of 1953 the Soviet Air Force accumulated a stock-pile of atomic bombs for a force of obsolescent medium bombers.

Nevertheless, in the three years of the Korean War Soviet strategic attack regiments expanded rapidly. Early in 1953 General Nathan Twining, then United States Air Force Chief of Staff, estimated the Soviet long range bomber force at about 1,000 obsolescent *Tupolev* four-engined non-jets. However, there were all the signs that before long the USSR would have a genuine strategic jet bomber force skilled in flight refuelling, capable of carrying hydrogen as well as atomic bombs, and of reaching most North American target areas and returning to base. Mikulin, Svetzov, and Klimov combined their jet engine experience and it was Mikulin's co-axial jet engine design which was put into large-scale production to power the new *Tupolev* and *Ilyushin* jet bombers. The static thrust achieved by Mikulin's engines increased to over 10,000 lb and by 1954 to 15,000 lb or more. The USSR was now making as powerful jet engines as any other country in the world. It was producing hydrogen bombs and test-firing successfully two-stage rockets. It was clear by then that

Western supremacy in strategic air attack was potentially threatened once the USSR began to build the new jet bombers in large numbers.

And, sure enough, in 1954 came the evidence that the USSR was engaged in series production of two long-ranged four-jet bombers and a twin-jet medium range bomber. At the same time she was developing a fleet of 'in flight refuelling' tankers and expanding the airfield and dispersal facilities for ADD bombers in the Arctic regions which provide the USSR with her shortest air route to North America.

The medium-ranged twin-engined bomber was a Tupolev jet design which NATO have dubbed the *Badger*. The average production of these planes has been estimated variously at ten to twenty-five a month over the last two or three years. This un-certainty has been due in part to the emergence of a civil version of it, the *TU 104* passenger airliner, which has now been in airline service with AEROFLOT for two or three years. The *TU 104* has similar (but derated) engines and its wings, and in part its fuselage, stem from its military counterpart the *TU 16* or *Badger*. The military engines of Mikulin design have a rating of 15,000–18,000 lb static thrust. The radius of action of the *Badger* is about 1,500 miles at a maximum speed of about 600–625 mph and a cruising speed of about 525 mph. It is the bomber weapon the Soviet would have used in their pre-IRBM rocket period to attack US air bases in the Middle East, North Africa, Britain and Japan. By the end of 1957 the Soviet long range bomber force was estimated to have between 350 and 500 of these, according to various US and British estimates, i.e. much fewer than the US and British equivalent bombers. But the production of Soviet IRBMs anticipated in 1955 and 1956, and confirmed by British and American official statements in 1957 (e.g. Mr Duncan Sandys' speech on the British White Paper on Defence early in 1957), indicate that these aircraft are considered obsolescent. The Soviet decision in 1956 to undertake large-scale production of the *TU 104*, not only for Russia's own civil airlines but for those of Czechoslovakia, Poland and China, is a firm indication that the *TU 16* is being phased out of the ADD command and that reliance is being placed more and more on the Soviet atomic war-headed IRBMs such as the *J 2* and *J 3*, with a range of up to 1,500 miles. These weapons appear to be considered the chief means of attack on

Western bomber or rocket bases in Europe and the Middle East and bases in and near Japan.

A similar but later switch from bomber production to transport production has been noted in the case of the two other Soviet bombers at present intended to carry the hydrogen or other bombs to North American targets. These bombers are called the *Bear*, a four-jet turbo-prop bomber and the *Bison*, a four turbo-jet bomber. Both have been designed by Tupolev with the help of Myasishchev, Ilyushin, Antonov and other heavy-plane designers. The turbo-prop engines of the *Bear* are attributed to the Soviet engineer Kutznetsov and members of his staff, and are claimed to give 12,000 lb shaft-horse-power each. If they do, they are the most powerful engines of their type in use anywhere. The *Bear* has a radius of action of over 4,000 miles and a maximum bomb load of over ten tons. Its top speed is probably about 500 mph, perhaps a little less. It was the first Soviet jet bomber with the ability to drop a hydrogen bomb on any target in North America. It could on the return journey rendezvous over fairly safe Arctic territory and be refuelled in flight. It was in service at the beginning of 1954. But because it was a turbo-prop bomber it could not be developed to achieve high subsonic or supersonic speeds. It is not surprising to learn that after 1956 it was being developed as a tanker for the faster four-jet *Bison* bomber. And in 1956–7 came the news of a civil and military transport version, the *Rossiya TU 114*. There are probably less than a hundred *Bear* bombers in the ADD, and perhaps only fifty. Its future is clearly in the field of tanker, transport and passenger operations.

The fastest of the long range jet bombers of the Soviet DA (as the ADD is now called) is the *Bison*.[1] Estimates of production since 1955 have ranged from fifteen to twenty a month. With its *Mikulin* axial jet engines giving a thrust of over 20,000 lb (probably with after-burner) the *Bison* has a top speed of about 625 mph, a radius of 3,000—4,000 miles and a bomb load of about ten tons. It is thus, broadly speaking, comparable with the US *B 52*, though it has not got quite the same range. The expansion of Soviet long range bomber bases in the Arctic in the middle of the 1950's was in preparation for the development of the new long range jet bomber air regiments equipped with the *Bison* four-jet bomber.

[1] A supersonic delta-wing bomber may soon be in service.

Flight refuelling, though not always over safe neutral areas, will give it the range to attack any target in North America, and it can carry a hydrogen or atomic bomb to its objective.

The majority of the four-jet bomber units of the Soviet long-range bomber command are based on the Arctic front, with the head-quarters near Magadan on the sea of Okhotsk. The units are under the command of General Kapitsa, but General Sudets is the Commander-in-Chief at the Moscow Headquarters. Between twenty and twenty-five new jet bomber bases are reported to have been constructed in the last few years from Murmansk in the west to Anadyr in eastern Siberia. There are new bomber bases on the Arctic islands of Novaya Zemlya, Severnaya Zemlya and Frans Josef Land, and in the Talmar peninsula. A special air transport organisation exists in the Arctic, equipped with long-ranged four-engined transport planes such as the *TU 70*, and entirely concerned with flying supplies, spares, men, fuel and equipment to the area. These cargo and troop carrying aircraft have been supplemented by turbo-prop jet *Ilyushin 18 Moskva* planes during the last year. Railway communications are being gradually improved in the area. Radar and weather stations have been added each year since 1950.

It is clear that any major bomber or rocket attack on North America would come from long range Soviet strike forces in this area. The Soviet Air Force may dispose of over 250 *Bisons* based in this Arctic region, and a figure of ten batteries of ICBMs by 1960 has been suggested by US Intelligence.

Perhaps the most difficult thing to estimate is when and if the Soviet four-jet bombers will be replaced by the new Soviet Inter-continental Ballistic Missiles, the *T 3* and *T 4*, which are credited with ranges of up to 5,000 miles. The Soviet Union claims to have successfully test-fired one of these missiles in the summer of 1957. Within two or three months Bulganin and Khrushchev and their Air Chief Marshal Vershinin were saying that the long range bomber was obsolescent, and that the Soviet Union could destroy all Western cities and air bases with her long range nuclear and thermo-nuclear rockets. Even allowing for maximum speed in Soviet production methods, the above statements could not have made sense when the Soviet leaders first made them in the autumn of 1957. And, even in the future, it is doubtful if the Soviet long range bomber forces will be entirely eliminated by the use of ICBMs which are expected to be available to Soviet armed forces in large numbers between now and 1960. Indeed, it is most unlikely, for one of the main targets for Soviet long range bomber attack in any future global conflict would be the US atomic-engined submarines of the *Nautilus* class firing atomic or thermo-nuclear rocket intermediate ranged missiles such as the *Polaris* and US aircraft carriers from which atomic and hydrogen bombers can be flown.

These mobile ship targets cannot be dealt with by long range rocket attack and may call for a bomber-reconnaissance technique such as that used by the *Luftwaffe*'s Focke-Wulf *Condors* against Allied shipping, or by RAF Coastal Command against German U-boats in Second World War. It is a matter for speculation both in Washington and Moscow as to whether specially trained anti-shipping crews flying subsonic jet bombers are the best means of future attack on Western ships, or whether naval air squadrons fitted with *Beriev* jet-engined flying boats will be used for the purpose.

Because of her present lead in IRBMs and ICBMs, her spurt in the production of long range jet bombers in the early 1950s, her development of rocket-firing ocean-going submarines, and her resources for making the atomic and thermo-nuclear warheads she needs, the USSR has negatived the advantages in strategic air attack that the West enjoyed over them in the first five or ten years after the Second World War.

The Chairman of the US Joint Committee on Atomic Energy stated in 1954 that Russia would 'in three or four years from now be able to launch a saturation attack on our country. She possesses all four of the main ingredients of a strong atomic warfare pro-gramme: adequate material resources, including uranium, adequate scientific competence and adequate technological and productional capacity.' For these reasons it is possible to say that the existing air defence plans of Britain, Canada, the United States and Western Europe are obsolescent. The most modern jet and rocket fighters and their air to air missiles, like the ground to air missiles, were never intended to defend against long range rocket attack. While the ground to air guided missiles such as the US *Nike*, or the British *Thunderbird* and *Bloodhound* will be effective against Russian bombers, something faster and more powerful will be needed to intercept Soviet intermediate range rockets or ICBMs.

It seems that during the last five years the Soviets have made such progress in their development of airpower that at the moment they are equal to the West in the air. Later they may gain strategic air superiority.

Is there anything which can be done to limit the Soviet lead in intercontinental missile striking power? Scientists both in Britain and America consider that there is a good chance of being able to plot the path of this weapon and to destroy it with an anti-missile missile. The Jodrell Bank radio telescope plotted the path of the Russian satellites with great efficiency.

There seemed no practical defence in prospect against the German *V2s* in 1944 and 1945, because the problem could not be solved with the means available at the time. Today we are allowed a breathing space in which to solve the newer and more serious problem. It is not yet solved and so the deterrent power of our bomber, that can carry the H-bomb, is seriously threatened by long range rocket attack. To meet this difficulty dispersal and mobility must not be mere text-book expressions. The West must use all the facilities of its advanced bases in Europe and elsewhere, so that IRBMs can to some extent offset the Soviet developments of ICBMs. In addition, atomic and thermo-nuclear strategic bomber units must certainly be dispersed by flights over distances of hundreds of miles. At the moment strategic squadrons are crowded into single bases. Is not this an outmoded conception? The right distribution of our air forces would be to base part of the British V-bomber force in Canada, whence it could carry out frequent operational training flights to Australia. The same could be true of US strategic bombers, and the carrier-based air forces that can hide, for a while at least, in the ocean mists. It could be made a virtually insoluble problem for Soviet Intelligence to have an up-to-date picture of the location of Western long range retaliatory forces if they were mobile and dispersed to the maximum. Until the balance of strategic air power is restored, this dispersal might well be a major plank in Western air policy.

Turning our eyes from the skies to the depths of the sea, it is at once apparent that the progress Russia has made in creating a very large submarine force, with its potentialities for high speed, long periods at depth, and armed with the IRBM, is perhaps the most serious threat to Western security.

By making use of designs that the Germans were perfecting in 1945, Russia has submarines that can achieve twenty knots while submerged, and maintain this speed for considerable distances.

Tremendous Soviet activity is now going on in these vessels: activity which threatens the West far more than the aerial earth satellite. Submarine craft may well replace surface fleets in the future and intermediate range ballistic missiles can be delivered in force by these fleets. At present the range of the Soviet *Komet* IRBM is believed to be about 500 miles, but a later version can carry a distance of 1,500 miles.

But before these missiles can be discharged effectively it must be possible for submarines to navigate with accuracy, even when continuously submerged. At present it will be generally agreed that nobody among the Allies can reliably claim to know the ocean bed sufficiently well for this purpose. That is to say that no allied submarine commander yet possesses maps which will guide him to a point, fathoms deep in the ocean, from which he can direct accurate fire at a land target many hundred miles away. But the Russian Naval Staff may already be on the way to possessing this information.

Fortunately the Russians are not alone in this line of submarine research. The West is planning the use of submarine merchant vessels, as well as rocket-firing submarines, in the not so remote future. These ships have great advantages over the ordinary surface vessel: higher speed, greater stability, greater carrying power and, particularly, the use of atomic energy to drive them.

But the crux of this situation is the urgent need for accurate maps of the sea-beds of the oceans of the world. Missile or freight carrying submarines will have to know that no submarine volcano or uncharted reef lies between them and their destination. Apart from a large number of soundings carried out by survey ships in the past, the true shape of the sea-floor of the principal oceans is barely known.

It is very likely that while the *Sputnik* holds our attention, Russia's submarine fleet is busily engaged in this work of mapping the bottom of the seas. The 'Schnorkel' air breathing device enables it to remain submerged for weeks at a time. It is even possible to coat this *Schnorkel*, where it protrudes from the water, with a radar absorbing material that greatly reduces the response and so provides an additional handicap to the search aircraft or long range radar equipment.

There have been a number of well authenticated reports of Soviet submarine activity in waters where trade routes converge. The most recent comes from the west coast of Canada, where two unidentified U-boats are supposed to have been refuelled by a Russian cargo tanker and where rumour suggests that they are planting submarine 'light-houses' that emit radio signals.

The Russians have always been good chess players. One of the attributes of a master of the game is the ability to build up attack into an obvious threat while, undetected, preparing the death blow that will be administered later. Something like this is going on in the vast game of power politics now being played between the East and West.

Admirals are very vocal on the subject of Russian submarine strength, with emphasis on atomic power units. But the problem is even more serious than the admirals believe. Underwater mapping will add to the ability of an enemy submarine to navigate successfully in protected waters. The intermediate range ballistic missile, with a range of 1,500 miles, can unquestionably be fired from under water. A vessel so armed and able to position itself accurately while hidden in the depths, has every large town in Britain, and a very large proportion of those in America, entirely at its mercy. The accuracy of the IRBM is good, particularly at shorter ranges of, say, 500 miles. It is by far the most dangerous weapon of all. Yet Russia, with her satellite and her intercontinental ballistic missile, has wrested our gaze from the seas and turned it upwards. Meanwhile, the quiet planning of the master stroke, that will come from under water, goes ahead, no doubt to our future discomfort.

To sum up: in the past the whole trend of thought in the Soviet Air Force has been towards the tactical support of the Army. Today, the picture has changed completely. Not only has the USSR made tremendous strides in the design and production of the most modern types of aircraft, but she has leaped ahead in long range rocketry on land and at sea, and hence in the strategic employment of air power. The advantages that the West possessed a few years ago have almost disappeared. It will need a major effort on the part of the democracies to regain the lead they have lost. They have the knowledge and skills: what they seem to lack is a purpose. It would appear to be essential that certain anti-submarine measures should be put into force at once. Patrolling of focal areas by air and sea forces is the first step needed. This should be followed by research into detection devices, the range of which must be measured in miles and not, as now, in yards. The air forces and navies of the West must be supplied with adequate numbers of anti-submarine aircraft and vessels. Lastly, research into all aspects of the problem presented by this new threat must be intensified.

CHAPTER 7

STRATEGIC AIR DEFENCE

Asher Lee

SOVIET AIR POLICY in nearly all its aspects emerges from military factors which are common considerations for all major air powers. There is a view that this or that aspect of the Kremlin military policy is Stalinist, Leninist, or Marxist. But the main elements that constitute the amalgam of Soviet air strategy are also those which go to make the air strategy of the Western powers. They are the geography of the USSR, the potential air threat to its territories, the air weapon developments in the countries of its likely opponents, the competing technical and economic requirements of the Soviet military machine, and, to a much less extent than in the West, the competing views of its military and political leaders.

Until the end of the Second World War there was no real threat to the Soviet Union of a strategic long range bomber or rocket attack of any magnitude. Neither Germany nor Japan had built a really substantial force of long range bombers and once these two powers were heavily committed to the wars in Europe and the Pacific, it was clear that Britain and the United States would absorb most of the bomber attack which Germany and Japan could administer. It was also clear that the *Wehrmacht*'s balance of air power would have to be spent in supporting the German armies in their hard battles on the central and east European fronts. The Soviet High Command had early and significant evidence of the strict limitations of the German long range air attack potential within a month of the outbreak of the war. In order to attack Moscow in July and August 1941, the *Luftwaffe* had to draw not only on its twin-engined *Junker* and *Heinkel* bombers engaged against the Russian Army on the northern and southern fronts, but bomber units had to be withdrawn from France. And yet, despite this concentration of forces, after about six night attacks

on the Soviet capital, with average raiding strengths of 120 to 150
twin-engine bombers, the attacks had to be called off, because of
the need to redeploy all available *Luftwaffe* bomber forces on the
more important job of giving tactical support to the *Wehrmacht*
ground divisions. A few months later came Pearl Harbour, and
with the entry of Japan and USA into the Second World War, the
need of the Soviet Air Force to build up large scale strategic air
defence forces was virtually ended.

It is perhaps worth considering some of the problems which faced
the Soviet Air Force in building up her air defences against long
range air attack during the Second World War, for some of them
persisted into the post-war period, and explain why the PVO
command[1] was slow to gain strength and recognition in the Soviet
armed forces even in the decade after the war. Indeed it was not
until 1955 that the Kremlin took the decision to form a really
strong independent anti-aircraft air command under Marshal
Biryuzov and to give it a status equal to the other Soviet major air
arms, with control over its own radar units, fighter squadrons, and
guided missile and artillery units.

The most severe limitation on the development of the PVO in
the Second World War has often been stressed. It was the strong
Soviet emphasis on tactical air power to support the army in its
ground battles and the policy of concentrating the best artillery
and artillerymen to support the Soviet armies in the field. While
the *Luftwaffe* controlled much of the German artillery *élite* resources
and could divert them to air defence or ground support as required,
the best Soviet artillery resources were bound up in Red Army
ground battles. The same was true of Soviet single-engined fighter
resources. The first year of air fighting on the eastern front had
shown that the German *Messerschmitt 109* single-seater fighter was
technically superior to the *I 15* and *I 16* Soviet machines and the
early *MIG* and *YAK* fighters. In 1942 the emergence of the *Luftwaffe*'s
FW 190 fighter, one of the best fighters in the Second World War,
created a further threat to the Soviet Air Force and its prospects of
securing and maintaining local air superiority in the battle-zones.
And so the new *YAK 9*, *YAK 3* and *Lavochkin 5* fighters had to be
sent as quickly as possible to the fighter regiments in the tactical
air divisions engaged in the battles against German tanks, artillery

[1] PVO stands for anti-aircraft defence.

and ground troops so as to ensure local air superiority over the battle zones for the Soviet armed forces.

Perhaps even more important: the Soviet Air Force lacked a long range early warning system without which modern strategic air defence can be powerless. The Battle of Britain had underlined the vital role which radar has to play in this aspect of air warfare. The disaster at Pearl Harbour had provided an even more dramatic example of the crucial importance of radar. Unhappily for the United States it was a negative example. Soviet electronics, including radar, was well behind German, British and American and Japanese development in the Second World War. Soviet early warning methods then in use have been graphically described by French fighter pilots who fought alongside Soviet air units in the German-Soviet War.[1] There was a kind of observer corps in the Soviet PVO and sometimes it worked effectively. In the night attacks on Moscow for instance when the *Luftwaffe* returned to the same target each time, Soviet sound detectors were of value. But in the 1944 surprise attack on the Soviet air base at Poltawa by German *Heinkel* bombers, the US *Flying Fortresses B 17* bombers which were based there suffered heavy casualties because Soviet anti-aircraft guns fired blindly into the night air and the *Petlyakov* night fighters had no ground-control or airborne radar equipment to beam them onto the oncoming raiders. In the battle zone itself, local bells were sometimes rung when enemy aircraft were diving to the attack and these were often the only early warnings available for fighter take-off.

But the Soviet Air Force maintained the framework of the PVO in the Second World War. The *Luftwaffe* attacks on Moscow had been a useful warning of the inadequacy of Soviet Air Defence. When the attacks came in the summer of 1941, the Kremlin rushed some of its best artillery units to defend the Soviet capital and produced one of the greatest concentrations of anti-aircraft fire ever assembled to protect one target area. The heavy barrages certainly deterred the weary German bomber crews and reduced the damage they caused. These attacks also stimulated the Kremlin to produce a few *PE 2* night fighter squadrons and to experiment later with anti-aircraft rocket units. But the lack of blind-flying training and radar equipment made Soviet night fighters ineffectual.

[1] See, for instance, Richard Sauvage's *Un du Normandie Niemen.*

Their poor performances at Poltawa in defence of US bombers was probably a fair reflection of their general fighting capacity. Strategically the USSR was pathetically unprotected from heavy bomber attack in the Second World War for most areas of the Soviet Union were entirely without means of local air defence. Aircraft and tank factories were a general exception to this rule.

In the event, strategic air defence was a vital aspect of modern air warfare in which the USSR had virtually no experience in the Second World War. The umbrella of British and American air power enabled the Soviet Air Force to neglect this air arm without any great danger to the homeland, although Russia's wide open spaces would have provided easy runs for a modern strategic bomber force unopposed by a long range radar early warning system. But at the end of the Second World War the world strategic situation called for a major re-orientation of Soviet air policy. For the first time in Soviet history the Kremlin planners had to consider the possibility of defending the USSR against atomic bomber attack which could wreak much greater devastation than the damage inflicted on Germany and Japan in the Second World War. Soviet staff officers who visited these two countries in 1945 reported in documented detail on the damage and dislocation which American and British bombers had inflicted. It was clear that Russia had now to look urgently to her strategic air defences. She was helped by two major factors in the early post-war period: the disarmament policies of the Western Powers which cut their long range bomber forces to ribbons and the enormous technical inheritance in strategic air defence equipment which she acquired from Germany. The great speed with which the Soviet Air Force built up a radar early warning network and a large force of defensive jet fighters in the five years after the Second World War was the best sign that, for the first time in her history, the USSR was looking seriously at the problem of strategic air defence. The technical development of these jet fighters is dealt with in Chapter 8.

Thanks to help from British and German jet engine designers of Rolls Royce, Junkers, and the Brandenburg Motorenwerke, the Soviet Air Force was technically level with the West in its jet fighter aircraft performance by the early 1950s, and has maintained approximate parity ever since. But the development of a long range early warning system and of airborne and ground radar aids to help

The *Yak 25*, a subsonic all-weather jet fighter which will soon be replaced by a supersonic twin jet

The *Sukhoi* delta wing fighter, a recent supersonic addition

The *Mig 19*, the first supersonic fighter in general use

The *Bison* long range
jet bomber, which will
soon be replaced by a
supersonic bomber

The *Tupolev 20* ('*Bear*')
which is becoming ob-
solescent

The *Tu 16* bomber, a
forerunner of the *Tu 104*
jet air liner

both day and night fighting was an even more crucial requirement. In this field, electronics, the Soviet technical debt to Germany is a particularly heavy one.

Although Germany had been behind Britain in developing an early warning radar system in the early part of the Second World War, by 1945 she had in operational use nearly all forms of modern radar equipment both for guiding night fighters and night bombers, for providing long range beam guided navigation, and for giving long range warning of the approach of enemy planes. Of these various electronic assets, the Soviet Air Force acquired a considerable number of samples of earlier warning German radar such as the *Wurzburg* and *Freya* apparatus. These had been in production in East German and Polish factories which could not be evacuated in time in the retreat of 1945. In addition trained personnel from the German Air Force signals organisation which had manned the early warning systems in Roumania, Hungary, and Poland and East Prussia were pruned out from the hordes of German prisoners of war and sent to train Soviet personnel at Leningrad, Kiev, Riga, Moscow and elsewhere in the art of assessing the meaning of radar blips on cathode ray tubes. At the same time, hundreds of radar technicians from the firms of Siemens Telefunken and Askania, which had moved their factories eastwards between 1943 and 1945 to avoid the devastation of Anglo-American bomber attack, were now moved farther east to Soviet electronic factories to help design, check and produce the first models of Soviet radar equipment. Air Marshal Kliment Vershinin, then (and now) Commander-in-Chief of the Soviet Air Force, was fully alive to the urgent need to develop an early warning system as a vital preliminary to a real Soviet strategic air defence system. By 1946, the first radar early warning units were being trained and set up to give long range warning of the approach of unfriendly planes along the Baltic coasts or over the frontiers of central and eastern Europe. By the outbreak of the Korean War, there was a skeleton radar organisation in the Far East along the coast lines of the Maritime Provinces near Vladivostok and farther north in the Magadan region opposite Alaska. The Soviet General Staff knew that it would take years, perhaps a decade, to man, train and equip a nation-wide radar organisation which could provide the vital early warning defence in depth, which became more essential as the US stock-pile of atomic bombs grew.

E

That the Soviet equipment was manned by skilled operators is proved by the successful interceptions of Polish and Czech planes trying to escape to the West. That the system was not watertight (as indeed no early warning system can be) was shown by the planes that avoided the radar scanners and landed in Austria or Denmark to make good their escapes.

But it was the Korean War itself which provided the first real, large-scale test under operational conditions of Soviet manufactured early warning radar equipment and the Soviet signals personnel who used it. On the whole, they came out of that campaign with enhanced experience and reputation. If the *MIG 15s*, supplied in thousands to the Chinese Communist Air Force, did not gain much glory in combat against United States *Sabres*, this was mainly due to the superior operational training and the higher pilot qualities of the United Nations flying personnel. But Soviet radar did give the Chinese and North Koreans adequate and consistent early warning of the approach of UN bomber and fighter planes, both by day and night, over a period of three years: a warning which enabled the Communist fighter air units to be airborne in time and frequently to reach an advantageous tactical height permitting the *MIG 15* fighters to dive out of the sun on their US and British opponents. What was lacking in the Korean campaign on the Communist side was two vital pieces of radar equipment which showed clearly that the Soviet still had a great electronic leeway to make up. These were ground controlled and airborne radar to help night fighter interception or daylight fighter interception, and radar gun-sights, which were then so important for automatic firing in the high speed fighter combats of the jet age. Finally it was interesting to see that none of the German defensive guided ground to air missiles: the *Wasserfall*, the *Schmetterling* or the *Rheintochter*, which had been part of the vast Soviet air booty taken from Germany between 1945 and 1949, had reached the operational stage in the Korean War. If they had, they would surely have been tested to the maximum under combat conditions. The Spanish Civil War had been made the testing ground of Soviet, German and Italian air equipment prior to the Second World War. In the main it was a test of tactical air weapons, of fighters, dive bombers and light and medium bombers. But for the USSR, the Korean War provided a major opportunity to test some of its weapons of strategic air defence. We can be certain that if the batteries of guided missiles had been ready and if the *MIG 15s* could have had radar gun-sights and the German radar *Lichtenstein* and *Naxos* aids to night fighting had been ready for use, these would all have played a prominent part in the Korean War between 1950 and 1953.

Thus although much had been achieved to develop a Soviet strategic air defence system by the end of the Korean War, much remained to be done. With the *MIG 15* and *MIG 17* the Soviet Air Force had achieved technical parity with the West in defensive jet fighters. It was to maintain this position, broadly speaking, in the supersonic age of the next five years with the *MIG 19* fighter and its successors the *MIG 21*, the *MIG 23* and *Sukhoi* delta wing fighters which are in the 1,500–2,000 mph class and have rocket engines to give superior performance at high altitudes, radar gun-sights, air to air guided missiles and airborne radar. But the Kremlin knew that it would take years to develop a complete radar early warning defence organisation in depth covering about one fifth of the world and they realised that the ground launched defensive guided rocket might soon be taking precedence over the jet fighter as a key element in local air defence. Especially was this true for the defence of their growing long range jet bomber and rocket bases in the Arctic areas, where much of the long range atomic and thermo-nuclear hitting power of the Soviet Union has been concentrated in the past few years.

The Soviet debt to German scientists and engineers in the field of defensive guided missiles is referred to in detail in Chapter 15. Technical details of some of the German strategic defensive rockets are given, but some further elaboration of the importance of this aspect of the *Luftwaffe* legacy is perhaps called for. The German rocket defensive missiles such as *Rheintochter, Wasserfall, Feuerlilie,* the *HS 298, Taifun,* and *Schmetterling* gave the Soviet Air Force almost immediate post-war technical parity with the West in this weapons field, for in 1945 no country in the world had had any substantial operational experience in the use of defensive guided weapons, though both British and US gunners had successfully fired anti-aircraft shells fitted with radar proximity fuses in the air defence campaigns against the German V-bombs and the Japanese *Kamikazi* suicide attacks on shipping. The most advanced of these German rocket defence missiles was the *Schmetterling*, a ground-launched radar guided weapon with a range of about twenty miles, a ceiling of about 50,000 feet, and a top speed of about 625 mph. Clearly, by current standards, this is an obsolescent weapon, but the point was that the Soviet authorities inherited from German resources, with little or no research effort on their own part, all the raw materials required to develop large-scale production of defensive guided rocket weapons including suitable propellants, rocket designs, an infra-red detection system, an operational proximity fuse, an air to air guided weapon (the *HS 298*) and finally the trained factory personnel to manufacture gyroscopes, radar instruments and guidance mechanisms. In this area of modern air defence the USSR certainly owes its flying post-war start to German invention and skill.

Thus in all the main fields of strategic air defence weapons, the Soviet air debt to Germany in the first ten years after the Second World War was most marked. The first generation of jet fighter planes such as the *YAK 15*, the early warning radar equipment, the radar guidance of fighter planes both from the ground and in the air, the prototypes of most of the first experimental ground to air and air to air guided weapons, these are what the USSR owes in whole or in part to German scientific and technical engineering genius. But it naturally took many years to profit to the full from German tutelage. There were Soviet factory and air force technicians to train, German equipment to be adapted to Soviet aircraft and rocket standards, new plants to be installed, many thousands of rocket and electronic specialists to be schooled in the Soviet Air Force and the Red Army. And so not surprisingly, for some years after the war, electronic equipment for the Soviet Air Force guided missiles and early warning radar continued to be made in factories in Poland, Czechoslovakia, Hungary and East Germany, especially in the latter territory.

By 1955 all the elements of a first class strategic air defence organisation were available in the Soviet Union. Thousands of highly and specially trained fighter pilots, a first class supersonic day fighter the *MIG 19*, a good subsonic radar equipped night fighter the *YAK 25*, a comprehensive radar early warning system which gave defence in depth and in particular an elaborate three-tier defence scheme from the Arctic Ocean offshore of the USSR down to the line Warsaw-Moscow-Omsk-Novosibirsk-Irkutsk-Vladivostok. In addition the first operational batteries of defensive ground to air and air to air guided missiles were coming into service. Fairly reliable radar equipment for ground controlled interception of bombers by jet fighters was in series production. Radar gun-sights or air to air missiles were gradually coming into squadron use. But perhaps most important of all was the realisation of the Soviet High Command, prompted perhaps by the hydrogen bomb, that more stress must be laid on strategic air defence. The PVO which had been a Cinderella department of the Soviet armed forces before and during the Second World War had now become a major military arm of the Soviet defence forces. For the first time in Soviet military history anti-aircraft defence became a separate independent service, equal in status, for instance, to the tactical air force or the long range air command. Marshal Biryuzov, its present Commander-in-Chief, is a deputy to the Defence Minister, Marshal Malinovski. He held this same high position in the Kremlin in the days of Defence Minister Marshal Zhukov. The new PVO has roughly half a million *élite* and well-trained personnel, a force of over 10,000 radar guided anti-aircraft guns and dozens of batteries of ground-launched guided missiles which will probably increase to hundreds in the next few years. There are more than twenty regional PVO commands each under an Army or Air Force general spread all over the USSR. In the Arctic north, there are anti-aircraft PVO headquarters near Murmansk, in the Taimyr peninsula and further east in Kolimsk and the Kamchatka peninsula. There are also regional commands near Leningrad and Moscow, in the Crimea, at Baku, Astrakhan, Omsk, Stalinabad, Alma Ata and in the Soviet eastern areas of Ayan, Komsomolsk and Vladivostok.

Although Biryuzov had only limited operational experience in the Second World War, he is, nowadays, a figure of considerable standing in Soviet military circles. In the early years of the Second World War he was an artillery commander with the Far Eastern Air and Land Forces and was not brought into any of the campaigns of the Red Army against the *Wehrmacht* until the beginning of 1944. Then he was transferred to the White Russian front and his gunners did good work in supporting the Soviet ground advance into Poland. When the war in Europe ended, he was switched back to the Far East and took part in the brief campaign in which the Red Army destroyed the Japanese 5th Kuantoong Army in Manchuria.

He had now reached the senior rank of Colonel-General and was transferred to the artillery department of the Soviet General Staff. At the end of 1945 he was given the job of planning and re-organising the enlarged post-war PVO which he now commands. During the war, Biryuzov had got to know Lieutenant-General Nikita Khrushchev, now Premier of the USSR and chief of its Communist Party, as well as other Soviet leaders such as Bulganin and Zhukov. Biryuzov is a typical member of the Soviet military-political aristocracy, a heavily built man in his late fifties who should survive long enough to bring the new Soviet strategic air defence command to its full fruition.

Some idea of Marshal Biryuzov's energy and status can be gained from the relative independence of his new anti-aircraft command. Soviet Army control over regional defence matters has been predominant throughout the forty years of Soviet military history. But now the structure and status of some of these forty-year-old Red Army regional commands have been modified to meet the needs of the new and expanded PVO strategic air defence organisation. Previously all Soviet armed forces within a region were subordinate to the Army Commander. Now the PVO has its own independent headquarters, sometimes within the Army region, sometimes side by side with the Army organisation; for instance in Moscow and Baku. But in the northern PVO regions of the Arctic Circle where there is the vital first line of strategic air defences ranged against potential US strategic air attack across the North Pole, there are no military regions and the PVO reigns supreme side by side with the Soviet DA long range air rocket and bomber attack commands.

How effective is the PVO branch of the Soviet armed forces? Like most aspects of Soviet air and rocket power it is uneven in performance and must needs be so. The early warning system is far from complete according to an article in a Soviet military journal published in 1957 by Major-General Kornyenko, a senior staff officer. He remarked naïvely that the problems of a future war would be different from those of the 1941–5 war. He said that the USSR must establish a chain of radar stations hundreds of kilometres outside her borders in order to get fifteen to twenty minutes' warning before the development of an enemy air attack over Soviet territory. General Kornyenko, incidentally, went on to stress the importance of the signatories of the Warsaw Pact as part of the outer early warning defences of the USSR and oddly enough singled out Hungary and Albania for special mention. 'The importance for us,' he wrote, 'lies above all in the fact that these countries are watchtowers.'

Quite apart from the uncertain efficiency, for political and other reasons, of the Soviet early warning radar equipment based in Hungary and Poland, all the Soviet outer and inner strategic air defences suffer from the same kind of deficiency, the same order of problems that face NORAD, the early warning defence scheme of the North American continent which stretches from the polar DEW line down to the Mexican and Florida coasts with their 'offshore' early warning lines. Both the Soviet and North American systems have taken a decade to build. Both the USA and the USSR are confronted by the fact that, having spent billions of dollars or roubles on radar, jet fighters and defensive guided missiles from 1946 to 1956, they must now solve a whole new series of air defence problems created by the long range atomic and thermo-nuclear rockets which have made even the very latest strategic air defence weapons virtually obsolescent. The latest jet fighters and ground to air guided missiles of the world's leading air and rocket powers operate at speeds in the 1,000–3,000 mph range. The long range attack rocket operates in the 5,000–15,000 mph and even 20,000 mph range. What would the air defenders of Britain, Germany and Japan have said in the Second World War if they had been presented with a speed disadvantage of several thousands of miles an hour? But that is the position of the latest *MIG 19*, *MIG 21* and *23* jet fighters of the PVO when they face the threat of NATO's *Thors*, *Jupiters*, *Atlases*, *Titans* and the submarine-launched *Polaris*. General Earle E. Partridge, Commander in Chief of the North American Air Defence, stated a year or so ago: 'If the aggressors' weapon is the long-ranged rocket, the continent stands today almost as naked as it did in 1946 for I have no radar to detect missiles and no defence against them.' Were the Kremlin to allow Marshal Biryuzov, General Partridge's opposite number, to speak as frankly he might well have echoed the US General's statement. The USSR has built over 20,000 miles of fairly continuous air fencing around its metropolitan territory. Like the US strategic air defences it has extensive airborne, sea-borne and ground radar early warning equipment. Like NORAD it is working on the development of long range anti-missile radar with a search capacity of 2,000 miles or more.

But one must assess Soviet strategic air defence in terms of its current and immediate potential. It is true that ground to air and air to air guided missiles have been developed in the USSR at a pace comparable with that of US defence equipment in this category. The Soviet *M 100* air to air missile has recently been reported to have improved its performance from a range of about five to about eight miles and its top speed from Mach 1·5 to Mach 2·5. Thus it is, broadly speaking, the equivalent of the British *Firestreak*, the French *Matra* or the US *Sparrow*. But it would be impotent against such US weapons as the *Jupiter*, the rocket that launched the first US earth satellite, or the *Thor* which should soon be in service in western Europe or the submarine-launched *Polaris* rocket. As for the Soviet ground to air defensive guided rockets, like their US and British opposite numbers, they suffer from a major tactical weakness. They do not function well against low-flying bombers: but supersonic fighter-bombers such as the US *Super Sabre* and its successors can carry a tactical atomic bomb attacking at tree-top height. This weakness of Soviet defensive guided rockets is a serious tactical problem. The Soviet *T 7* and *T 8*, both inspired in their experimental days of the early 1950s by the German *Wasserfall* and *Rheintochter* ground to air missiles have perhaps a range of about twenty and forty miles respectively. The *T 7* which has an effective infra-red detection guidance system, is roughly on a par with its British and US opposite numbers. No doubt the range of Soviet defensive guided missiles will increase in the next few years, atomic warheads will be added and anti-missile missiles will be tested and developed: but the basic air defence problem remains. Even if Soviet long range radar detects US long range rockets soon after take-off, it will be highly vulnerable to jamming especially from submarines and so cannot know when it is to be relied upon. And even if Soviet radar were immune to jamming there are radar deception ruses apart from jamming which can undermine radar efficiency which is itself subject to recognition hazards even when unharassed by enemy counter-measures. Mr Gromyko, in a 1958 speech, referred to confusion on a radar screen between meteorite blips and rocket or bomber flights. He could have thrown in flocks of birds and friendly Soviet bombers to add to the confusion. Radar is a major contribution to all aspects of warfare in the atomic and thermo-nuclear age but it is not a watertight device, yielding one hundred per cent results. Airborne radar equipment suffers from the assaults of temperatures especially at heights of 20,000 feet and above and on the ground. It is not a push button device but depends on judgements of the human eye applied to a small dark flickering screen on which the movements of small dots and lines have to be assessed.

What then is the value of Biryuzov's PVO organization? The fighter elements are dealt with in Chapter 8 mainly from the point of view of technical performance. The crew flying standards of these planes are likely to be high and comparable with those in the US Strategic Air Command, for the PVO fighter units have the pick of Soviet fighter pilots compared with those in the tactical air regiments of the VVS. The potential weakness of ground and airborne radar equipment has been noted. Refugee Hungarian Air Force personnel and returning Germans who have test-flown the airborne radar sets have said it is not reliable in some cases, though this is a technical weakness which must occur in all air forces. Marshal Biryuzov has been striving to create a strong signals branch in the PVO. This he has almost done and has secured for it independence of the Central Signals Administration of the Soviet armed forces. He has his own 'technical regiments' which provide maintenance and transport for fighter defence airfields and defensive rocket battery sites. But even he suffers from a dichotomy in command decisions for the over-all rocket supervision in the USSR is in the hands of the KGB secret police forces under A. Shelepin and this divided command may well hinder the quick automatic reflex reaction which modern air defence demands.

To sum up, the Soviet PVO is modern, extensive and powerful in the armed forces hierarchy at the Kremlin. It could do well against the manned bombers of the RAF *V* bomber and US *B 52* squadrons. But even here it is doubtful if it can prevent catastrophic destruction, for that means the ability to shoot down three quarters or more of the raiding bombers and that it is unlikely to be able to do. This is one of the many reasons why the Kremlin despite its political outbursts must aim to keep the peace and succeed by political and economic infiltration including the generous provision of Communist-built arms. The advent of US long range rockets underlines the necessity for the Kremlin to travel at a more cautious pace in carrying out this latter policy.

CHAPTER 8

THE DEVELOPMENT OF JET FIGHTERS
AND FIGHTER BOMBERS

William Green

THAT RUSSIAN FIGHTERS have now achieved parity with those of the West is still very much a matter for conjecture, but there can be no doubt that one of the most remarkable aspects of the post-war Russian aviation scene has been the rapidity with which the Soviet aircraft industry has assimilated Western fighter design techniques and adapted them to meet Russia's particular requirements. No more outstanding example of the Russian ability to assimilate the work of others can be seen than in the *MIG 15* which, combining German aerodynamic research with a proven British turbo-jet, gained the distinction of being the first swept-wing jet combat aircraft in the world to attain quantity production status. It was undoubtedly the Soviet aircraft industry's first post-war *pièce de résistance*: not only did it signify the turning point in Russia's long struggle to attain world standard with her combat aircraft, but it revealed to the Western world that Russian military aviation had cleared the first hurdle towards technical parity. It indicated that the remarkable speed with which the Soviet aircraft industry had completed the task of copying and placing in quantity production the Boeing *B 29 Superfortress* bomber was no fluke. Russia had produced a jet fighter comparable in every way with the best that the Western world had to offer and, what is more, this advanced fighter had entered service within a year of the flight of the first prototype.

Until the début of the *MIG 15*, Russian fighters had been looked upon as crude machines about a half-decade behind their Western contemporaries. While this opinion was soundly based, it tended to give the impression that Russian fighter designers were incapable of original thought and slavishly followed Western trends. Nothing could be further from the truth, for the Russian fighter designers were displaying considerable inventiveness and design ingenuity long before the outbreak of the Second World War. Russia was, however, an industrially backward nation, and no amount of design ingenuity can completely overcome lack of production skill. The Russian fighter designer also lacked suitable power plants for his progeny, a deficiency which has bedevilled Soviet fighter development until quite recently. Nevertheless, there were several outstanding examples of design farsightedness as long ago as the mid 'thirties. For instance, before the *Messerschmitt 109* and the *Hawker Hurricane* (generally looked upon as the progenitors of the high-powered, single-seat, low-wing fighter monoplane) were preliminary drawing-board studies, the veteran Russian aircraft designer, the late Nikolai N. Polikarpov, was building the *TsKB 15* which flew for the first time on 1st September 1934. A low-wing fighter monoplane with a retractable undercarriage and a relatively high-powered liquid-cooled engine (an 840 hp Hispano-Suiza *12Y*), the *TsKB 15* was of extremely advanced conception. A second prototype, the *TsKB 19*, powered by an *M 100* engine, a Russian copy of the Hispano, was displayed at the 1936 International Aeronautical Exhibition held in Paris where Western observers severely criticised the heavy crudity of the engine, the low standard of riveting and the poorly varnished fabric covering. Nevertheless, the *TsKB 19* might have been seen as the writing on the wall; an indication of what Soviet aircraft designers might be able to do with modern production facilities. Despite the crudity of its construction, the *TsKB 19* attained a maximum speed of 304 mph, a maximum cruising speed of 273 mph, a range of 497 miles and an initial climb rate of 3,400 feet a minute. Its armament was remarkably heavy for the period, consisting of four wing-mounted 7·62 mm machine-guns and one engine-mounted 20 mm cannon. A production development of the design, the *TsKB 33*,[1] entered service with the Soviet Tactical Air Forces (VVS-RKKA) as the *I 17*, although the fighter's complex composite structure appears to have proved too much for the Soviet aircraft industry to cope with at a time when quantity was of greater importance than quality, and so only limited numbers were built.

By the late 'thirties, the Soviet High Command had learned much from the operation of Russian fighters in the Far East against Japan

---

[1] *TsKB33* was its TsAGI (or Central Aero and Hydrodynamic Institute) design number.

and in Spain against the Nationalists and their supporting Italian and German elements, and entirely new fighter requirements were drawn up. These requirements placed the accent on production and maintenance simplicity, and demanded performances comparable with those of the fighters entering service with the Western nations. Russia was short of light alloys, and wooden or composite wood and steel structures had to be used. Although the Russians were aware of stressed skin techniques, they demanded too high a standard of manufacture and maintenance. A fine finish was later to be obtained by the simple expedient of coating the wood and steel fighters with a thick layer of polish which was found to stand up remarkably well to the wear and tear of operational service.

The first of the new generation of fighters in the Second World War was the *I 22*, a neat and extremely robust little fighter monoplane of wooden construction which was flown for the first time on 30th March 1939. Developed for quantity production as the *I 301* (later redesignated *LAGG 3*), this fighter marked the début of Semyon A. Lavochkin, whose fighters were to play a leading role in the coming conflict with Germany. Simultaneously, the partnership of Artem I. Mikoyan and Mikhail I. Gurevich was perfecting the *I 61* which was later to appear in service as the *MIG 1*, and another young designer, Alexander S. Yakovlev, who had already achieved some prominence with sporting and training aircraft, was putting the finishing touches to the *I 26*, which saw extensive service and was called the *YAK 1*. These fighters were simple to build and lightly armed; their equipment was taken to the limits of austerity and instrumentation was extremely limited, no gyroscopic instruments being installed. They could, however, be produced rapidly by plants employing a high percentage of unskilled labour, and their performances were fairly adequate by current world standards.

The exigencies of the war years were the primary factors in influencing Russian fighter development. The *Lavochkin* and *Yakovlev* fighters were progressively developed to take improved power plants and armament, and the necessity for maintaining the highest possible output did not permit any major change in the Soviet fighter concept. The Russian aircraft industry was not unaware of the development of jet propulsion in the West, however, and laboured under no delusions as to its importance. The possibilities of rocket propulsion as a means of boosting the climb and combat speed of fighters had been investigated as early as 1934 when six *M 22* solid-fuel rockets had been mounted under the wings of a *Tupolev I 4* fighter, and research intensified as war approached. In 1939, requirements for a rocket-propelled target-defence interceptor fighter were drawn up and the design of three different rocket fighters was initiated. Simultaneously, interest was shown in the possibility of boosting the performance of fighters by fitting them with auxiliary ram-jet units underwing. The first tests were conducted on 25th January 1940 when a *Polikarpov I 15B* fighter biplane was flown with a *Merkulov* ram-jet under each lower wing. Further tests were made with an *I 153* biplane and, some time later, with a *YAK 7B* fighter monoplane. The *Merkulov* ram-jets boosted the maximum speed of these fighters by 10 to 15 per cent, but this was not thought to be enough to justify the loss in manœuvrability.

To power the proposed rocket fighters, L. S. Dushkin was developing a liquid-fuel unit which, for initial flight tests, was installed in a *Korolev* single-seat sailplane. The first rocket flight was made on 28th February 1940. The sailplane was towed to an altitude of 6,500 feet and cast off from its tug before the rocket unit was fired. Tests were sufficiently promising to warrant the further development of the *Dushkin* rocket motor which, at that time, was giving 660–880 lb thrust, and power plants of this type were installed in the prototypes of the three target-defence interceptors, the *Polikarpov Malyutka*, the *Tikhonravov 302* and the *Berezniak-Isaev BI 1*, which had been designed to meet the requirements of the Committee for the Defence of the State (GOKO). In July 1941, the Committee selected the *BI 1* as the most promising of the three fighter designs and ordered a pre-production series of five machines. The *BI 1* was a single-seat low-wing monoplane of mixed construction with a nosewheel undercarriage and a nose-mounted armament of two 20 mm cannon. On 10th September 1941, gliding trials with the first prototype *BI 1* commenced, the little fighter being towed into the air by a twin-engined *PE 2*. Eight months later, on 15th May 1942, the first Soviet rocket-powered aircraft flight was made. The *Dushkin* rocket provided 1,100 lb thrust, and the *BI 1* possessed a powered endurance of eight to fifteen minutes. The *Polikarpov Malyutka* and the *Tikhonravov 302* were also test-flown in 1942, but like the *BI 1* their endurances were extremely limited and were considered insufficient for operational purposes. Attempts were made to augment endurance by providing an auxiliary combustion chamber. The arrangement was extremely complex, however, and increased the weight to such an extent that the rocket-powered fighter offered little performance advantage over the orthodox piston-engined fighter, and further development of the rocket target-defence interceptor was abandoned.

In 1943, Artem I. Mikoyan evolved a mixed-power fighter, the *I 250(N)*, which had a 1,600 hp *Klimov VK 107* piston engine in the nose and a ram-jet in the rear fuselage, the intake for the latter being situated under the fuselage nose. The *I 250(N)* was flown for the first time in March 1945, and during the course of flight trials attained 497 mph in level flight, but by this time the Soviet technical institutes were already experimenting with captured German turbo-jets. During 1944, several *Lavochkin LA 7* piston-engined fighters were fitted with a liquid-fuel rocket motor in the rear fuselage for boosting combat performance, while several *LA 9s* were fitted with a pair of such units underwing, and the exploits of Lieutenant-General Savitskii in one of these machines were widely publicised, possibly in an effort to disguise Russia's shortcomings in the opening field of jet propulsion. The fact that Savitskii's machine was merely an adapted piston-engined fighter was not, of course, revealed.

Jet fighters were not necessary for Russia's retention of aerial superiority in the east during the closing stages of the Second World War, but the fact that the Soviet Union, alone among the major combatants, had failed to develop a successful turbo-jet engine was a thorn in the side of the Russians. Several leading Soviet aircraft engineers, such as Arkhip M. Lyulka, had been working on turbo-jet development from the early 'forties but had not succeeded in producing a unit of sufficient reliability to permit flight tests. As Russian forces advanced towards Germany's borders, however, examples of German turbo-jets fell into their hands and were hastily shipped back to Russian experimental establishments where preparations began to adapt them for mass production in the Soviet Union. In this endeavour, the Russians were assisted extensively by German and Czech technicians who, possessing Communist sympathies, passed invaluable information on German production techniques to Soviet agents. Thus, some time before the final German collapse, work on adapting the turbo-jets for Soviet production had reached an advanced stage. The capture of factories in Poland and east Germany, producing *Junkers JUMO 004B* and *BMW 003A* units, together with numerous German turbo-jet engineers, expedited the Russian jet engine crash programme and, under the respective designations *RD 10* and *RD 20*, these power plants were leaving Soviet factories in 1946 to power the first generation of Russian production jet fighters.

The Mikoyan-Gurevich design partnership was early in the field, having initiated the development of an airframe suitable for two *BMW 003* turbo-jets several months before the end of the war. Called the *MIG 9*, this type was flown for the first time on 24th April 1946, although it is doubtful if it was, at that time, powered by Russian production engines. Nevertheless, production deliveries started before the end of that year. According to official Russian figures, the *MIG 9* attained a maximum speed of 590 mph, its maximum attainable altitude was 42,650 feet, and its loaded weight was 11,177 lb. Assuming the Russian figures to be accurate, the *MIG 9*'s maximum speed was slightly superior to Britain's contemporary *Vampire F 1* and America's *F 80A Shooting Star*. The *MIG 9* had the advantage of twin turbo-jets although this was offset by the dubious reliability of the *RD 20s* which were disposed side by side in the fuselage: an arrangement to which the Mikoyan-Gurevich team was to return about seven years later in designing Russia's first supersonic jet fighter to enter service, the *MIG 19*; this was again dictated by the lack of a single turbo-jet engine of sufficient power to provide the desired performance. The *MIG 9* was armed with two 23 mm Nudelmann-Suranov and one 37 mm Nudelmann cannon, an armament which was to be standardised by all Mikoyan-Gurevich fighters until the mid 'fifties, and the fighter was the first Soviet production combat aircraft to feature a retractable nosewheel undercarriage. No details of the equipment and instrumentation of the *MIG 9* are yet available, but these are likely to have been primitive by Western standards.

For the early post-war period, Alexander Yakovlev had developed a turbo-jet-driven fighter but, unlike his compatriots, he merely adapted the basic airframe of his *YAK 9* piston-engined fighter to take a single German *JUMO 004B*, alias *RD 10*, turbo-jet, exemplifying the haste with which the Soviet aircraft industry made use of the German turbo-jet legacy. The turbo-jet engine was attached to the fuselage below the wing main spar, being fed by a circular intake in the nose and exhausting beneath the wing trailing edge; the rear fuselage was protected from the exhaust gases by a concave steel 'bath'. The original tailwheel undercarriage was retained, and the nose-up engine-revving approach for landing, combined with the indifferent view from the cockpit, must have rendered the fighter somewhat tricky to handle. Reports current at the time of the fighter's service début suggested that, in addition to its unpleasant take-off and landing characteristics, it had a tendency to spin at the least provocation. Despite its shortcomings, the fighter entered limited production as the *YAK 15* and, although it had less than 2,000 lb thrust available, it attained level speeds of the order of 520–540 mph. The *YAK 15* soon gave place to the *YAK 17* which was essentially a progressive development of the earlier fighter embodying a nosewheel undercarriage, redesigned tail surfaces, and an improved version of the *RD 10* developed by A. M. Lyulka's design bureau. Neither the *MIG 9* or *YAK 17* was looked upon by the Russians as anything more than a stop-gap, but these fighters did enable the Soviet Air Forces to build up a nucleus of trained jet fighter pilots and also infused an element of modernity into the Russian fighter scene while captured German research data were being evaluated.

By 1947, several parallel fighter research programmes were under way. Some of the products of these programmes offered little advance over their predecessors; one of the earliest of these fighters was the *SU 9* evolved by Pavel O. Sukhoi which, weighing 12,787 lb loaded and powered by a pair of *RD 10* turbo-jets underslung on the wings, bore a marked resemblance to the *Messerschmitt ME 262A* and attained a maximum speed of 560 mph. The *SU 9* was one of the first Soviet jet fighters to use rocket-assisted take-off and a tail braking 'chute to reduce landing runs. Of greater interest was an experimental fighter designed by Semyon A. Lavochkin which bore the design bureau designation *LA 160*. The first Russian fighter to embody wing sweep-back, the *LA 160*, was powered by a single 1,760 lb thrust *RD 20* turbo-jet which was installed in a similar fashion to the *RD 10* of the *YAK 15*. Weighing only 8,950 lb fully loaded, the *LA 160* utilised 35° sweep-back on the wing leading edge, and attained 653 mph in level flight. A Mach number of 0·92 was attained in a dive during flight testing.

In the late 1940s several fighters of extremely advanced concept were under development in the Soviet Union but the principal stumbling block was the lack of a turbo-jet engine of sufficient power and reliability. A variant of the basic *RD 10* axial-flow turbo-jet with a two-stage turbine and three extra compressor stages was being bench-run by A. M. Lyulka's bureau. This was expected to be delivering 4,400 lb thrust by mid-1947 and 6,000 lb thrust in its eventual production form by the end of 1948 or early 1949, and on these expectations several airframe constructors were developing fighters. Then, fortuitously for the Russians, the United Kingdom agreed to export to Russia twenty-five examples of the sturdy and reliable Rolls-Royce *Nene* centrifugal-type turbo-jets and, for good measure, thirty of the lower-powered Rolls-Royce *Derwents*. Had it not been for this unfortunate export the *MIG 15* might never have materialised, at least in the form in which it attained international fame in the skies above Korea. There can be little doubt that the supply of British turbo-jets to the Soviet Union saved Russia about two years' research in her fighter development programme.

The arrival of the British engines, which were immediately allocated to the leading fighter design bureaux, resulted in a frenzy of new activity in the Soviet aircraft industry. Airframe designers immediately began modifying their fighter projects to take the imported turbo-jets while top priority was given to the copying of the engines for production in Russia: the Rolls Royce *Nene* as the *RD 45* and the *Derwent* as the *RD 500*. Alexander Yakovlev was allocated examples of the *Derwent* for installation in the prototypes of the *YAK 23*, a relatively orthodox lightweight interceptor, while Semyon A. Lavochkin received this engine for use in the *LA 15*, also a lightweight fighter but embodying a shoulder-mounted wing swept 37° 20′ at the leading edge. The *YAK 23* was the first Russian fighter to be fitted with a trigger-actuated ejection seat, and flew for the first time during the last months of 1947. The production model attained a maximum speed of 568 mph, had an initial climb rate of 6,690 feet a minute, a ceiling of 48,550 feet, and an endurance (with auxiliary wingtip tanks) of two hours. Empty and normal loaded weights were 4,410 lb and 7,365 lb respectively, and the armament comprised two 23 mm Nudelmann-Suranov cannon. The similarly armed but more advanced *LA 15*, which flew for the first time during the early months of 1948, had a maximum speed of 638 mph, a normal range of 727 miles and a ceiling of 45,000 feet. The limiting Mach number of the *LA 15* was 0·92 and its loaded weight was only 8,488 lb.

Both the *YAK 23* and the *LA 15* were placed in limited production for the Soviet Air Forces, but the advances that they marked in Russian fighter development had been totally eclipsed by the début of the *Nene*-powered *MIG 15* prototype on 30th December 1947— two months after the first flight of the first prototype North American *Sabre* which was to oppose the Russian fighter in Korea a few years later. Like the *LA 15*, the *MIG 15* displayed strong Germanic influence, and design work had been initiated in 1946 to meet the requirements of a specification calling for a single-seat bomber interceptor with heavy cannon armament. Like its contemporaries, it was originally intended to take the Lyulka-developed axial-flow turbo-jet and, being rather heavier than either the *Yakovlev* or *Lavochkin* fighters, it was allocated the more powerful Rolls-Royce *Nene* turbo-jet. From the time that the turbo-jet was delivered for installation in the prototype, development proceeded at a phenomenal rate, matched only by the rapidity with which the *Nene* engine itself was adapted for Russian production; we were to witness amazing achievements in an aircraft industry then considered to be at least several years behind the major Western nations in technological progress. In its initial production form as delivered to the Soviet Air Forces late in 1948, the *MIG 15* was powered by a single 5,000 lb thrust *RD 45* turbo-jet and carried an armament of one 23 mm NS cannon and one 37 mm N cannon. With their external fairings, the guns marred the fighter's otherwise clean lines, and these excrescences, coupled with a relatively thick wing, prevented the *MIG 15* from reaching transonic speeds even in the most determined full-throttle dive. The *MIG 15* was, nevertheless, a fine piece of engineering design, and later examination of an example built at Factory No. 1, Kuibischev, in 1948, revealed that the Russian aircraft industry had attained an extremely high standard of workmanship with fine flush-riveting, and that the fighter was quite well equipped, even by Western standards, although no provision for gunsight radar ranging had been made at that time. Both the NS and N cannon had muzzle velocities of some 2,150 feet a minute; the smaller gun had a fire rate of 650 rpm while that of the larger gun was 450 rpm. This armament was evidently considered inadequate at a very early stage in the *MIG 15*'s production life for, by 1949, it had been supplemented by a further 23 mm NS cannon.

The year 1948 also saw the first Russian attempts to produce jet all-weather fighters. A primitive form of airborne radar was fitted to a number of piston-engined *PE 2* night fighters during 1945 and 1946, and there were several reports of a two-seat radar-equipped all-weather variant of the experimental *Sukhoi SU 9* fighter, although there has since been no certain evidence of this development. Pavel Sukhoi was, however, instrumental in developing the *SU 15*, a large, twin-jet machine with a cone-type housing above the nose air intake presumably intended to accommodate AI radar. The *SU 15* weighed 22,050 lb in loaded condition, and attained a maximum speed of 652 mph. Two axial-flow turbo-jets (probably derived from German designs by Arkhip Lyulka) were installed side-by-side in the fuselage and exhausted beneath the tail boom. The *SU 15* did not progress further than the experimental stage. Another experimental fighter design stemming from the Sukhoi bureau, the *SU 17*, is claimed to have been Russia's first supersonic fighter. The *SU 17* appeared in 1949, and featured sharply swept wing and tail surfaces and a capsule-type cockpit which could be jettisoned in an emergency.

By 1950, the production tempo of the *MIG 15* had reached a rate at which some deliveries of this fighter could be diverted to the satellite air forces and, before the end of 1951, substantial numbers of these fighters, bearing the insignia of the Sino-Communist Air Force, were appearing over Korea and the first jet-versus-jet combats in the history of aviation had taken place. In combat with the North American *F 86 Sabre* the *MIG 15*'s appreciably lower loadings as compared with the American fighter endowed it with several advantages. It was soon discovered that the *MIG 15* was faster than the *Sabre* above 32,000 feet; its rate of climb was superior and climb angles could be maintained at which *Sabres* would stall if they tried to follow; the *MIG 15* could hold formation at 50,000 feet whereas the *Sabre* experienced trouble at 5,000 feet below this altitude; the Russian fighter enjoyed a 15 per cent smaller turning circle and its acceleration was superior to its American counterpart. Conversely, the *Sabre* possessed superior high Mach dive characteristics at all altitudes; the *MIG 15* suffering from severe directional snaking above Mach 0·86 which reduced its effectiveness as a gun platform; some fore and aft instability could result in a snap roll and spin when its pilot attempted too tight a turn, and its relatively low fire-rate cannon, combined with an elementary type of mechanical gun-sight, placed it at a disadvantage in fighter-versus-fighter combat. The *Sabre*'s radar gunsight and better high Mach characteristics rendered the American fighter the better weapon whereas the *MIG 15* was the better flying machine.

The *MIG 15* was progressively improved during the Korean con-flict; boosted ailerons were introduced and a more powerful version of the basic *Nene* engine, the *Klimov VK 1*, was installed. Featuring scaled-up internal gas passages, larger combustion chambers, longer and wider turbine blades, the *VK 1* offered 5,950 lb thrust as com-pared with the 5,000 lb thrust of the original *Nene* copy, the *RD 45*. During USAF flight evaluation of one of these later production *MIG 15s* in 1953, it was discovered that the Russian fighter was slightly slower than the *F 86F Sabre* in level flight at all altitudes below 35,000 feet; that it possessed insufficient stall warning and its lack of automaticity was liable to divert the pilot's attention during combat.

The Russians were already aware of the *MIG 15*'s shortcomings, however, and late in 1951 or early in 1952 high-ranking Soviet Air Force officers and leading Russian aircraft designers reputedly held a conference to study the combat deficiencies of the *MIG 15* revealed during the air war over Korea. The direct result of this conference was the *MIG 17*. This fighter, although bearing a close over-all similarity to the *MIG 15*, was an entirely new design. It retained the *Klimov VK 1* turbo-jet of the late production *MIG 15*, but the fuselage was of improved fineness ratio and the wing was entirely redesigned; the sweep-back on the inboard sections being increased to reduce the thickness/chord ratio and raise the critical Mach number, and the overall span being increased by some three feet. The initial pro-duction model of the *MIG 17* began to supplant the *MIG 15* in 1954, and there is reason to suppose that provision was made in this fighter for gun-sight radar ranging: several *Sabres* were captured by the Communists in North Korea and presumably the radar gun-sights obtained from these aircraft served as a basis for Russian develop-ments in this field. Early *MIG 17s* evinced a noteworthy performance improvement over the *MIG 15* which had been capable of a maxi-mum speed of 683 mph at low altitude (Mach 0·89) and a service ceiling of 51,000 feet. The newer fighter was still incapable of exceeding Mach unity in a dive but was capable of very high subsonic Mach numbers of the order of 0·975 and level speeds of the order of 590 mph (Mach 0·9) at 50,000 feet, while operational ceiling was raised to approximately 53,000 feet, this altitude being attained in ten minutes. The introduction of the *VK 1A* turbo-jet with a short afterburner, which boosted available thrust to 6,990 lb, further improved the *MIG 17*'s performance characteristics, speeds very close to the fighter's maximum Mach number being attainable in level flight; operational ceiling being increased to about 58,000 feet, and climb to 50,000 feet taking only about six minutes.

The *MIG 17* was obviously only a stepping stone between the *MIG 15* and Russia's first service fighter capable of supersonic speeds in level flight, the *MIG 19*, which appeared (in prototype at least) in 1953. Although Arkhip Lyulka was awarded a Stalin Prize in 1950 for an axial-flow turbo-jet claimed to offer 9,900 lb thrust, the Soviet aircraft industry still lacked turbo-jets suitable for fighter installation in the 10,000 lb thrust category. The Mikoyan-Gurevich team had, therefore, reverted to the power layout adopted for their first jet fighter, the *MIG 9*. The *MIG 19* employed two slim axial-flow turbo-jets mounted side by side, each offering 6,500 lb thrust dry and 8,800 lb thrust with afterburning. Initial production machines carried a 23 mm cannon in each wing root and a 37 mm cannon in the port side of the fuselage. Later production machines had this built-in armament augmented by a further 37 mm cannon in the starboard side of the fuselage. In addition, underwing attachment points were provided for four rocket pods each housing eight 50 mm folding-fin unguided air-to-air missiles based on the German *R 4M*. The normal loaded weight of the *MIG 19* was reportedly 19,800 lb, and the fighter could attain Mach 1·4 (925 mph at 36,000 feet) in level flight. Later production *MIG 19s* featured a central aerodynamic shock cone in the air intake which presumably housed search and tracking radar.

While the *MIG 15* had brought about a very marked advance in the day interception capabilities of the Soviet Air Forces, the all-weather interception capabilities were almost non-existent until the appearance of the *YAK 25* in 1952. Interceptors like the *Sukhoi SU 15* apparently proved abortive; perhaps because of Russia's failure to develop effective airborne interception equipment rapidly. As a stop-gap, all-weather variants of the *MIG 17* were produced, both with and without afterburning. These carried radar-ranging equipment, a fire-control scanner in a central nose cone and an extended lip over the air intake; but the limited visibility interception capabilities of these conversions are believed to have been poor. The *YAK 25*, however, was a very different matter. Powered by two slim axial-flow turbo-jets each offering approximately 6,500 lb thrust and presumably similar to those installed in the single-seat *MIG 19*, the *YAK 25* featured a capacious, circular section fuselage indicating substantial internal fuel capacity, and a large nose radome which suggested the employment of quite advanced AI equipment. The appearance of the *YAK 25* in squadron service in 1955 also marked the first employment of a built-in rocket armament in a Russian fighter, a large rocket tray of the snap-opening type in the fuselage belly housing 50 mm FFAR missiles. In addition, two semi-externally packaged 37 mm cannon were carried. Carrying a crew of two in tandem-mounted ejector seats, the *YAK 25* was believed to be capable of speeds of the order of Mach 0·95 in level flight and a tactical radius in the vicinity of 800 miles.

At the present time, the single-seat *MIG 19* and the two-seater *YAK 25* equip a large proportion of the Soviet Air Forces' first-line interceptor elements. Both now reputedly carry several types of air to air missiles underwing, including infra-red homers, and their cannon are believed to be improved versions of the guns used by the *MIG 15* over Korea, although new high fire-rate revolver-type cannon are known to have been introduced on later fighters and may be installed in current production models of the *MIG 19* and *YAK 25*. Present radar limits Russian interceptors to 'Lead Pursuit' attack methods, although the Soviet Union is undoubtedly making strenuous efforts to perfect 'Collision Course' techniques similar to those used by the interceptors of the USAF Air Defence Command. It is not generally believed, however, that any fully automatic form of interception has yet been introduced.

During 1956, a considerably refined version of the *YAK 25* was shown in public. Aerodynamically improved in several respects, and featuring lengthened engine nacelles which are believed to denote the use of afterburners, the improved *YAK 25* has a longer, pointed radome and extended inboard wing sections. These changes, combined with the additional power, are expected to boost the level flight performance of the fighter to the vicinity of Mach 1·0. Other

1956 débutantes included the *MIG 21* and three different fighters from the drawing-boards of Pavel O. Sukhoi's bureau. The *MIG 21*, which is reportedly entering service with the Soviet Air Forces at the present time, is estimated to be capable of level speeds of the order of Mach 2·1 (1,386 mph at 36,000 feet). Powered by a single turbo-jet which is thought to offer some 11,000 lb thrust dry and 16,000–17,000 lb with afterburning, the *MIG 21* carries AI radar in a central intake cone and what appears to be the standard built-in armament of all new Russian single-seat interceptors: three 37 mm cannon probably of revolver pattern. The semi-external packaging of these cannon and the whip-type radio antenna appear to be anachronisms on a fighter of the *MIG 21*'s performance capabilities, but there can be little doubt that it is potentially a formidable interceptor fighter. The present production status of the trio of *Sukhoi* interceptors is very much a matter of conjecture. The official Soviet designations for these fighters are not yet available; reference has been made to the *Sukhoi SU 23* but this designation may apply to any one of the three interceptors. NATO identification names *Fitter*, *Fishpot* and *Fishbed* have been allocated to the trio. The *Fitter* appears to be a relatively orthodox swept-wing interceptor powered by a single afterburning turbo-jet and capable of maximum speeds of the order of Mach 1·6. The *Fishbed* appears to share a common fuselage with the *Fitter* but employs a 60° delta wing, while the *Fishpot* uses this wing combined with a new fuselage. The latter fighter is thought to be fitted with a full fire-control system and be capable of speeds in the vicinity of Mach 2·0.

The decade that has elapsed since the prototype *MIG 15* made its début have been years of striking progress in the Soviet aircraft industry, and in no field has this progress been more marked than that of the interceptor fighter. It would be the height of folly to assume that the Western technological lead, in this category at least, is more than marginal, and it is probable that the Russians have attained parity in performance. It is apparent, however, that the Russians do not yet consider that their air to air missiles have reached a stage where the classic cannon armament can be entirely dispensed with, and it appears feasible that the interception equipment installed in US fighters still gives them the edge over their Russian counterparts.

The foregoing gives an impression of the development of aircraft equipment of the PVO Strategic Defence Command of the Soviet Air Force, which is dealt with more generally in Chapter 7. Numerically, the tactical air forces which give close air support to the Soviet ground forces are still the most important part of Soviet air power, comprising some 10,000 aircraft, that is, about half the present operational strength of all Soviet air squadrons. The tactical air formation, commanded by General Loginov, who is a deputy of the Soviet Air Force Commander-in-Chief, Marshal of Aviation Konstantin Vershinin, has recently been renamed, but its functions and equipment have not changed as a result. Indeed it is equipped almost entirely with the jet fighter type aircraft of which the main technical details are given in this chapter. But it has always been Soviet air policy to make its interceptor fighters do the dual purpose job of air defence and tactical close support. Thus the *MIG 15* (*Fagot* is its NATO designation) which was primarily an interceptor fighter in 1950 and 1951, is now one of the chief close-support props of the air regiments of the 'Frontal Aviation' as the tactical units are called. Its operational strength of 280–300 regiments also includes large numbers of *MIG 17* and *MIG 19* fighters but the latest *MIG 21* jet is likely to equip the PVO strategic defence units for the next year or so. Apart from the *MIG 15* tactical bombers, of which there are over 1,500, the main light jet bomber equipment is the twin-engined *Ilyushin 28* and the fighter-bomber *MIG 17*, which have been supplied in large numbers to the air allies of the Soviet Union. It is to be expected that a supersonic tactical support jet bomber will shortly be in service in large numbers, either a re-engined *YAK 25* or an *Ilyushin* supersonic plane which NATO has designated *Blowlamp*. Although there were still some air regiments of obsolescent *Ilyushin 10* piston engined bombers in service at the beginning of 1958 these are likely to have been replaced by *IL 28s* or later equipment by the end of the year.

It is fashionable nowadays to consider the long range bombers and rockets of the Soviet Air Force and the Strategic Air Defence fighters and guided missiles as the primary air concern of the West. In fact the tactical air units of General Loginov's 'Front Aviation' may well play the major part in any future war simply because it is likely to be of the so-called 'limited' variety. If this is so, then it should be borne in mind that many of his air regiments have the capacity to drop tactical atomic bombs and that his fighters can be reinforced at short notice by *MIG 21* and *YAK 25* air regiments of General Klimov's Fighter Aviation Air Defence Command, which is part of Marshal Biryuzov's general PVO anti-aircraft strategic defence command. It is easy to forget that the Soviet Union, despite recent pronouncements by Marshal Vershinin and Mr Khrushchev, is still making more advanced manned fighters and that these could decide to what extent NATO land forces will be able to use their atomic artillery and anti-tank guided missiles, tactical air forces and ground to ground guided weapons. If the Soviet Air Forces gain local air superiority through their large force of modern supersonic jet planes, then their tactical air forces could do to the airfields and roads of western Europe what the Anglo-American air power did in the summer of 1944. In current defence debates on the future of the manned fighter, the tactical air spaces over Europe and elsewhere rather than the business of the metropolitan defence of Britain or the United States should be considered.

CHAPTER 9

SOVIET MISSILES

Asher Lee and Richard E. Stockwell

WHILE THE RUSSIANS were not first in the development of military rockets and make no claims to such fame, there can be little doubt that they have long been interested in them. Now, in the second half of the twentieth century, they are in a position to exert leadership and dominance in this field and can use missiles as the means to develop and extend their current military doctrine in all spheres.

As long ago as the first half of the nineteenth century Russian military engineers built war rockets charged with gunpowder which gave good performances for their time. Late in the nineteenth century Konstantin Tsiolkowsky and Ivan Mesherhsky laid the foundation for this new science when they wrote of 'rocket dynamics and the mechanics of bodies with variable mass'. Today Tsiolkowsky is a hero in Russia: as Thomas A. Edison is a hero in the United States and Faraday in England. Tsiolkowsky's name is on the lips of most Russians, as it properly should be. He produced the blueprint of a rocket that burned hydrogen and oxygen in 1903, and in 1915 he wrote of using hydrocarbon fuels with oxygen. A few years later, he produced the conceptual design of a three-stage rocket.

But for all of Tsiolkowsky's early conceptual work, the Russians did not do much in this field until after the old man had died in 1936 at the age of 79. True, they did send up some all-metal meteorological rockets as early as 1933, and in the late 1930s they were working on a rocket-powered glider. However, little seems to have come of these efforts other than the milestones they contribute to Russia's rocket history.

Nevertheless, Tsiolkowsky's pupils and rocket colleagues, Soviet scientists like Rynin, Perelman, Petrovich, Scherchevski, Zander, Tichhof, Wetchinkin and Seylinger worked in the 1920s and 1930s at the Tsagi rocket research centres in Moscow, Leningrad and Kazan, doing experimental work on both large fuel rockets and small solid propellant rockets. The works of Herman Oberth, the German mathematician, on rockets and space travel, were translated and closely studied. In fact the Soviet literature and bibliography on rockets and astronautics was probably more prolific than that of any other country between the two World Wars. Professor Nikolai Rynin's book on the subject published in 1931, for instance, contains a virtually complete list of all the reference material available in any language on rocket research and space travel. In Willie Ley's *Rockets and Space Travel*[1] the number of books given in a rocket bibliography published in Russian in the USSR between 1925 and 1933 is impressive and much greater than of those published in France or Germany in the vernacular. *Osoaviakhim*, the Soviet para-military youth organisation of the pre-war period, provided lectures on long range rockets and travel space and were encouraged to make Tsiolkowsky one of their national heroes. These things do not add up to the production of Soviet rockets for military purposes; but they do indicate that Soviet interest in this field is of very long standing and that, before German influence intervened on such a large scale in 1945 and 1946, there was a useful core of Soviet rocket scientists and technicians who could profit immediately from the German rocket missile legacies.

When the Second World War broke over them in June 1941, the Russians were every bit as far behind Germany in rocket development as the United States. They did have some rockets in production however, and by the time of the battle of Moscow in the winter of 1941–2 they were ready with the first version of their *Katyushka*, a powder rocket fired in multiples from a truck-mounted launcher. It was so successful that the Germans protested against the use of such weapons, while the Russians rushed production for *Katyushka*'s next large-scale use, which was to be in the Battle of Stalingrad.

This was its major application in the Second World War. Batteries of these rockets, with explosive warheads, were mounted on Studebaker trucks. The drivers, who steered their vehicles by peering through slits in steel plates that covered the windshield, drove as close to the front lines as possible, pointing their trucks at the enemy lines. The batteries of *Katyushka* rockets were then raised and fired forward, over the truck cab. The result caused panic among the German troops. This success helped foster the use of rockets by other countries.

[1] Chapman & Hall, London, 1948.

But the Russians had no large long range military rockets at the end of the Second World War, and they developed none. They limited themselves to small-size powder rockets a few inches in diameter, some of which were installed on *Sturmovik* aircraft and used also as anti-tank weapons.

Russian ideas of warfare up to then were limited largely to 'battle area' concepts. They had not generally accepted the importance of long range aircraft that could hit an enemy far behind his lines. This naturally affected their thinking about rockets; and precluded their use as long range weapons. Limited land and sea war was still very much the pattern of Soviet military thought during the Second World War.

But in Germany there was a small military group that saw the rocket in a much larger sense, and were putting their dreams into hardware. They saw it as a military tool that could strike at bomber distances, without the need for a pilot or crew. Under Hitler, the Germans developed their rockets slowly. The Nazis saw no great need to speed the work unduly, for they, too, were fighting a short, 'limited war' in the initial stages of the Second World War. Only after the war got out of hand, and spread around the world, did they begin to take the rocket-missile work at Peenemunde really seriously.

The story has been told many times of how the Germans gradually perfected rocket technology, after many failures that have since been repeated with monotonous similarity in the United States. Near the end of the Second World War they were ready with their *A 4* missile, known as *V2* to the Allied Powers. It had a range of at least 200 miles, and was equipped with a TNT warhead. While the Germans were certainly capable of developing an atomic bomb during the Second World War, they did not do so. Equipped with even a small atomic warhead, the *V2* would have caused real havoc and might have marked a late turning point of the Second World War. Appreciation of this fact was lost on the West a few months later in the full flush of victory.

After 1945 there was a period of weapons-loot hunting. The Russians were most assiduous and persistent in this game.[1] The Red Army had destroyed much that was valuable as it marched into Germany, including most of the facilities at Peenemunde and the *Luftwaffe*'s research institute in Berlin. Factories were wantonly

---

[1] For further details see Chapter 15, 'The German Legacy'.

blown up by the Reds. Only after the dust began to settle did the Russians try to re-assemble the pieces of the modern German war machinery. They put Peenemunde together again as best they could and special teams were sent in to see what could be done to re-assemble German aircraft engine and missile research facilities.

A rocket-engine testing site at Lehesten was taken over. In Thuringia, the Mittelwerke GmbH facilities in Niedersachswerfen and Klein-Bodungen ended up in Soviet hands. So did the Walter Raketentriebwerke (Walter Rocket Works) in Prague, which once had been at Kiel, only to be transferred when Allied bombing became too severe. It was turning out rocket powerplants for the *Messerschmitt ME 163*, and the same rocket engine was adapted to missile use. Similarly, BMW rocket powerplants fell into Soviet hands. The country was scoured for German scientists and technicians. Special offers were made to those who had moved into the Western zone to induce them to return to East Germany.

And then, finally, in October of 1946, all those available were scooped up and shipped to the USSR. For the Soviet Union the equipment and talent they got in Germany were like a flask of water to a man who had been in the desert too long. Their aircraft, jet engine and missile technology got a tremendous shot in the arm. Soon they undertook an intensive and growing programme to build bigger and better rocket missiles. The Germans had had years of successfully developing long and short range missiles, and these the Russians took over and began to copy, manufacture and develop almost immediately. The *V2* was one of the key weapons. In it they had a more or less proven powerplant and aerodynamic body. Over 4,000 of them were fired mostly at London and Antwerp between September 1944 and the end of the Second World War. They had only to perfect an atomic warhead and improve its range to get a good intermediate ballistics missile, an IRBM.

From the German concept of the two-stage *A 9*, the *A 10*, the USSR secured drawings and test data for a longer range weapon that could more than double the range of the *V2*. And from there they could go on to more stages and the kind of multiple-staged vehicles envisioned by Tsiolkowsky. That old gentleman, buried with simple honours in 1936, came back into the limelight in the USSR, as if returning from the dead.

From 1946 onwards the Germans worked at Khimki, outside

Moscow, and elsewhere designing and improving the *V2*. Another group worked on problems of guidance at Ostahkosh. Others worked on rocket fuels at Leningrad; work on rocket powerplants took place at Kuibischev. The work went ahead quietly, carefully screened from the Western world, while the work on jet aircraft was given more public prominence.

Though some of the returning Germans (like Dr Tellman) were to warn the West many times of Soviet progress in missiles, until 1957 most Western eyes were turned to the more visible Russian aircraft.

Most of the currently published information about Soviet post-war progress in developing long range rockets belongs to the 1957–8 period. But even before the outbreak of the Korean War, published eye-witness reports had testified to the development of an improvement of the German *V2* going through firing trials from Soviet submarines and of the development of long range rockets at Irkutsk and Kuibischev. In 1951 and 1952 there were reports of an improved *V2* going into large-scale production, using liquid fuel propellants, having a range of up to 500 miles and weighing about $12\frac{1}{2}$ tons. This is probably the rocket subsequently referred to as the *T 1*. By 1955 there were reports of a two-stage rocket going into production with a range of over 1,000 miles; some sources put the range at 1,500 to 2,000 miles. Even if these reports were premature, other sources made it clear that in 1954 and 1955 there were a large number of test firings in the Soviet Union of missiles in the IRBM category. These probably included the final testing of the *T 2* IRBM, which then had a range of over 1,000 miles.

One of the most detailed and authentic statements on the progress of Soviet missile development has come from Dr Walter Dornburgher, who in the Second World War was the major-general in command of the German Army Missile Experimental Station at Peenemunde. He had spoken to a number of his German long range rocket colleagues, who had worked from 1946 until the early 1950s at Soviet rocket development centres and firing sites. His view, expressed early in 1955, was that the USSR was well ahead of the United States in the early 1950s and by 1955 had produced large numbers of rocket missiles which could be launched from Soviet rocket land bases in Europe at European cities or NATO military targets. Dr Dornburgher had, at the time, had twenty-five years of practical experience in the field of rocket weapons and, through his German contacts, was probably in a good position to assess the time-table of Soviet long range rocket progress. One of his sources reported that one Soviet rocket of the 1949–50 period (presumably of the *T 1* type) had a range of at least 300 miles, could be accurate to within 1,500 feet and could carry an atomic warhead.

Dr Dornburgher also expressed the view early in 1955 that the Soviet Union had been developing a submarine-launched missile with a range of several hundred miles, though he was not sure if it was yet in service. The Soviet naval authorities owe part of the inspiration of this weapon to German developments in the Second World War. Peenemunde projects, inherited by the USSR, included a submersible launching platform about 100 feet long in the form of a large container, housing a *V2* rocket with a gyro-stabilised firing platform which could keep the missile steady regardless of the swell of the sea. Each container weighed about 500 tons and a submarine could tow three of them. No doubt the Soviet authorities have now developed submarines which can fire a dozen or more *Komet* or *Golem* rockets and so the German devised system of towing is obsolescent. But the realisation that it could be practical warfare to fire missiles against a city from a submarine lying hundreds of miles out in the ocean may initially have entered into Soviet strategic thinking as a result of its Peenemunde inheritance.

Dr Dornburgher's remarks on the German two-stage *A 9/A 10* long range missile are also an interesting pointer to the Soviet potential development of IRBM and ICBM rockets. In 1945 there was a German expectation that by 1950 the *A 9/A 10* rocket could be ready for operations and reach New York from sites near Hamburg, that is a distance of 3,800 miles. The German rocket scientists then estimated that an initial rocket power of 440,000 lb thrust would be required for such long range rockets of the two-stage type, firing distances of 3,000 miles or more. It is now clear from the *Sputnik* performances that the Soviet Union has an even more powerful rocket engine than this. Some sources have reported that even at the beginning of 1955 she had a rocket motor with a thrust of 240,000 lb and the use of two such power units in combination would provide the required initial thrust for IRBM rockets and even ICBM rockets. Even allowing that the Russians might not be able to develop an IRBM as quickly as the Germans, especially working as they were in 1944-5 under the supreme pressure of war, it seems reasonable to suppose that if the Soviet rocket scientists were at work on the German *A 9/A 10* project by 1946-7, they could have brought the weapon to a pitch of operational efficiency by say 1955-6, and so, by now, have three or four years of series production behind them.

Certainly the large number of long range rocket sites reported both inside and outside the Soviet Union during the past two or three years has been impressive. Despite Mr Khrushchev's insistence to the contrary, the east and central European allies of the USSR would appear to have permitted the construction of IRBM sites and bases in their countries. The reports have come from the territory of every member of the Warsaw Treaty pact. From Roumania and Bulgaria, there have been reports of sites near the Black Sea coast and the Carpathian mountains. From East Germany sites have been reported near Erfurt and on the island of Ruegen. From Czechoslovakia there are reports of sites near Karlsbad, Reichenberg, Olmutz and Javorina near the Czech-Polish border. From Poland comes evidence of sites near Kolberg on the Baltic and several sources have reported them near Kaliningrad (Konigsberg) in East Prussia. The Hungarian reports have come from near Lake Balaton.

From the USSR itself reports of both long range rocket production and test-firing have persisted since 1956. In western Russia they have come from Latvia, Estonia and Lithuania, Riga, Kronstadt, Kiev, Smolensk, Chernyakovsk, from Kraskino and Stavyanka, south-west of Vladivostok in the Far East, from Nikolaevsk and Komsomolsk in the same area, from Stalingrad, Omsk and Tomsk, from the Caspian Sea area north of Persia, from Novosibirsk and Irkutsk, from Novoya Zemlya in the Arctic Ocean, from Severnaya Zemlya in the same area, in fact from virtually every region of the USSR. According to one source the Soviet Union had test-fired over 100 IRBMs by the end of 1957. There has been more than one report that the Soviet had produced as many as 20,000 intermediate ranged ballistic missiles by the summer of 1958. Clearly these figures cannot be regarded as firm or even approximate but they do suggest that the Soviet Union is far ahead of the United States in the large-scale production of intermediate ranged rocket missiles and probably in tactical missiles of less than 500 miles range. Dr Dornburgher

ht: The *Yak 24* helicopter. It has been in
rvice for several years. *Below:* The *Mil 6,* the
gest helicopter in military use. *Centre:* The
shin 18 four-jet turboprop, in regular service
military air transport units. *Bottom:* The
114, the largest air liner in the world. Its
boprop engines are very powerful.

Soviet long range rockets mainly for use against ground forces and other tactical targets

One of the chief anti-aircraft rockets defending Soviet cities

reports the large-scale manufacture of these later weapons as far back as 1949. Even if his quoted figures of 2,000–3,000 *V2* type rockets a year are a considerable exaggeration, the indelible impression remains that the USSR post-war plans for long range rocket development have matured at least two or three years earlier than those of the United States in the field of tactical and intermediate range offensive rockets. As Dr Dornburgher puts it, the USA and the USSR began the post-war era at about the same level of inexperience but their approach was different. While the United States used the information and rocket technicians they obtained from Germany as a broad scientific basis for long range and long-term improvement plans for more modern weapons, the Soviet authorities launched a crash programme with a 'do it as soon as possible' approach. By using and copying German tools and facilities they were able to get the new rocket weapons, both offensive and defensive, into operational units more quickly than the Americans. Thus for instance, the ground to air missiles based on the radio-guided German *Wasserfall* (Waterfall) and *Rheintochter* (Rhine Daughter) have been ready for use to defend such key centres as Moscow, Leningrad, Stalingrad and the atomic weapons development centre at Ulan-Ude since 1953, while the US equivalent, the *Nike*, was not in service until a year or so later.

These developments of course are not necessarily crucial to the balance of strategic air and rocket power between the USA and the USSR. The intercontinental ballistic missile, the number of submarines, with trained crews and which can use long range missiles, and the operational efficiency of the Soviet long range jet bomber force are the key factors in modern strategy and modern politics.

The Soviet Union has been developing all these facets of her strategic air power in the 1950s. The intercontinental ballistic missile has had its component rocket engines test-fired probably since the beginning of 1955. In 1957, in full radar-sight of USAF tracking stations in Turkey, the Russians began firing ICBMs. Not long after the US began to track them, the Russians told the world of their ICBM achievement to have test-fired a rocket of this kind successfully. A few short months later they pulled off an even more dramatic achievement, the launching of *Sputnik I*.

This was a short-lived satellite, and was followed soon by *Sputnik II*, carrying a dog. Finally, they performed a feat still marvelled at,

F

the launching of a satellite that still is in orbit and that weighs over 2,900 pounds: *Sputnik III*.[1]

In themselves, *Sputniks* are not military weapons; though in the field of propaganda they may be the equivalent of whole armies. But the *Sputniks* clearly indicated the technological level which the Russians had achieved, and pointed directly towards a guided missile programme of considerable size.

The question naturally arises, where are the Russians in missiles today? Some data are available, and inferences can be drawn from what the Russians have said and shown of their equipment.

When they took over the German *V2*, the Russians continued its production, phasing in new ideas and improvements as they went along. This was the basis of the missile that became their *T 1*, a single-stage rocket burning oxygen and alcohol.

They set out to improve it almost immediately. It was too short-ranged in concept and design to suit the growing need for long range strategic weapons. They tried a winged version and increased the range to 990 miles. Even this was far from adequate and attention was turned to a more advanced design, the *T 2*. It was test-fired in the late 1940s. A genuine IRBM, it is now one of the standard weapons of the Soviet armed forces. A two-stage missile, it probably has a range of 1,200 to 1,500 miles.

The propellants used by the Germans, liquid oxygen and alcohol, were used as fuels for the *T 2*. It employs a simple inertial guidance system. The engine of the first stage provides some 268,000 lb of thrust and the second stage has a thrust of 78,000 lb: the same as the *T 1*. Like most Russian missiles, it is somewhat unsophisticated and over-powered for the job required of it. However, gigantism is a recurrent virtue in Russia, and it is doubtful if the Soviet Army, which so far has had general jurisdiction over the tactical use of missiles, has been much concerned about the inefficiencies.

The *T 2* was far short of the range the Soviets were ultimately aiming for, i.e. an intercontinental ballistic missile, but it did provide the basis for a missile that could achieve such a range. This is the *T 3*, with a power system known to the Russians initially as the *M 104*. This missile, on which work began about 1948, was mostly a Russian project. The guidance system is believed to be

[1] The launching of the 'moon' rocket earlier in 1959 indicated the use of even more powerful rocket motors.

German in origin, but the rest is virtually all Russian. Again, the Russians insisted on a lot of thrust either because they had not yet devised ways to reduce the size of the nuclear warhead such as was made possible in the US by a breakthrough in research in 1953, or because they wished to deliver a much larger warhead on target.

The first stage is reported to have about 480,000 lb of thrust. This lifts a 176,000 lb missile. The second stage appears to incorporate $T 2$ hardware and has a thrust of 268,000 lb. The third and final stage resembles nothing so much as the $T 1$, with a thrust of 78,000 lb. Burning time for the three units totals 315 seconds, and the range is just short of 5,000 miles.

There are other versions of this missile, but the most important today is known as the $T 3A$, the ICBM which the Russians are now making operational. The thrust of the first stage has probably been increased to 517,000 lb, while the second and third stages remain the same as in the $T 3$.

The $T 3A$ is reported to have a top range of 6,000 miles, which means it could be launched from a great many points in the Soviet Union against targets in the United States.[1] It stands about 95–100 feet high and has a diameter of 12 to 15 feet. This is not much larger than many Western long range missiles. It would appear that the $T 3A$ delivers more thrust than Western missiles in terms of its size because the Russians are using hydrogen and oxygen as fuel. These deliver about 85 per cent more thrust than equivalent amounts of lox and alcohol. Hydrogen is something the Russians have long worked with in their research laboratories. Peter Kapitsa, top Russian physicist, has done extensive experimental work with hydrogen and it is possible that the Russians have found a way to stabilise it and simplify its handling for missiles.

Next of the Soviet missiles is the $T 4$, believed to be in the experimental stage. Launched from a mobile ramp, it uses liquid oxygen and hydrazine as fuel. Reputedly this missile will give the Soviets a weapon of great accuracy, capable of hitting pinpoint targets. It employs a directional gyro to guide it and carries a TNT warhead rather than a nuclear type, simply because the former would be more suitable for limited targets, such as dams and railroad bridges or yards. It is a two-stage affair and the first stage develops 82 metric tons of thrust, the second develops 24 metric tons.

[1] A later ICBM has been reported with a range of up to 8,000 miles.

More interesting is a special evolution that has taken place from this missile. Designated the $T4A$, it is a winged-type vehicle that employs the boost-glide principles first publicised by Dr Eugen Saenger. Saenger worked for the Germans during the Second World War and wrote a paper on his boost-glide rocket-powered vehicle that could be developed to a high altitude rocket bomber capable of ranges up to 10,000 miles. Saenger reasoned that such a vehicle could be made to skip almost half-way around the world and could drop its load of bombs on target while on the way over a continent inhabited by the enemy. As recounted in a later chapter, the Russians, and especially Stalin himself, took a special interest in Saenger's ideas. They evidently went ahead with the project on their own, and developed a three-stage rocket bomber. The first two stages probably have thrusts of 120 metric tons each while the third produces 35 metric tons, and is of polished stainless steel so as to have the necessary strength-to-weight ratio for the high stresses and high heat caused by passing through varying densities of the atmosphere at high speed. To date, indications are that the Russian $T4A$ is intended to be unmanned, though it would not be surprising if a manned version appeared in the Soviet technological arsenal in the future.

The Russian $T5$ is an improved German *Rheintochter* missile developed late in the Second World War. It is now in the Red Army's arsenal for use against targets from 25 to 100 miles away from launching. A four-stage affair, it is one of the few Soviet missiles that employs solid fuels.

The $T6$ is a two-stage anti-aircraft missile, truck-mounted. It is believed to have a proximity fuse and may be employed against targets within a twenty-five miles radius. $T7$ is a meteorological rocket used for experimental work, and $T7A$ is a special version employed as a surface to surface weapon. The latter has a range of about 100 miles.

$T8$ is an infra-red seeking anti-aircraft missile now said to be available to defend major Soviet targets. It has a range of about twenty miles.

The Russians have not limited themselves to non-air breathing types. At least three missiles employing turbo-jet engines or ramjets have been experimented with and carried into the development stage. These are winged vehicles: the first is the $J1$; the second is the

J 2 designed to be launched from submarines, and the third, the *J 3*, has swept wings as if it were capable of transonic speeds. These missiles are not believed to have a major role to play in the Soviet arsenal.

Pulsejets, such as the Germans used in their *V1* missile, have also interested the Kremlin. They took over the more sophisticated German pulsejet testing centre during the Second World War and have since developed some missiles employing this engine, though it is doubtful whether such missiles are important to the Red Army today. Similarly, while work has been done on ramjets, there is little to indicate that the Russians are now using them to power missiles.

As stated earlier, the Germans had carried out some experimental work in 1945 in launching long range missiles underwater from submarines and the Soviet authorities went ahead from where the Germans at Peenemunde had come to an abrupt stop at the end of the Second World War. The information available suggests that two series of long range rockets have been developed, the *Golem* and the *Komet* series. The *Golem* rockets, of which three different types have been developed, are thought to be the ones to be fired when the submarine is travelling well below the surface while the *Komet* series are more dual nature in purpose and can be used as both ship-launched and land-launched weapons. The *Golem 1* is the submarine-launched equivalent of the *T 2* rocket. It is a liquid fuel rocket giving an initial thrust of some 50–60 tons and a range of some 300–400 miles. The *Golem 2* and *3* are the operational equivalent of the US *Polaris* missile and are two-stage rockets with an operational range of perhaps 1,200–1,500 miles. While the *Golem 2* is reported to have liquid fuel rockets the *Golem 3* is stated to have solid fuel engines which may give it increased range up to 2,000 miles. The *Komet* rockets are also believed to have solid fuel propellants, the *Komet 1* having a range of, perhaps, 150 miles and the *Komet 2*, 600–700 miles. It is also reported that a two-stage *Komet 3* is under development with a range of, perhaps, 1,800 miles.

While the impact of these submarine-launched long range rockets on both Soviet and American strategy will be considerable in the 1960s and 1970s, at the moment they must rate second in importance to the long range strategic attack potential of the *DA* jet bombers and the land based long range rockets. While the Soviet Union may have hundreds of ocean-going submarines, it is doubtful whether she has at the most more than a few dozen fitted to fire long range rockets and manned by trained crews whose navigational standards permit them to reach an action station with pin point accuracy after cruising, perhaps, thousands of miles underwater. Despite all that has been written and is likely to be written about the future influence of rocket-firing submarines on contemporary strategy, the subsonic and supersonic bomber is a much speedier, more flexible and more accurate method of delivering atomic and thermo-nuclear loads. It may, therefore, remain the main spearhead of Soviet strategic attack for several years yet. But with each year that passes, the long range attacking power of Soviet submarines will become more important to over-all Soviet strategy.

In launching their *Sputniks*, the Russians apparently employed special versions of the *T 3* and *T 3A* rocket engines. According to information reaching German sources, these were the *CH 9, CH 10*, and *CH 11*, used to launch *Sputniks I, II* and *III*. It is believed that a three-stage rocket was used to launch *Sputnik I*, and that it had a take-off weight of 211,200 lb. The first stage engine produced about 451,000 lb of thrust and the second and third stages had 264,000 lb and 77,000 lb respectively. *Sputnik II* was heavier, and the total launching weight was 228,800 lb, according to the best information available. The first stage engines produced 517,000 lb of thrust and benefited from solid fuel boosters that produced another 140,000 lb. The second and third stages were similar to the same stages for *Sputnik I*. Less is known of the launching of *Sputnik III*, though a three-stage rocket was used. There have been any number of reports that the Russians have built an 800,000 lb thrust rocket engine and have tested it. If so, it is logical to suppose that it was used in launching *Sputnik III*.

From the size of *Sputnik III*, and with its weight established at 2,900 lb, it seems likely that the Soviets have developed enormous missile powerplants beyond the size of those currently available in the West. The Russians, however, may not have put all of the sophistication found in Western missiles and earth satellites into their ICBMs and *Sputniks*. At the moment of writing, this trend is all too evident in the earth satellite programme. The highly sophisticated *Vanguard* has failed repeatedly to get into orbit. The less sophisticated *Explorer* has been put into orbit by the US with far more success.

It is our opinion that the *Sputniks* are even less sophisticated than the *Explorers*. This is partly based on the observation of one of us who examined replicas of the *Sputniks* at the Academy of Sciences Pavilion at the Agricultural and Industrial Exhibition in Moscow in 1958. There the guidance system of *Sputnik III* was explained in sufficient detail for its principles to become self-evident. They were based simply on rate of climb data obtained from accelerometer equipment, and angle-to-the-earth data taken from a magnetometer or refined version of the dip needle used in high school physics classes. The two types of data, fed into a computer, gave *Sputnik*'s position relative to the earth and when this matched certain pre-programmed points along the trajectory the first and second stages were cut off and finally the cap over *Sputnik III* was sprung free as it went into orbit. Corrections could be fed into a finned second stage as necessary to achieve the orbit which the third stage ultimately achieved. This is a far cry from the type of guidance being worked on in the West. Admittedly, the more sophisticated type of development ultimately leads to a finer product, but within a given time period it may result in the West not having a superior weapon in hand at the time that the Soviets do.

It is unlikely that the Soviet Union will have any appreciable numbers of intercontinental ballistic missiles or of ocean-going submarines capable of firing the latest *Golem* and *Komet* long range rockets much before 1960.[1] Even then they will not be able to attack US rocket or air bases with sufficient accuracy to ensure the effective neutralisation of NATO deterrent air and rocket forces. Soviet sources claim for their ICBMs an accuracy of about plus or minus five miles. This in practice is likely to be optimistic. By further dispersal and further mobility, NATO can neutralise the advantages in strategic attack which the USSR may enjoy in the early 1960s, especially if the plans to step up the number of US rocket-firing submarines are implemented.

[1] US Defence Secretary, McElroy recently estimated a total of 1,000 Soviet ICBM's in the early 1960s.

CHAPTER 10

SOVIET AIRBORNE TROOPS

J. M. Mackintosh

IT HAS BECOME a recognised fact in military history that the Soviet Union was the first to plan, organise and integrate parachute troops and airborne units into the armed forces. The birth of parachute troops is generally assigned to the years 1930 and 1931, when two Russian Air Force commanders were sent to the United States to examine American safety parachutes and to select those most suitable for military purposes. It was in 1930 that a Soviet military publication wrote: 'The parachute is no longer a lifebelt, but an offensive weapon of the future.'

In 1931 there were already two small units of professional parachutists in the Red Air Force, and it is reported that in the previous year a small group of individual parachutists made a successful landing at manoeuvres in the Moscow Military District and seized a Corps Headquarters. First experiments were made with a device in which the parachutist lay in a kind of coffin attached to the underside of the fuselage of an aircraft. When the dropping ground was reached, the pilot pulled a lever, the coffin turned over, and the parachutist fell out, his parachute opening automatically by static line attached to the coffin. This device was tried on various types of aircraft, the *TB 1*, the *ANT 9*, and the *R 5*, but was found to be impracticable, and Soviet parachutists began to be trained to jump from their aircraft. At first the need was for instructors and these were chosen from air force personnel. Gradually, infantrymen began to be selected for parachute training; at first they were returned to their infantry units after qualifying, for it was not until 1932 that the first airborne brigade was formed and called the 'air brigade for special employment'. Its training area was near Leningrad, it consisted of 450 trained parachutists and about nine aircraft of the *TB 1* type, and the same number of *R 5s*. After successful experiments had been carried out with this 'brigade', it was decided to create small units of parachutists in other Military Districts, for instance White Russia, Kiev, and the Far East. Training and exercises concentrated mainly on dropping small parties of parachutists for reconnaissance and sabotage, and on the transport of weapons and ammunition. The Air Force, meanwhile, was carrying out experiments to find the best type of aircraft for the airborne units. In 1934 they introduced the *TB 3*, a four-engined transport plane with six openings for simultaneous jumping.

By the later summer of 1935, the development of airborne forces had reached the state at which the Soviet High Command believed that they could be put through their paces in front of foreign military observers. In that year the main manœuvres were held in the Kiev Military District. Suddenly, foreign service attachés saw a fleet of *TB 3s* appear and drop 600 parachutists, who, on landing, formed a roughly circular defence perimeter. A few minutes later, another group of planes appeared, landed within the perimeter, and took off again after unloading a unit of fully armed infantrymen. A third wave of aircraft followed bringing artillery, ammunition and supplies. In the same year, a whole rifle division of 14,000 men, with all arms, supplies and equipment, was transported by air from Moscow to Vladivostok: not only a technical achievement, but a warning to the Japanese in the Far East at a time when Soviet-Japanese relations were becoming strained.

The successes of the 1935 manœuvres encouraged the Soviet advocates of airborne forces, and in 1936 parachute drops were shown to the public twice: in the manœuvres in the White Russian Military District and in the Caucasus. In White Russia, where the airborne unit had been brought up to the strength of a brigade (two battalions of 300 men each), the drop included light weapons brought to earth on parachutes, and the introduction of the double parachute for increased safety. In 1937, it was clear from the manœuvres in the Moscow Military District that the problems of individual parachute descents by small units had been largely solved (some Soviet parachute pioneers were recording jumps of over 10,000 metres), and the attention of the High Command turned to the transport of tanks and other equipment by air. Experiments were tried involving the attachment of vehicles, guns and light tanks to the underside of the fuselage by steel hawsers, and it appears that, by

1937–8, a device of this kind had been constructed which could hold the Soviet army tank current in 1937, the *T 37*.

At this point, however, the Soviet policy of regular display of progress in airborne development ceased. This may have been due to the fact that experiments were entering more technical fields of weapon transport, or to the appearance of unsuspected difficulties; whatever the reason, the era of spectacular novelty was over. The Red Army purge of 1937 and 1938 may also have had an effect on progress in this field, involving, as it did, the Deputy Commissar for War, Marshal Tuchachevski, who was believed to have been the organising brain behind the development of airborne forces. Certainly at least one prominent officer who was later connected with airborne troops, General Gorbatov, was thrown into prison in 1937, as Khrushchev revealed in his secret speech in February 1956. On the basis of Khrushchev's accusations against Stalin, it is logical to assume that the progress of this new arm was slowed down by the purge as were the other arms of service in the immediate pre-war period.

However, numerically and in organisation the Soviet airborne forces did increase and develop after 1937, and certainly there was no lessening of official encouragement to young men and women to take up parachute jumping as a sport in preparation for army service. This preliminary training was carried out in the para-military youth organisation *Ossoaviakhim*, founded in 1927, to help to prepare the people of the country for defence, by interesting them in flying, sharpshooting, athletics, and later, parachute jumping. Literally thousands of young Soviet citizens underwent elementary parachute training and great publicity was given to individual feats. In 1940, a Major Kharakhonov completed his 599th jump from a height of 13,025 metres, falling 11,755 metres before pulling his rip-cord.

Publicity was, however, denied to the airborne units in the forces as they grew in size and strength. In 1938, the airborne troops were reorganised into four brigades of 1,000 men each, one brigade being stationed in each of the Leningrad, Kiev, White Russian and Far Eastern Military Districts. In the next year, 1939, the airborne forces had their first baptism of fire—as infantry. During the Soviet Japanese clashes in July and August 1939 along the Manchurian frontier, the 212th airborne brigade, stationed in the Far East, was thrown into the battle as infantry, and fought a number of bitterly contested local actions against the Japanese. This initial use of carefully trained airborne units as infantry was, in fact, an ominous pointer to the future for the Soviet airborne forces.

Within a month, the Second World War broke out, and on 17th September 1939, Soviet troops, including some parachute troops, entered eastern Poland. In November, the Red Army invaded Finland, and here the High Command attempted to use the airborne forces of the Leningrad Military District to seize important military objectives ahead of the land armies. The intense cold and impossible flying conditions cut down these operations to the minimum, and by the later stages of the Soviet-Finnish war the airborne troops found themselves once more employed as infantry.

The years 1940 and 1941 witnessed a thorough overhaul of the Soviet armed forces, partly because of the failures in the Finnish war, and partly as a result of Soviet studies of German tactics and experience in the campaign against France and the Low Countries, and later of the airborne operation against Crete. Soviet military experts who had been in Spain during the Civil War had returned with the impression that there was little future for large mobile formations such as armoured corps or mass airborne assaults, and the Soviet High Command had, in consequence, restricted the size of such formations. But after the German successes in France and Belgium in 1940, in which massed armoured and airborne forces played so vital a part, Soviet military planners changed their minds, and began the re-establishment of large mobile groups. Early in 1941 the first Soviet tank corps were activated (only very few were ready and fully equipped when the German assault came in June), and in May, airborne forces of the key western military districts were reorganised as airborne corps. They were deployed as follows:

> 3rd Airborne Corps in Kiev
> 4th Airborne Corps in the Minsk area
> 5th Airborne Corps in Leningrad.

Each corps was meant to have three parachute brigades, but by the outbreak of the Soviet-German war, only the original brigade in each was fully equipped. They were subordinate to the Headquarters of the Air Force in Moscow.

On 22nd June 1941, the German invasion of Russia began, and

within a few weeks the Red Army on the western frontier had been driven back towards Moscow, Leningrad and Kiev with enormous losses in men and material. The three airborne corps became inextricably mixed up with the retreating land armies, and, being deprived of aircraft by the collapse of Soviet air power during the frontier battles, were thrown into the front line as infantry. One airborne brigade, the 214th, broke out of German encirclement near Smolensk in July 1941, and its personnel, presumably acting on orders from Moscow, acquired civilian clothes, merged with the local population, and formed the nucleus of a partisan unit. At the end of August 1941, a small detachment was organised from the scattered remnants of the 3rd Airborne Corps in the Ukraine, and dropped into besieged Odessa, where the parachutists succeeded in reinforcing a dangerously weak sector of the line. Another airborne brigade survived to fight at the approaches to Moscow in November 1941, and during the Russian counter-offensive in the Crimea at the end of the year, parachutists from bases in the North Caucasus landed behind the German lines on the Arbat peninsula, and helped marines to re-occupy the towns of Kerch and Feodosia.

These were, however, individual operations by small units which had survived the early disasters of the summer of 1941. It seems clear that the Soviet High Command was not discouraged, and as early as August 1941 decided to re-create a powerful force of airborne troops for employment in the 1942 campaigns. In October 1941, the activation of ten airborne corps began in the Caucasus and the lower Volga region, and in spite of great difficulties such as shortage of training aircraft from which to make parachute jumps, by the end of the year, the first corps, numbering about 8,000 to 10,000 men each, were deployed in reserve in the Moscow area. By the middle of February 1942, all ten airborne corps were grouped in or near Moscow, and plans for their intervention in the Red Army's winter offensive were well advanced.

At this time, the Soviet airborne forces had been removed from the command of the Air Force, and placed directly under the Commissariat of Defence as an independent arm of service, under Major-General V. A. Glazunov. In operations, each corps came under the direct command of the Front or Army-Group Commander. First of the new airborne corps to go into battle was the 4th, whose brigades were dropped in the rear of the German defence position at Vyazma, west of Moscow. Here, in January 1942, a mobile group composed of cavalry, tank brigades and ski troops operating under the command of Major-General (now Colonel-General) P. A. Belov, had broken through the German lines and was harassing German communications between Vyazma and Smolensk. More than 10,000 airborne troops were dropped to help Belov's operations, in what has been described in the Soviet press as the biggest airborne operation of the Soviet-German war. In temperatures of 40° C of frost, units of the 4th Airborne Corps led by Colonel Kazankin and Lieutenant-Colonel Onufriev joined General Belov's raiding columns, which, although they were unable to effect any major strategic gain such as the capture of Vyazma, continued to cause considerable losses to the Germans right up to the end of the winter snows and the spring thaw in April. In the later stages of General Belov's raid, units of the 3rd and 10th Airborne Corps were also dropped as reinforcements, and it is interesting to note that when casualties became heavy, the raiding troops were able to obtain replacements from among partisans in the area, some of whom were themselves ex-paratroopers.

A change of fortune on the battlefield, however, brought this brief period of airborne activity to an end, for in June and July 1942, the Germans broke through the Russian front in the Ukraine, and raced eastwards towards Stalingrad and the Caucasus. So urgent was the need for ground forces that the Soviet High Command withdrew its ten airborne corps from service, and converted them into infantry divisions and armoured corps, and rushed them southwards to the Don to take part in the Battle of Stalingrad. During this period, only one airborne operation took place: the seizure of an airfield near Maikop in the foothills of the Caucasus in October 1942, followed up by the landing of a small unit near the Black Sea port of Novorosiisk.

At the end of 1942 another attempt was made to resurrect the ten airborne corps, but an initial plan to employ parachute troops against the German fortress in the Demyansk salient in February 1943 was considered too costly and in April 1943 a new policy for airborne forces was adopted. The ten corps were reorganised as ten 'Guards Airborne Rifle Divisions', and sent into front-line armies as infantry formations, though preserving their distinctive name and prestige. They continued to figure in major land battles up to the end of the war, and took part in the capture of Budapest and Vienna in 1945. But they ceased to be in any way connected with airborne operations.

In April 1943, a new kind of airborne force came into being, the Guards Parachute Brigades, subordinate to the Commissariat of Defence. About fifteen or twenty of these brigades were formed by the end of 1943, and each contained four parachute battalions, together with engineer, signals, anti-tank and machine-gun units. The brigade strength was just over 3,000 men. The airborne forces did not have their own aircraft, but used those of the Long-Range Air Force and the Civil Air Fleet. These were usually *PS 84s*, a transport plane resembling the American Douglas *DC 3*, adapted to carry twenty-five parachutists each with full equipment.

Employment of the new brigades was attempted in the autumn of 1943 during the Russians' crossing of the river Dnieper. The most important of these operations was that carried out in September 1943, near Kanev, south of Kiev, by 5,000 parachutists under the command of Lieutenant-Colonel Sidorchuk, drawn from the 1st, 3rd and 5th Guards Parachute Brigades. It does not seem to have been very successful, and was, in fact, the last attempt by the Soviet High Command to use parachute troops on any scale in the Second World War. It is true that parachutists were dropped on towns in Manchuria during the brief Soviet-Japanese War in August 1945, but their use has been described officially as 'small scale air-landing operations'. In fact, the independent parachute brigade of the period 1943–5 went out of commission shortly after the end of the war, and it is one of the puzzles of the Soviet-German war that whereas 1945 brought a highly efficient and well-accepted airborne divisional formation in both the British and the American armies, the Soviet Army was apparently not able to find a satisfactory organisation capable of tackling tasks beyond those of a tactical nature, or sabotage and co-operation with partisan forces. It is possible, and has indeed been suggested, that the airborne operation at Kanev in September 1943 was intended to be on a much bigger scale, and might have led to the re-establishment of airborne corps, had not the operation failed to come up to expectations. Indeed, looking back on the role of Soviet airborne forces during the Second World War, it is difficult to avoid the conclusion that they were at their most dangerous during their period of co-operation with General Belov's battle group behind the enemy's lines in 1942, in conditions where they could, if necessary, merge into the local population, in order to carry on the fight as partisans, reappearing as regular troops if necessary. Parachutists could conduct major sabotage operations, assist the partisans, and keep them supplied with arms and explosives. But in the larger strategic uses of airborne forces (the seizure of key positions, bridgeheads and lines of communications by major formations such as the Western allies achieved in the crossing of the Rhine in 1945), Soviet airborne forces did not seem to have found success. Nor did any outstanding commander of airborne forces emerge in the Soviet Army in 1944–5.

The fact that Soviet airborne techniques and experience developed along different lines from those in Western armies should not blind us to the fact that their speciality is sabotage, partisan work, and other activities behind the lines. Although the Soviet forces have been reorganised into divisions in the post-war period (the generally accepted estimate seems to be about ten divisions of three regiments each, with about 10,000 men to a division), each division has a unit trained and equipped for this kind of work. While the wartime activities of the Soviet airborne forces are by now fairly well documented, official secrecy prevents any reliable description of this arm of service as it exists today. Very little is known about the position of the command of the airborne forces within the Ministry of Defence, or its relations with its original parent, the Soviet Air Force. The most probable organisation is that of an independent headquarters staff, responsible directly to the Ministry of Defence, and headed by a marshal. The headquarters probably controls a number of subordinate staffs dealing with the airborne divisions themselves, with the aircraft supplied to the airborne forces, with technical supplies and equipment, and so on. The headquarters certainly has its political directorate, and probably also an inspectorate. It deals directly with the divisions which, according to German sources, consist of one parachute regiment, one air-landing regiment, whose equipment includes gliders, and the special sabotage regiment of which mention has already been made. One thing is certain: that the parachute troops themselves are *élite* troops in the highest category, as regards both physical fitness and intelligence. Many of the rank and file would certainly be senior NCOs and warrant officers in infantry units, and the training which they undergo is extremely demanding. In addition to the technical training of parachute jumping, Soviet parachutists have to qualify in swimming, cross-country running, ju-jitsu and unarmed combat.

It seems likely that the airborne forces now have their own aircraft complement, though they can call on the resources of the Civil Air Fleet, whose aircraft strength is believed to be about 8,000. One of the most interesting of recent developments has been the change-over to modern helicopters as the means of transport for the air-landing units of the airborne forces. It was in June 1953, on Air Force Day at Tushino airfield that foreign observers first saw helicopters used in this way, when a flight landed troops and motor-cycles swiftly and effectively. The Soviet Army paper *Red Star*, of 28th December 1957, described how helicopters took part in recent manœuvres. A unit of airborne troops was ordered to seize a target area on the other side of a river, and to hold it until relieved by a tank battalion. As soon as the helicopters landed, the target area was quickly secured and sealed off, while the remainder of the unit unloaded guns and equipment. The area was successfully held until the arrival of the tanks.

Indeed, it is likely that helicopters will play an increasingly important part in the development of Soviet airborne forces. In 1954, at the Air Day Parade thirty-six large helicopters took part, and unloaded military vehicles and small guns. In the following year, twin-rotor helicopters, *YAK 24s*, were shown, out of which a complete truck and anti-tank gun drove, ready for action. One of the leading constructors of light helicopters is N. I. Kamov, who has built a machine which can land on a 3 ton truck; M. L. Mil is another constructor who has built standard machines for the airborne forces. The Russians are particularly interested in jet-propelled helicopters, and press articles have quoted with approval the published data on the *MI 6*, and also the future possibilities of helicopters fitted with automatic pilot mechanisms.

As in most branches of the Soviet armed forces, technical details are difficult to obtain, and guesswork is frequently misleading. However, the future of the airborne arm of the Soviet forces has been described by the man who may well be the commander of the field forces, Hero of the Soviet Union Lieutenant-General V. Margelov. In *Red Star* on 28th December 1957, he wrote: 'The experience of the Great Fatherland War, and the development of military science and military technology have injected new blood and importance into the role of airborne forces in modern war. This role has increased still further because of the appearance of weapons of mass destruction. The employment of airborne forces in conditions of the use of weapons of mass destruction opens wide possibilities for deep offensive movements, and for speeding them up. Air landings will be widely used in the future for the seizure of important areas, river lines and crossings, mountain passes, and ridges, and in order to remove obstacles in the path of the advancing armies. They will also be used for the destruction of targets deep in the enemy's rear, such as centres of communication. These tasks impose on all ranks the need to perfect the battle readiness of their units.'

It is difficult to tell to what extent General Margelov's words in 1957 represent the dream of the military theoreticians in the Ministry of Defence: a dream which may be as difficult to put into practice as were the probable plans for using large airborne formations in the Ukraine in 1943. According to some eye-witnesses in western Hungary, Soviet airborne forces carried out an unopposed parachute drop near Veszprem, west of Lake Balaton on 4th November 1956, with speed and precision. This is the only known occasion when Soviet airborne forces were used in semi-operational conditions. All that can be said at this stage is that the Soviet armed forces do possess about ten divisions of highly-trained well-equipped airborne forces, each of which could represent a serious and extremely dangerous opponent both in the mass and in individual units. Perhaps, in spite of training, of equipment, and of morale, in conditions of modern war, the Soviet airborne force might find its most effective role once again as a link between partisans and the Centre, as groups of saboteurs, or as small, individual battle groups operating on their own initiative, whose mopping up could cause their opponent much damage and loss.

CHAPTER II

SOVIET AIR POWER
ORGANIZATION AND STAFF WORK

Dr Raymond L. Garthoff

THE ORGANISATIONAL STRUCTURE of the air forces of a state is a valuable key to understanding its underlying military strategic concepts and doctrine. Soviet military leaders are fully aware of this structural reflection of doctrine. Lieutenant-General of Aviation Zhuravlev, for example, noted some years ago that: 'The relationship among the various forms of aviation of the air force of any country permits one to judge the content of its military doctrine on the role of air power.'[1]

Soviet military strategic concepts have broadened in recent years, to provide greater importance to the long-range offensive air arm and to air defence, and the Soviet air establishment has similarly been expanded. This significant development has not, however, led to a lessening of the traditional Soviet attention to providing powerful tactical air power for support of the surface forces. As Marshal Zhukov authoritatively declared: 'In the post-war construction of the armed forces we are proceeding from the fact that victory in future war will be achieved only by the combined efforts of all arms of the armed forces and on the basis of their co-ordinated employment in war.'[2] This remains true since his ouster, and the organisation of the Soviet armed forces does, indeed, reflect this continuing doctrinal principle.

The basic organisational structure of the Soviet armed forces is their unity in a single powerful Ministry of Defence. The Army and Navy have previously alternated between separate and unified ministerial representation; the Air Forces have never had cabinet

---

[1] Lieutenant-General of Aviation N. Zhuravlev, *Vestnik vozdushnogo flota* (Herald of the Air Fleet), organ of the Soviet Air Forces, No. 1, January 1952, p. 67.

[2] Marshal G. Zhukov, cited in *Krasnaia zvezda*, 23rd March 1957.

representation. Under the Minister of Defence are a series of 'administrations' and 'chief administrations'. Among these are six major operational commands: the chief administrations of the Air Forces, the Ground Forces, the Naval Forces, the Air Defence Forces, the Long Range Aviation, and the Airborne Troops. Among the First Deputy and Deputy Ministers of Defence are the Commanders-in-Chief of the Ground Forces, the Air Forces, the Naval Forces, and the Air Defence Forces. Their functions, however, vary; the commanders-in-chief of the naval forces and air defence forces have a direct operational *command* relationship over all their component forces, including respectively the naval aviation and interceptor aviation components of these commands.

The Soviet Air Forces in the Second World War

Let us begin with a brief look at the Soviet Air Forces in the Second World War. The organisation of military aviation was divided among a number of air forces: the Army Air Force (VVS-KA), Navy Air Force (VVS-VMF), the Interceptor Air Defence Forces (IA-PVO), and from April 1942 until December 1944, a separate Aviation of Long Range Operations (ADD). The main component was the Air Force of the Red Army, VVS-KA, which sometimes had up to 90 per cent of all military aircraft. Correspondingly, the Main Staff of the VVS-KA was the central air force staff, though the other forces noted also had their own main staffs. The Main Staff of the VVS was of course closely tied to the dominant General Staff of the Red Army. In the field, the main organisation was the 'Air Army', which was the air support force for a Front (Army Group). The Air Army Commander was under the Commander-in-Chief and Main Staff of the VVS-KA, but he was also *operationally* subordinate to the Front commander, a ground forces general or marshal. The Air Corps, Divisions, Regiments, and Squadrons were subordinated hierarchically (in that declining order) to the Air Army. The Main Staff of the VVS controlled basic aviation training, material replacements, etc., for *all* of the air forces excepting the Naval Air Force. During the war, it was not inaccurate to say the Soviets had a unified air force: the tactical, supporting Army Air Force was virtually the whole of Soviet air power. As we have noted, in December 1944, the Long Range Air Force was 'merged' into it as the 18th Tactical Air Army, and beginning about the same time the air defence fighter force declined as the front moved away from the USSR.

In March 1946, the first post-war development of significance occurred: the war-time high command under Chief Marshal of Aviation Novikov, a young and capable officer, was disbanded, and some of them (including Novikov) were arrested. The Long Range Air Force was re-established and the Air Defence Force began to grow. But rather than chronologically tracing developments, let us turn to the present organisational picture.

The Air Force High Command

The Commander-in-Chief of the Air Forces (an office that has existed since 1937) *represents* all the air forces in the Military Council of the Ministry of Defence, for certain aircraft and ordnance development and procurement and personnel training. But operational command is limited to the tactical air forces and this is shared with the corresponding superior Army units in the field. As we have noted, the Long Range Aviation is an autonomous command, and the Navy, Air Defence, and Airborne Troops aviation components are part of combined commands.

The present Commander-in-Chief of the Air Force is Marshal of Aviation Konstantin A. Vershinin, the ninth incumbent of the office in the past twenty years, and in the post since January 1957. This marks the second tour in the office for Vershinin, who occupied the post from March 1946 to July 1949. Chief Marshal of Aviation Pavel F. Zhigarev served in the interim period from 1949 until 1957 (the second tour for him also; he had briefly and unsuccessfully held the office from July 1941 to May 1942). Zhigarev now heads the Civil Air Fleet, and in listings of governmental officials is usually accorded a place higher than his successor, despite the evidently lesser real importance of his new post. Chief Marshal of Aviation Aleksander A. Novikov, war-time chief of the air force (from August 1942 until March 1946) was imprisoned after his sudden relief by Stalin in 1946 until 1953. For a time in 1954 he served as a deputy to Zhigarev, but he is now in retirement. Marshal of Aviation Sergei I. Rudenko has been First Deputy Commander-in-Chief since 1949, and Chief of Staff of the Air Force Staff for most of this period.

CHART ONE

The Administrative Structure of the Air Forces

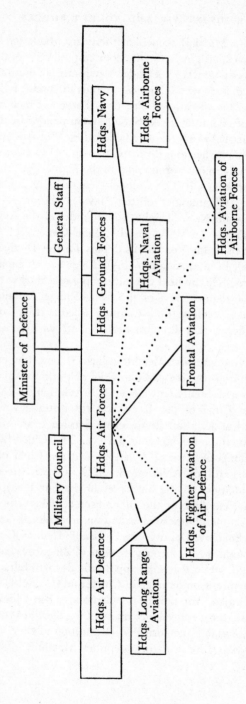

The Headquarters of Air Defence, Air Forces, Ground Forces, and Navy are headed by commanders-in-chief; those of Long Range Aviation and Airborne Forces by commanders; and those of Naval Aviation, Fighter Aviation of Air Defence, and Aviation of Airborne Forces by commanders subordinate to the intermediate commands.

—————— Direct subordination.
— — — — Partial subordination.
· · · · · · · · · · · No subordination, but responsibility for initial training, servicing, supply, etc.

In addition to Marshal Rudenko, there are about ten 'Deputy Commander-in-Chiefs', including the four commanders of the active air combat forces who were not under Vershinin's operational command, and the deputy who in fact commands the tactical air forces, which are under his operational direction. These five men currently are: Marshal of Aviation V. A. Sudets, Commander of the Long Range Aviation (DA) (and former Chief of Staff of the Air Forces under Vershinin's earlier tour, from 1946 to 1949); Colonel-General of Aviation I. D. Klimov, Commander of the Fighter Aviation of the Air Defence Forces (IA-PVO); Colonel-General of Aviation Ye. N. Preobrazhensky, Commander of the Naval Aviation (A-VMF); Marshal of Aviation N. S. Skripko, Commander of the Aviation of the Airborne Troops (A-VDV); and Colonel-General of Aviation Ye. F. Loginov, probably Vershinin's deputy for the Tactical, or, as it is now termed, Frontal Aviation (FA). These are all capable and experienced men; Klimov held the same command during the war; Skripko was the deputy chief of the Long Range Aviation (then ADD); Rudenko, Sudets, and Loginov filled varied command and staff positions; and Preobrazhensky had various naval air commands.

The other five deputies to Vershinin head responsible services of the air forces. One is the inescapable chief of the Political Administration, at present Lieutenant-General of Aviation A. G. Rytov. The incumbent Chief of the Rear Services is unknown to me. Colonel-General of Aviation Engineering Service I. V. Markov is Chief of the Aviation Engineering Service. The Chief Inspector, probably a Colonel-General of Aviation, and the Chief of Training, Colonel-General of Aviation S. A. Krasovsky (from 1947 until 1953 commander of the air forces in the Far East), are the other two deputies. Among the other senior officers in the Air Forces' High Command deserving attention are Colonel-General of Aviation I. M. Sokolov, Deputy Chief of Staff; Colonel-General of Aviation F. A. Agal'tsov, a former associate of Zhigarev's, and for a time Chief of Staff while Rudenko apparently devoted full attention to being First Deputy Commander-in-Chief; and Colonel-General of Aviation P. I. Braiko, Assistant to the Commander-in-Chief.

Gone from the scene, retired, are many of the Second World War chiefs who rose, and fell, meteorically. In addition to Chief Marshal of Aviation Novikov, his war-time deputies Marshals of Aviation

CHART TWO

Operational Command of the Air Forces

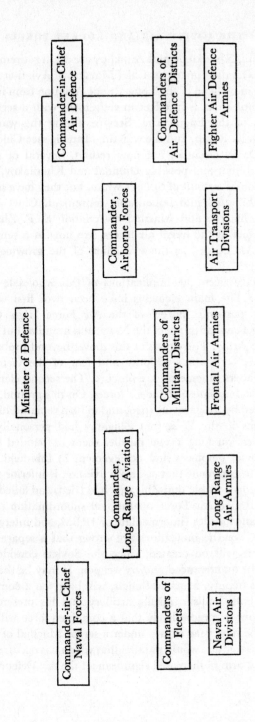

Defensive rocket batteries are subordinate to Commanders of Air Defence Districts. Long Range Offensive Rockets, pending further expansion and development, are probably part of the responsibility of Headquarters of Artillery Arm on the General Staff, with special supervision by the Ministry of Defence. Presumably Headquarters of the Navy are also directly concerned.

(Editor's Note)

Vorozheikin, Khudiakov and Astakhov are all in retirement (as was Falaleev, who died in 1955). Chief Marshal of Aviation Aleksander Ye. Golovanov, head of the Long Range Aviation from its initiation in 1942 until 1948, is in effect in retirement with a serious illness. The chief of the Engineering Service during the war, Colonel-General A. K. Repin, and the war-time Intelligence Chief, Colonel-General D. D. Grendal, are now retired. Several of these men, Novikov, Repin, and possibly Grendal and Khudiakov, fell victim to repression as a result of Stalin's whim, but they have now at least been rehabilitated into honourable retirement. Chief Marshal of Aviation Zhigarev and Marshal of Aviation S. F. Zhavoronkov, wartime chief of the naval air forces, are now in a sense 'retired' from the Air Forces, as the two chiefs of the growing Civil Air Fleet.

What have been the implications of this wholesale change of command? The main elements have been two: first was Stalin's immediate post-war 'purge' of the Air Force High Command, paralleling a similar purge of the Navy, and a similar but less drastic shift in the Army. The causes of this move, beyond probably sound speculations on Stalin's jealousy and fear of the victory-flushed military leaders in general, are obscure. The second element was a drive for modernisation of the air forces. On this ground, Vershinin was replaced by Zhigarev in 1949, and in turn replaced him in 1957. Speculations in the West that Zhigarev had personally favoured greater stress on long range missiles seem ill-founded in view of evident Soviet emphasis and achievement in this field, and Vershinin's own comment that strategic aviation is inferior to missiles. But it remains possible that Zhigarev had tried, and failed, to get for the Long Range Air Force operational subordination of the long range ballistic missiles (intermediate or IRBM, and intercontinental or ICBM). For the indications are strong that a separate ballistic missile force will be created, since the Soviets consider ballistic rockets to be an advanced *artillery* weapon. It may be that Marshal Vershinin's deputy, Marshal Sudets, will be given a combined one including both ballistic missile artillery and his present strategic bombers; but it is more likely that a combined force will be established in the next year or two under a senior Marshal of the Soviet Union. This solution would parallel that which has occurred with the other major arm of increased significance: the Air Defence Forces.

CHART THREE

Headquarters, Air Forces (GU-VVS)

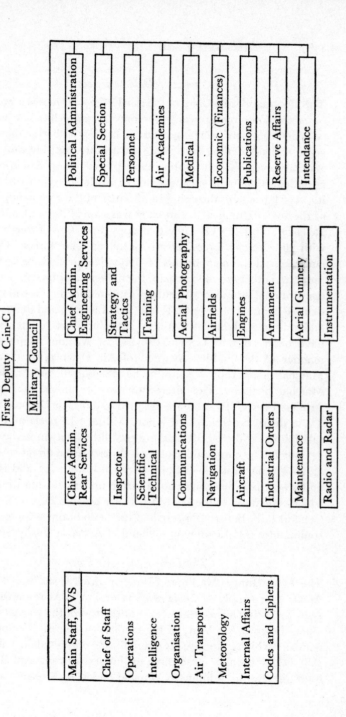

Commander-in-Chief
First Deputy C-in-C

Military Council

Main Staff, VVS

Chief of Staff
Operations
Intelligence
Organisation
Air Transport
Meteorology
Internal Affairs
Codes and Ciphers

Chief Admin. Rear Services

Inspector
Scientific Technical
Communications
Navigation
Aircraft
Industrial Orders
Maintenance
Radio and Radar

Chief Admin. Engineering Services

Strategy and Tactics
Training
Aerial Photography
Airfields
Engines
Armament
Aerial Gunnery
Instrumentation

Political Administration

Special Section
Personnel
Air Academies
Medical
Economic (Finances)
Publications
Reserve Affairs
Intendance

The Air Defence Forces

The Commander-in-Chief of the Air Defence Forces is a post which has existed for many years, but only recently has it come to be considered of particular importance. During and after the war, the commanders of this force were invariably anti-aircraft artillery generals, even though fighter-interceptor aviation had come to be regarded as the main means of active air defence by 1946. In 1955, in accordance with the rising importance of the command, Marshal of the Soviet Union S. S. Biryuzov was named its head, and the Air Defence Forces (PVO) came to occupy a position of rough equality with the ground forces, naval forces, and air forces. The PVO embraces all the components of the active air defence system: the radar and other warning system, the fighter aviation component, the conventional anti-aircraft artillery (still retained on a wide scale, in marked contrast to recent UK and US practice), and the new rocket and missile anti-aircraft artillery introduced in recent years. We have observed that Colonel-General of Aviation Klimov, Commander of the Fighter Aviation of Air Defence, is a deputy to Marshal of Aviation Vershinin; he is simultaneously a deputy to Marshal Biryuzov. The interceptors are organised in Fighter Air Armies (IVA-PVD), and are assigned to joint Air Defence Districts. These districts overlap and ignore Military Districts and political subdivisions of the USSR, and are established only in key areas to be defended. The commander of each district is the direct superior for all air defence installations and forces in his district, and is directly under Marshal Biryuzov, who in turn is under Marshal Malinovsky. The Commander of the key Moscow Air Defence District is Colonel-General P. F. Batisty (for much of the period from 1946 to 1953 the commander was Lieutenant-General of Aviation Vasily Stalin).

The Long-Range Air Force

The Long Range Air Force (formerly *Aviatsiia dal'nego deistviia* or ADD; now simply *Dal'naia aviatsiia* or DA) was re-established in 1946, following a two-year period at the end of the war when it was made the 18th Air Army of the tactical air forces. The long range bombers which comprise its strength are organised in Air Armies (VA-DA), of which some three or four exist at present. These are each directly subordinate to Marshal Sudets in Moscow, and he in turn to Marshal Malinovsky. The acquisition of the *TU 4* (*B 29* type) four-engine bombers in the period from 1947 to 1953 gave this force its first real reason for existence. The subsequent modernisation and procurement in large numbers of the twin-jet *Badger*, four-jet *Bison*, and four-turbo-prop *Bear*, long range bombers has made this force a potent threat to the United States as well as to the United Kingdom and other Western powers. As we have suggested earlier, the introduction of long range ballistic missiles may lead to a combined forces organisation, probably entirely independent of Vershinin's air forces. (Submarines equipped for launching missiles against strategic targets may also be taken from the navy and assigned to such a combined strategic striking force.)

Airborne Forces

The Aviation of the Airborne Troops (A-VDV) has been under Marshal of Aviation Skripko since 1950. It is exclusively transport aviation, recently including large helicopters as well as aeroplanes. The 500 or so aircraft assigned provide a substantial airlift. More and more will be four-jet transports in the next few years. They are organised in air transport regiments.

Naval Air Forces

The Naval Air Forces have always been an integral component of the navy, and they so remain. There are no aircraft carriers, nor any planned, in the Soviet Navy.[1]

The fleet air forces are each subordinate to the corresponding Fleet commanders (Northern Fleet, Baltic Fleet, Black Sea Fleet, North Pacific Fleet, Pacific Fleet), and under the naval aviation chief in Moscow.

Frontal Aviation

Frontal Aviation is the somewhat awkward title the Soviets have used to re-christen their tactical air forces. Over half of all Soviet military aircraft are in the twelve or more Frontal Air Armies (FVA). Usually a Frontal Air Army includes about three fighter, three fighter-bomber or ground support, and three light-medium bomber air divisions. Thus the total force may be twenty-seven air regiments.

---

[1] For further information about Naval Air Forces see Chapter 9 of *The Soviet Navy*, edited by Commander M. G. Saunders.

One such Air Army is ordinarily assigned to each Front (Army Group) of the ground forces, to provide cover, support, interdiction, and reconnaissance for the appropriate sector of the front. In peacetime, those military districts designated for activation as Fronts in wartime are generally each assigned a tactical air army. The other, especially interior, military districts have an 'Aviation of the *N* Military District' to administer such tactical and training air force units and installations as are found within the given district. All Frontal Air Armies are administered from Air Force Headquarters in Moscow, but operationally subordinate to the senior ground force commander (Front, Group of Forces, or Military District commander).

Headquarters of the Air Forces

The Chief Administration of the Air Forces (GU-VVS) is composed of the Commander-in-Chief, the Military Council (composed of his senior deputies), the Main Staff or General Staff, the Inspector, the Chief Administrations of Engineering Service, and Rear Services, and a host of other subordinate administrations for personnel, aircraft, engines, armament, aviation academies, maintenance, intendance, navigation, meteorology, strategy and tactics, aerial photography, airfield servicing, industrial orders, training, communications, medical services, and still others.

The Main Staff of the VVS (as it was officially called in 1957, although in 1955 it was termed the 'General Staff of the VVS') is composed of seven sections: Operations, Intelligence, Organisation, Air Transport, Meteorological, Internal (Administration), and Ciphers. The work of these sections is generally self-evident. They are in most instances in close touch with the superior General Staff of the Armed Forces (the former General Staff of the Soviet Army re-christened to reflect its combined military forces representation and competence). Thus, for example, the Intelligence Section is closely tied to the Intelligence Division of the General Staff for many of its sources of information and for co-ordination. The Operations Section is responsible for tactical air forces and training forces operations: but within the framework of the joint service programme established in the Operations Division of the General Staff (under General of the Army M. S. Malinin). The other sections are more autonomous in their relation to the superior staff by virtue of their duties, although liaison is of course necessary.

The Chief Administration of the Rear Services has very wide responsibilities for the whole supply and maintenance infra-structure. It is co-ordinated with the Rear Services of the Ministry of Defence as a whole (under Marshal Ivan K. Bagramiam). The Chief Administration of the Aviation Engineering Service has important lateral ties with the research and development agencies of the Ministries of Aviation and Defence Industry, as well as those operated by the Air Forces and under its direction.

The Chief Political Administration has dual subordination. Lieutenant-General of Aviation Rytov is a deputy to Marshal of Aviation Vershinin, and a deputy to Colonel-General F. I. Golikov, head of the Chief Political Administration for the whole armed forces (who, in turn, has dual subordination to Marshal Malinovsky and to the Military Section of the Central Committee of the Party). Also, a separate organisation with subordination external to the Ministry of Defence is the 'Special Section', which is staffed by secret police counter-intelligence officers.

The Headquarters of the VVS has occupied approximately the same place, and performed the same functions, throughout the post-war period. Its importance has increased as the importance of the air forces in general has risen in the Soviet military establishment; but it also has reflected the continuing dominance of the ground forces marshals in the Ministry of Defence. The precise role of the air forces headquarters has even been subject to confusion by the Soviets themselves. The title of the Air Forces has been given in official published Soviet sources inconsistently, sometimes as 'the Air Forces of the Soviet Army' and sometimes as 'the Air Forces of the Armed Forces'. Yet the inconsistency cannot be explained by a change in name (unless one were to suppose they are constantly changing the title back and forth) or by different contexts (for example, Vershinin's title has been given both ways in the same document). When I had an unusual opportunity to inquire of a senior Soviet Air Force officer about this inconsistency he replied that it didn't make much difference, 'it all comes to the same thing since with us the Army is the main force'. And indeed Soviet official decrees continue to specify 'the Soviet Army and Navy' when obviously the armed forces as a whole, including the air force, are the subject of the reference.

Staff Work

As in other countries, some air force officers tend to command careers and others to staff careers. Both command and staff personnel attend the aviation schools, and the combined services Frunze Academy. A distinction is made for aviation engineering personnel who attend special academies such as the famous Zhukovsky Air Engineering Academy at Moscow (and others at Leningrad, Riga, and elsewhere).

Let us assume that an air force colonel has completed staff courses at the Monino Air Academy, and also the Frunze Academy higher staff course. He is doubtless a veteran of the war, when he may have held a squadron command, and later an air regiment staff position. Since the war he may have held primarily field staff positions, but also served as an air regiment deputy commander. Let us say that our hypothetical officer has now been assigned the duty of Chief of Staff of the Air Staff of a Military District, a very responsible post.

The Air Staff is a junior partner of the combined, but predominantly Army, Staff of the Military District (which is probably headed by a lieutenant-general with long staff experience, including service on the General Staff). The role of the Air Staff which our colonel heads is to establish plans, including contingent war plans if the district is on the periphery of the USSR, for the training and employment of the air forces in the district, on the basis of the Military District staff plans when they have been confirmed by the district commander (a colonel-general, general of the Army, or even a marshal). Of course, our colonel participates in the drawing up of the over-all plan, as well as preparing the specific implementing plan for the air forces.

The Military District plans, for training and for contingent wars, of course, in turn implement the general war plans and training plans for the whole of the Soviet Union. Hence our colonel and his commanding officer will be directly in touch with, though not under the control of, the Main Air Staff in Moscow, just as the superior Military District commander and staff are associated with the General Staff of the Armed Forces.

The question of direct training and other assignments of specific air units in the district will be decided upon by the district Air Force commander (perhaps an Air Army commander, or else an equivalent) on the basis of the air staff's plan drawn up under the supervision of our colonel.

This, then, is the general pattern of staff work at all levels.

The Civil Air Fleet

The growing Soviet civil aviation is a Chief Administration (GVF) under the Council of Ministers, independent of the Ministry of Defence and VVS. During the last war, and until 1948, it was subordinate; in any future war it would doubtless either be subordinated or largely merged in the military Air Forces. Now headed by Chief Marshal of Aviation P. F. Zhigarev, with Marshal of Aviation S. F. Zhavoronkov and Lieutenant-General of Aviation N. A. Zakharov as his chief deputies, it is staffed to a large extent by military or reserve military airmen. While its chief function is the current peacetime expansion of air transport, it would be readily available to provide strategic airlift and supply in time of war. The new turbo-prop and jet aircraft used as transports can be readily converted to military use.

Organisational Summary

For an organisational summary, three diagrams outline (1) the administrative relationships among the Headquarters Air Forces and the other air force headquarters; (2) the operational subordination of the various military air components; and (3) the internal organisation of the Air Force Headquarters.

As these charts illustrate, the Chief Administration of the Air Forces (GU-VVS-SA or GU-VVS-VS) and its Commander-in-Chief, Marshal of Aviation Vershinin, have very *far-reaching administrative responsibilities* for the various aviation components of the military establishment, but *no operational command over any of the five military air forces*. None the less, direct responsibility for the tactical air forces extends directly down to the field level subordination of these forces to Front and Military District ground force commanders. Also, a degree of authority over the Long Range Air Forces may be exercised in practice. Finally, Vershinin represents the air forces in highest level general decisions taken by the Minister of Defence with his Military Council.

Organisation of the Air Armies

The Air Army is the largest operational aviation unit. It is composed in turn of air corps, divisions, regiments, and squadrons. As we have noted, there are Frontal (tactical), Long Range (strategic), and Air Defence (interceptor) Air Armies. The latter two are simple in their functions: each is composed of only one form of aviation (though, of course, the former has heavy turbo-jet, heavy turbo-prop, and medium turbo-jet bomber types; and the latter has various all-weather and day turbo-jet fighter types).

The Long Range Air Armies, operating under orders direct from Moscow, will be organised for wartime combat missions in 'task force' formations of varying size depending upon the targets and a host of operational considerations. No details on the organisational form of these mission flights are available.

The Air Defence Fighter Air Armies are merely administrative organisations, with the interceptor Air Divisions the actual field command unit, under the Air Defence District commanders. Again, the wartime operational employment will depend entirely on the scale and form of attacking aircraft and missiles. Here, unlike the case of the long range bomber air armies, the combined-arms district commander and staff have authority, and co-ordinate all air defence forces, though the districts in turn also are directly under a central command in Moscow.

The Fleet Air Forces of the Soviet Navy are essentially the arms of the various Fleet Commands, and here too the Air Division is the basic unit.

But the largest air force, the tactical air force, has a much more complex command and staff structure to meet the wide range of missions it must perform, and the wide variety of aviation components necessary to perform these tasks.

The 'type' or model Frontal Air Army totals about 1,400 aeroplanes. It has three Air Corps: one Fighter Corps, one Attack (or Fighter-Bomber) Corps, and one Light Bomber Corps, each of which in turn has three air divisions. The corps would be 'mixed', with different components; the attack corps and bomber corps would each have two attack or bomber divisions and one fighter division. The fighter corps would have all fighter divisions. From the level of division and lower, only one aviation type is included (a bomber division has only bombers, etc.). Each division has three regiments, and each regiment is composed of three squadrons. This is the *model* tactical air army. In practice, there are wide variations, especially in wartime, and the average size is not over 1,000 aeroplanes. Since each air army is assigned to a given ground army group (Front), the Soviet solution to the problem of the continually shifting requirements for concentration of air power is simply to take away air divisions or regiments 'on loan' for assignment to another air army. Thus some air armies may be 'stripped' of even the major part of their forces for an extended period, while others are much augmented.

The Commander of an Air Army is the deputy for air to the corresponding ground force Front Commander. At all lower echelons the air force commanders are responsible through their own channels of command to the Air Army Commander, not to the corresponding ground force commanders. On the basis of the general decisions of the Front command, the Air Army Commander and his staff work out a detailed 'Operation Plan for the VVS (Air Forces)' for the employment of various units for particular missions. This plan designates precise missions for each corps (or even for each division). It is then presented to the Front commander for approval, before being issued. The Air Army Commander has considerable authority in apportioning the air forces to defensive cover, interdiction, and close support; but the Front Commander has the final word.

The staff of the Air Army includes a deputy commander, a political affairs deputy, and a chief of staff who controls operations, intelligence and reconnaissance, communications, meteorological, security (codes), and other sections paralleling the Main Staff of the Air Forces. There is also a Ground Servicing Staff with two deputies, one for the rear services, and one for the engineering-technical service. The former controls all supplies, airfield servicing, and similar units; the latter ordnance and repair facilities.

The Command Post of the Air Army is ordinarily located in proximity to the Staff of the Front; and the Air Army Commander is ordinarily there (or, if not, his deputy there is acting commander).

During the last war, and so far as I know continuing now, Soviet employment of tactical air power was organised on the basis of either of two principles, called 'support' and 'assignment'. 'Support' is the usual form of employment of tactical aviation and is based on

G

centralised command and direction at the Air Army level to permit the utilisation of aviation against the most important targets at the most important moment. 'Assignment' connotes the subordination of air units to the commander of a specific ground formation, limited to particular units at particular stages of an operation. This principle was employed to strengthen combined troop units, especially those acting on a flank or in operation depth, that is, separated from the main mass of troops. This most frequently involved armoured troops in an advance. In this case the commander of the air unit received his missions from the commander of the ground unit he was assigned to support, locating himself at or near the command post or observation post of the ground commander. This form of close support was used relatively infrequently.

If the commander of an air unit was operating according to the principle of 'assignment', the selection of targets was made primarily by the ground force unit commander. When operating on the principle of 'support', he was assigned missions by the Commander of the Air Army, in accordance with orders of the Front Command. In practice, the Air Army Commander often changed or augmented the missions, if the circumstances on the front so demanded.

An air regiment, division, or corps, acting according to the general plan of the Air Army, was always given clearly defined targets in a definite region. The commander of a squadron was always given definite targets to attack and, also, an alternative objective. Nevertheless, rational initiative was encouraged. If the commander of an attack group (six or eight planes) saw a new non-stationary target which, in his opinion, was more important at the given moment, he might direct his group to the new target, immediately informing his senior commander. In an attack on a stationary target, the commander of a group was not permitted to change the objective of attack. In certain cases he might attack the assigned alternate target: for instance, if the airfield he was ordered to attack was not occupied by aircraft, or if weather conditions did not permit an attack on so precise a target as a bridge or rail intersection. In the case of a sharp change in the situation, all commanders, from the commander of a squadron upward, could direct their air units to new targets, immediately informing their senior commanders. This was true even of air units in close combat support of ground formations. However, as is general in the Soviet armed forces, the use of such initiative was fraught with danger to the commander responsible, particularly if the result was unsuccessful. Exercise of initiative was thus infrequent and was sometimes lacking in situations demanding such action.

Co-ordination at intermediate and subordinate levels was achieved by liaison officers of the Air Army assigned to the corresponding ground force units.

Conclusions

The Soviet Air Forces are organised in a loosely co-ordinated whole, with the major functional missions being autonomous either as independent commands (the Long Range Air Force) or components of such 'mission' commands (the Fighter Aviation of the Air Defence Forces; the Naval Aviation; the Aviation of the Airborne Troops). The major force in size, today, remains the Frontal (tactical, or Army) Air Force, with about half of the total number of active aircraft. It is operationally subordinated to the Army ground force commanders at the Army Group (Front), Air Army level, as at the Ministry level. But below this level, air force channels in the field directly control subordinate air units except under particular temporary tactical circumstances.

The organisation of the Soviet Air Forces, and of the Soviet Armed Forces as a whole, shows the degree of change (but also of continuity) as the nuclear-jet-missile era has transformed the strategic role of aviation.

CHAPTER 12

THE TRAINING OF PERSONNEL

George Schatunowski

IT IS SCARCELY feasible to cram within the compass of a few thousand words a comprehensive survey of air training and technical education in the Soviet Armed Forces. It involves millions of Soviet citizens and it is virtually impossible to give a representative account even if all the relevant data were available. In Chapter 4 on 'Soviet Air Strategy' Hanson Baldwin makes the point that the performance of Soviet air power in the Second World War varied greatly from air regiment to air regiment. The education and training of Soviet air and rocket personnel must inevitably suffer from the same unevenness in equipment and instruction as no doubt the personnel of Western air and rocket forces do. The ability to instruct and to absorb is a constantly changing variable depending on such local factors as the weather, the availability of equipment and spares, the experience and personality of the instructors and not least in the USSR, the degree of interference from the MVD and KGB political/military troops who vary from area to area in their definition of political police duties.

The first general point which needs to be made is that, basically, the training of Soviet airmen and rocket personnel is similar to that found in NATO countries. A fairly comprehensive account of the Soviet air schooling methods used during and before the Second World War can be found in 'The Soviet Air Force'.[1] However, much has been done in the last decade to modernise the Soviet air and rocket training schools so that they can meet the needs of the new air weapons and equipment such as radar, defensive and offensive rockets, long range jet bombers, atomic and thermo-nuclear rocket weapons, guided missiles, helicopters, and the new medium and long range jet transport aircraft of the Soviet Air Transport forces.

[1] Published by Duckworth, London, 1950. See also 'Polygon' article on Soviet Air Force training. *Aeroplane*, issue of August, 1948.

Before considering some of the major aspects of Soviet air and rocket training something needs to be said about general scientific and technical education in the Soviet Union. In the last few years much has been written on this subject. Gordon Dean, Chairman of the US Atomic Energy Commission from 1950–3, wrote[1] in 1954 that from the '900 or so higher educational institutions about 200,000 Soviet people graduate every year and about 100,000 of them are scientific or technical students, a figure roughly equal to the number of scientific or technical students who graduate annually in the United States'. Mr Dean estimated that in 1952, about 30,000 engineers graduated from Soviet schools and this figure is currently thought to have increased to 40,000 or 50,000 annually, that is nearly twice the number in the USA. In his report of 1954, Mr Gordon Dean said he thought the quality of professional training in the USSR was very good and that there were about 3,500 technical schools turning out about 250,000 trainee engineers a year. Professor P. M. Blackett, Nobel Prize Winner in physics and author, gave it as his view, in April 1958, that the USSR was turning out more technicians than the rest of the world put together. Clearly all this did not happen in a decade. For more than thirty years scientists have been the chief household gods in the USSR. Before the Second World War, Sir Eric Ashby published a book, in the Penguin series, on science in the Soviet Union which foreshadowed much that has been written subsequently on this subject.

Since the early 1930s, Soviet youngsters have, from early child-hood, been encouraged to be technically minded and opportunities have been provided for organised instruction on aeronautics and electronics greatly in excess of those provided by Western countries. The OSSOAVIAKHIM organisation of pre-war days has been now replaced by DOSAAF, which is itself a merger of DOSAV (the Air 'Club'), DOSARM (the Army 'Club') and DOSFLOT (the Navy 'Club'). The merger, incidentally, is one of the many signs that the USSR has gone farther than the West in developing the trend of combining the Armed Services. When Army and Navy and Air Force youth instructional clubs are joint, and the Soviet Defence Ministry and Communist Party have supreme control of all military, naval and air forces, liaison, flexibility and combination in the three fighting services are bound to be easier, in some ways, than in the

[1] See *Report on the Atom*, Gordon Dean.

West. The DOSAAF flying clubs constitute a major pool from which the Soviet air squadrons of the VVS can and do draw their future pilots. They are, so to speak, the preparatory schools of the Soviet Air Force. Just as they shed their semi-military character to become bona fide military organisations in the 1930s, before the Second World War, so they have tended to become para-military in the 1950s. Not that the activities of the DOSAAF branches are concerned solely with aircraft and technical training. Considerable time is devoted to such things as boxing, athletics, literary and political readings and, of course, glider, aircraft and rocket modelling. Parachute jumping from *UT 2* planes (the *Tiger Moth* of the USSR) is also practised. DOSAAF have recently been given some of the new *MIG* primary jet trainers with an engine of about 1,000 lb thrust as part of the general modernisation of their equipment.

The main scheme of flying training in the USSR is, in its basic essentials, similar to that of any other major air force and is divided into primary *ab initio* training, the intermediate stage and the advanced operational schooling. Having reached the age of 17 or thereabouts and having shown enthusiasm for flying, probably at one of the DOSAAF clubs, the young Soviet lad or girl will be eligible for the Air Force (or Army or Navy) entrance examination which leads to the Soviet Air Force (VVS) training schools. In the jet age the medical standards have naturally been raised. In addition candidates have to take an examination in general subjects including aeronautics and also satisfy the 'credentials commission' about the political reliability of themselves and their family. *Komsomol*, MVD or KGB security officials take an active part in the selection of all candidates for the Air Force.

The full course at a VVS flying training school normally takes from two to three years to complete. The elementary training lasts about nine to twelve months. This includes the Soviet version of 'square bashing': drill and military discipline, a course in political study as well as courses on the technique of aircraft construction and maintenance, the study of radio-communications, including wireless, radar and the radio-telephone, a course on gunnery and navigation, lectures on rockets and an introduction to Soviet flight manuals. Until an examination in all these subjects has been passed no Air Force candidate can begin his flying training proper.

This elementary flying training is usually done under the guidance of a pilot instructor with experience in the Second World War. In the last few years there have been changes in the aircraft equipment used for elementary flying training. The long service *UT 2* (designed by Yakovlev in 1935) which was so extensively used in the Second World War and before, has been replaced by more modern types such as the *YAK 18 U*.[1] This machine is powered by an *M 11* 160 hp engine, has a top speed of 150 to 160 mph and a landing speed of just over 50 mph. Elementary jet trainer aircraft, including the above mentioned *MIG*, are being developed and may well be in general use within the next year or so. The *YAK 18*, designed by Yakovlev, can land in less than 300 yards and is convenient for the small airfields which abound in the USSR. This machine is a multi-purpose non-jet trainer used also for more advanced training in instrument and blind flying, a form of schooling which is now more ubiquitous in the Soviet air training scheme than in wartime and pre-war days. It is also sometimes used for parachute jumping instruction. Each Soviet pilot undergoing the elementary flying course has to make several parachute jumps. The basic trainer for parachute troops is of course Antonov's *AN 2* of which over a thousand have been produced in the last five to ten years. The *YAK 18* is being gradually replaced by the *YAK 20* of similar design and performance.

For the first twenty to thirty hours of dual flight the aspirant pilot is naturally closely watched by his instructor so that his operational potential can be assessed at an early stage. A further twenty to thirty hours of solo flying follows. At first the usual circuits and bumps and then comes the stage of cross-country flying. If the pilot fails to make the grade required he can ask to be transferred and trained as a navigator, provided he has completed ten years' schooling. If he has not, he can go to a Soviet technical air force school for training maintenance personnel. Radio and radar operators, rocket specialists or gunners are usually not recruited from unsuccessful *ab initio* pilot aspirants but from the initial intake into the Air Force if they fail to pass the stiff medical examination for pilots.

The most generally used intermediate trainer machine until a year ago was Yakovlev's *YAK 11* which he designed in the early post-war period and which came into general training use in 1947.

[1] *U* stands for training or instruction.

Fitted with a 650 hp *Shvetsov* radial engine this machine, roughly the equivalent of the RAF's *Percival 56*, set up a world record for closed circuit flying for machines in this class in 1950, achieving an average speed of 274 mph. Its maximum speed is about 295–300 mph. Another Yakovlev trainer used in the elementary and intermediate stage is the *YAK 14*. It is also a communications machine. With a landing speed of less than 50 mph and a range of over 600 miles, it is well suited to do the training jobs for which it is widely used in the Soviet Union. It is to be expected that Mikoyan or Yakovlev will produce an intermediate jet trainer, perhaps before this book is published.

After the first forty to sixty hours of dual and solo flying the Soviet pilot begins to specialise as a bomber, fighter, reconnaissance or transport crew member. Here of course the training schedule varies enormously in length according to the type of specialisation. Fighter pilots may be ready to go into tactical air squadrons after a further seventy to eighty hours' flying training. Once in the operational squadrons, they will continue to train and fly conversion courses, e.g. from the *MIG 17* subsonic fighter to the *MIG 19* and *21* supersonic fighters. Bomber pilots will probably be ready to fly the *Myasishchev* four-jets, the rough equivalent of the RAF's *V* bomber or the US *B 52s*, after 100–150 hours further training. But they may well be relegated to transport duties if they do not turn out to be first class long range pilots or if they find Arctic flying too much for them. If after the intermediate flying stage the pilot is considered fit to fly transport aircraft only, his operational training will again vary from a further thirty to forty to over 100 hours depending on whether he has to do routine cargo flights or specialist work for the Soviet parachute divisions or the special Arctic Air Transport Command. Specialisation for long range reconnaissance work is a new post-war feature but most of this training is done in the operational units.

The range of aircraft used for training in the advanced schooling period is of course extensive. Some of the wartime *MIG 3* and *Lavochkin 5* fighters are still in use; *PE 2s*, *TU 2s* and *IL 4s*, once operational bombers, are now used for bomber training. The tactical army support bomber pilots still train on wartime *IL 2s* and *IL 10s*. But the over-all tendency is to replace these machines by advanced jet trainer planes such as the *YAK 15* advanced jet fighter trainers, the *YAK 17* two-seater jet trainer and the *MIG 15* and *MIG 17 UT* trainer planes. Tactical bomber crews have a trainer version of the *IL 28* twin-jet plane. The letters *UT* incidentally are often found after Soviet trainer planes as well as the letter *U*. The *T* stands for *Trenirovochny* and means 'training' and the *U* for *Uchebny* which means 'instructional'. Operational long range bomber training is carried out on the obsolescent *TU 4* and *PE 8* four-engined non-jet bombers, and on twin-jet *TU 16* and the four turbo-prop *Tupolev TU 20 (Bear)*. The final stages of operational training are of course handled in the air regiments themselves at the peacetime bases. The *Bison* four-jet long range bombers do 5,000 mile Arctic flights using the latest navigational radar beam aids from their northern bases which stretch from Murmansk to Magadan. The tactical air regiments of fighters and fighter-bombers, still the strongest arm numerically of the VVS, train in annual manœuvres with the Red Army. Air transport regiments equipped with *Ilyushin* four-engined planes and *MIL* and *YAK* helicopters train continuously in disgorging artillery, tanks and troops. The PVO air defence units hold continual exercises of co-ordination with local radar and ground to air guided missiles units.

The training of scientists, technicians and engineers calls for special consideration in an age in which rockets, electronics and atomic energy dominate military weapons. The training and education received at Soviet educational technical institutes and universities are as relevant as those obtained in the schools of the Soviet Armed Forces. There is, for example, a scheme of training air navigators outside the framework of the Soviet Air Force. It is called VVP (*Vysshaya Vnevoiskovaya Podgotovka*) which stands for 'training outside the services'. The system was inaugurated in the early 1930s and still exists. It has been expanded in the post-war period to embrace a high proportion of the universities and high technical educational establishments in the USSR. I had personal experience of VVP during my education and training as a bomber-navigator at Kiev University. The idea behind the scheme is that university students are sometimes exempt from military service and go on to an industrial job after graduation in engineering or scientific work. But they are sometimes trained during the first two years at a university to become reserve navigational and engineering officers.

Incidentally the chairs of military science at Soviet universities are frequently occupied by officers appointed by the military. The university post is designated *Voyenny Rukovoditel* and the person who occupies it has the rank of major or above. He and his work are part of the VVP training scheme. The essential flying training is done by the university student officer cadets during the long summer holidays where they put in perhaps ten to fifteen flying hours annually. At the end of two years, VVP students are vetted by the 'credentials commission' and may become fully fledged reserve officers. In an emergency, about a thousand of them would be available. In 1941, I was one of a large number called up under the scheme and was shot down over Germany during the Second World War.

In order to appreciate the vast reserve of human and technical resources that Soviet air and rocket units can draw on, the training of scientists and engineers in the general system of education in the USSR must be briefly considered. During the last forty years some four million students have graduated from Soviet universities and higher technical institutes though many thousands of them were killed in the Second World War. The technical institutes are under a system of dual control. The Ministry for Higher Education approves the syllabus, appoints professors and teachers and the relevant industrial or technical ministry pays the salaries, the overheads and the cost of scientific and technical research. The teaching system is fairly uniform. Indeed, every student attends the same basic lectures and follows the same syllabus at all the universities and institutes in the USSR. During the first three years there are usually thirty-six 55-minute lecture periods every week and all lectures are compulsory. Practical work in the laboratory is in addition to the above substantial quota. During the fourth, fifth and sixth years at the university or higher technical institute there is a great degree of specialisation greater than in most Western universities. The student works under a Professor who holds a chair (called a *Kafedra*) which is narrower in concept than a British or US chair. The Moscow State University has about 170 of these *Kafedra* which gives some idea of the degree of specialisation. Apart from the final State examination students may have to take up to forty or fifty fairly extensive written and practical test papers during their higher technical studies. Even in specialised technical institutes, i.e. those doing nuclear physics or electronics, more than 10 per cent of lecture time is devoted to

Marx-Leninism, political economy, dialectical materialism and the history of the Communist Party in the USSR. I imagine that these courses have had no more effect on my fellow scientists at Kiev University than they had on me. Like the snow in Russia, the indoctrination was accepted as inevitable. But the main technical studies in science and engineering, with rare exceptions like the Lysenko theories, conform to Western canons of experiment and criticism.

The State examination nearly always calls for a thesis from the student. No degree is awarded though the standard reached is as high as and often higher than the graduate standards of the Western universities with which I have recently become familiar. After the State examination the successful student can take a job in industry, teach, do further research or take a post-graduate type of course called *Aspirantura* which after two years enables him or her to sit for the degree of 'Candidate of Science'. The Doctorate of Science would come next and the length of study and research naturally varies. The *élite* of the Doctors of Science provide the members of the USSR Academy of Sciences and also those of other scientific academies.

In addition to the trained personnel provided by the universities and technical institutes of the USSR the various military technical institutes and aviation institutes have an annual intake and output of over 500 specialist high grade officer engineers and the number is increasing. The syllabus for general subjects at the military and air technical institutes is on the general pattern of the civilian institutes and universities and is prescribed by the Ministry of Higher Education though they do not make the appointments which are naturally the concern of one of the personnel departments of the Soviet Ministry of Defence.

Perhaps the best known of the Soviet technical air academies are the Zhukovsky Air Force Engineering Academy and TsAGI. There is also the Mozhaisky Air Force Engineering Academy at Leningrad, the large Orjonikidze Aviation Institute in Moscow and similar though smaller air force engineering institutes in Kiev, Kharkov, Odessa, Kazan, Rybinsk, Voronezh, Noginsk, Komsomolsk and other major cities of the USSR. The Riga Air Force engineering College specialises in producing engine maintenance engineers and there is an expanding electronics Air Force institute in this newly

acquired Soviet city. The Kuibyschev Military Academy east of
Moscow does special courses on airfield construction and maintenance, rocket engineering and also jet and rocket engines. The Air
Academy at Monino like the Zhukovsky Academy in Moscow puts the
final staff polish on Air Force officers who have qualified and reached
fairly senior rank in an air regiment, division or corps.

Since 1946, a signals academy in Moscow has trained officers for
responsible posts in the radar units of the Soviet PVO strategic air
defence system. It is so to speak the air graduation college of the very
good electronics training schools in Leningrad, Riga, Novosibirsk,
Kiev and elsewhere, which provide the training in using and
servicing the radio and radar equipment of the VVS units.

The initial course at the electronics training school lasts about a
year and includes no formal flying training but naturally includes a
number of flights with the fighter pilots of the PVO air defence
command when the radar specialists are posted to an air regiment
particularly on the *IL 28* and *YAK 25* twin-jets. At school they
learn to service and work *RS1 6K* wireless transmitters, *RS1 6M 1*
aircraft and ground receiving sets, the ins and outs of the Soviet IFF
equipment and the use and importance of marker beacons. Like the
fighter pilot in his operational training they learn to understand
SKP (Startovy Kommandny Punkt) equipment for take-off and landing at
night or in bad weather: this is the Soviet equivalent of Western
GCA radar equipment. Like fighter pilots too, the radar technicians
of the VVS study AI radar procedure and have to familiarise themselves with the latest radar gun-sights used in the *MIG 19* and *21*
jet fighters and also have to study the control systems of the ground
to air guided missiles such as the *T 6* and *T 8*.

The use of modern electronic equipment in Soviet air training
schools and operational training units has of course raised the whole
standard of effectiveness of Soviet fighter and bomber operations.
The Kremlin was clearly dissatisfied with their training standards in
the Second World War when they were well behind the *Luftwaffe*,
the USAAF and the RAF in blind and night flying. Even some of
their crack Guards regiments had less than half their crews capable
of operating in such conditions because of training deficiencies.
Towards the end of the Second World War a group of over 100
pilots flying on the 1st Belorussian front, who had been trained
at schools at Sverdlov and Gatchina, had to be sent back for re-

training to Tashkent and there were many other analagous cases in 1944 and 1945. After the Second World War the Soviet Air Force Commander-in-Chief, Chief Marshal of Aviation Novikov, put his deputy, Colonel-General Sudets, in charge of the new modernised and expanded air training scheme in which theoretical lectures were reduced and practice in flying and the use of equipment was especially emphasised. In a speech at the Zhukhovsky Academy, Marshal Novikov said 'the school lessons must be taken out of the class-room and on to the airfield'. The new training scheme, backed by modern planes and equipment, has, roughly speaking, raised the flying standards of the Soviet Air Force to those of Western air forces in my view, though it is absurd to generalise about training and education standards in any air force. Other high ranking Soviet military and air leaders who led the post-war drive for higher training standards were General (later Marshal) of Aviation Rudenko and Colonel-General Golikov. As part of this post-war scheme, a drastic reduction in Soviet Air Force first line strength was made from over 20,000 in the summer of 1945 to about 15,000 in 1946–7. Three of the six air corps of the 1st Air Army stationed in Germany, for instance, were disbanded and the same reduction was made in General Krassovsky's 2nd Air Army stationed in Austria and Hungary. In the case of the 3rd Air Army in Roumania commanded by General Kamanin, two of the four air corps lost their operational status. In Belorussia and the Ukraine similar reductions were made and the units sent back to school. Training schools especially devoted to night and blind flying were established in the 1946–7 period near towns such as Chelyabinsk, Omsk, Irkutsk, Gorki, Michurinsk and elsewhere. The *élite* of the commanders of air regiments and divisions and the best graduates of the Soviet air academies, mentioned earlier in this chapter, were sent to command the new blind flying schools of which those mentioned above constitute only a proportion.

The commitment of training the satellite air forces of Czechoslovakia, Poland, Hungary, Roumania and Bulgaria, and after 1949, those of China, East Germany, Albania, Syria, Egypt, Indonesia and Afghanistan has acted as a stimulus to the improved post-war flying school standards. In the last year or so the effects of a decade of the new standards of training were seen in combined tactical air exercises in which Soviet, Czech, Polish and Hungarian air regiments took part. But as Asher Lee suggests in Chapter 18, ('Air Allies of the USSR') no major key operational role in future Soviet air plans is likely to be assigned to these satellite air forces. They may, however, serve useful purposes as European, Asian or Arab trouble shooters in the future.

Czech, Polish, Chinese and United Arab Republic air officers, sometimes specially selected for political reliability as much as for aviation skills, are also undergoing courses at Soviet Air Academies and training schools such as the Zhukovsky air technical academy in Moscow and the flying training schools at Kharkov, Saratov, Novosibirsk and Lipetsk. There are language problems at the moment and special interpreters have had to be recruited. It may be of interest to add that even these visiting pilots have not only received technical and flying training but also follow the Communist political indoctrination classes which are ubiquitous in the Soviet personnel and flying training system.

Something has been said earlier in the chapter about the pre-operational training of the Soviet long range jet bomber force which consists almost entirely of jet bombers based in the northern half of the USSR. Practice in flight refuelling techniques to expand the practical range of the *Bison* and its successor has been a cardinal feature of strategic bomber training in the last two or three years with the emphasis on the Arctic routes to North America. In his book, *Atomic Weapons and Foreign Policy*, Dr Kissinger has drawn attention to the flight refuelling problems of the *Bison* jet bomber if it is to reach all the targets in USA to which it may be assigned. One can be sure that the Soviet DA Long Range Flying Command is aware of these problems and is practising the techniques of flight refuelling, which may well include Soviet radio counter-measures designed to deceive would-be US fighter interceptors operating against refuelling rendezvous points. The use of Tupolev's *Bear* (*TU 20*) turbo-prop long range four-jet machine as a refuelling tanker for these exercises has grown in the last year or so. One must also anticipate further use in future of the new Soviet jet transport planes as tankers such as the four-jet *TU 110* or the giant long range four-jet turbo-prop *TU 114*. While Soviet statements have linked these two recent machines, like the four-jet *Antonov 10* and *Ilyushin 18* transport planes, with the civil operations of AEROFLOT, it would be absurd not to expect them to be used in a tanker flight refuelling role and as military transport planes for the operational training of parachutists and airborne troops in the next year or so.

With the increasing threat of the use of the long range atomic rocket *Polaris* from US submarines, the need for the USSR to train her long range attack planes in anti-submarine warfare becomes greater than ever before. If one has little hard news of operational training in this field, it may be that the Soviet authorities are hesitating whether to assign the role to their naval air forces which are carrying out operational training of this kind with the *Beriev* long range flying boats or whether to keep long range attack operations of all kinds under the ægis of the DA command. No doubt there will be further information on this point within the next year or so.

It is the training in the use of long range rockets from land bases and Soviet submarines which is likely to be the key factor in the military effectiveness of Soviet military operations in the unlikely event of a third world war. Trial firings of *V2* type non-atomic rockets from Soviet submarines were reported in the Baltic by eye-witness accounts published in the Swedish and Norwegian press as far back as 1950. Richard Stockwell's *Soviet Air Power*[1] provides a map showing some of the Soviet rocket sites which were used as training centres including Heidelage in Poland, the old *Wehrmacht* operational training centre for *V2s* and Kolberg in East Germany. It is ironic that in May 1958, the British Minister of Defence, Mr Duncan Sandys, said in answer to a question in the British Parliament that he had no official information that the USSR had long range rocket sites in Warsaw Treaty country territories outside the USSR. (The Soviet long range rockets are so mobile, both the land and submarine based, that, politics apart, both the question and the answer are scarcely relevant.) It is even more ironic that at a meeting of the Warsaw Pact countries in May 1958, Mr Khrushchev said Russia might be forced to station rockets in East Germany, Poland and Czechoslovakia, if NATO went ahead with its plans for missile bases in Germany.

In fact there is little to be said about rocket training and schooling in the USSR, for the successful operation of these weapons depends mainly on first-rate technical education, factory production, easy replacement of faulty parts and mobility and ease of movement of

[1] Published in 1956 in New York by the Pageant Press.

firing sites. We have touched briefly on the education and for the more curious reader Alexander Korol's *Soviet Education for Science and Technology*[1] offers a wealth of detail. The emphasis on rocket-firing submarines and the increase in the Soviet jet transport arm, dealt with more fully elsewhere in this book and in Commander Saunders' *The Soviet Navy*, are in themselves guarantees of constantly improving mobility in rocket-firing potential. The problems of servicing will, however, be awkward in a weapon which so far uses mainly liquid fuels which deteriorate in storage and which has many delicate electronic and gyroscopic parts liable to imperfections and errors in performance. One must remind oneself that even when they were fully operational many of the German *V2s* misfired and this rocket had relatively little delicate instrumentation.

The surprising gap in the Soviet air training scheme is the lack of emphasis on anti-submarine work. For a year or so now it has been apparent that US long range atomic submarines firing 1,500 mile atomic *Polaris* rockets may constitute eventually the chief Western deterrent or the chief weapon of war. The Soviet Naval Air Force has been a Cinderella for most of the forty years of its existence but there have been signs of modernisation and a new-look in the last year or so. It is hard to believe that between now and 1960 the Kremlin will not give higher priority to training and equipping its naval air forces for the duties of long range anti-submarine recon naissance and attack.

[1] Published in 1957 in London by Chapman & Hall.

CHAPTER 13

POLITICS IN THE SOVIET AIR FORCE

Boris Kuban

POLITICS ARE INSEPARABLE from the Soviet Air Force. All its personnel must constantly learn about political events in the Soviet Union and in the rest of the world as well. But they must study these events in the only way possible in the Soviet Union, in the way selected and adapted by the Communist Party.

The Party is the real and absolute ruler of the country and of its armed forces. That is the officially held principle behind all the facts of Soviet military life. Therefore it is quite natural that the air force, nowadays held to be the *élite* of the armed forces and the key to victory in any future war, has a carefully thought-out, all-embracing system of Party political control and the indoctrination appropriate to it.

The Communist Party is represented in the air force by a powerful network of political administrations and political sections. At the head of this system stands the Central Political Administration of the air force. It occupies an old-fashioned six-storied building in a quiet street off Gogolevsky Boulevard in Moscow. In this district are concentrated various high military organisations; the headquarters of the air force, the Ministry of Defence, the headquarters of the armoured troops, and the Central Political Administration of the Soviet Army and Air Force. The buildings of these organisations are all scattered along the chestnut shaded streets close to Arbat Square. Every morning hundreds of officers in full air force uniform stream into the building of the Air Force Political Administration. A stranger might find it very hard to tell the difference between them and ordinary flying officers of the Soviet Air Force, for they even wear the golden epaulettes, the badge of the flying personnel. In fact, hardly any of them have flying qualifications and many of them do not even have any military qualifications or training, since it has not been found necessary for them to go through the routine of an officers' school. They are Party political workers, serving in one of the many Political Administrations of the USSR, that of the air force.

From this organisation pour forth tens and even hundreds of thousands of instructions, orders, explanations and booklets. Some are praising, more are threatening in tone, but the majority assume a note of dull nagging, varied with stringent demands. There also pour into the building just as many secret reports on 'the politico-moral state' of air armies scattered throughout the Soviet Union and the satellite countries. The Central Political Administration is fed, round the clock, with the most detailed information covering every aspect of air force life. Résumés of all this information are also sent regularly to the immediately superior organisation, the Central Political Administration of the Soviet Armed Forces, at the head of which stands the veteran of political activities, the 'Party Appara-tchik' as he is nicknamed, Colonel-General Golikov. Despite his comparatively modest rank, he has more authority and influence than most of the Soviet marshals and generals, for they only speak in the name of the Ministry of Defence, while he speaks in that of the Party.

From General Golikov the Central Political Administration of the air force receives the current political orientations and rulings in general terms, which he in his turn has received directly from the Central Committee of the Communist Party of the Soviet Union. The main duty of the Air Force Political Administration is to digest and work out the details in the material received before sending it on to the subordinate administrations.

The first subordinate administrations are those of the air armies and independent air corps. They are in fact scaled down versions of the Central Political Administration in Moscow. Each possesses its own newspapers, printing works, and permanent staffs of agitators and propagandists, as well as large libraries of political literature, just like the Central Administration.

After having received their instructions, these administrations at army and corps level digest them and work out adaptations to suit local conditions. For example, if the Central Political Admin-istration received from General Golikov the following kind of 'orientation' as it is called:

'The anti-Party group of Molotov tried to weaken the strength of our armed forces,' then the Central Political Administration of the air force might send out to the armies and independent air corps something like this: 'The anti-Party group of Molotov tried to prevent us from receiving new equipment and to upset the production of new aircraft and rockets.'

The Political Administrations of the air armies would again work on these instructions before sending them to the Political Branches of the air corps incorporated in the armies. The corps would receive the orientation perhaps on these lines: 'The anti-Party group of Molotov tried to destroy the supply of new aircraft to our air force. They wanted to weaken our strength. Let us answer with the best possible training, and the best possible adaptations of new flying techniques.'

The Political Branches of the corps would also spend some time on this orientation before sending it on to the Political Branches of the air divisions: the divisions might then receive something like this: 'The anti-Party group of Molotov tried to weaken our striking power by depriving us of the latest Soviet aircraft. The best answer to these dastardly activities will be our supreme mastery of flying training. Let us reach the zenith of ability in night flying. Let us be the best unit in our military region.'

The Political Branches of the divisions would consider it carefully before sending it on to the air regiments. Political deputies to Commanding officers of the air regiments might receive this: 'The anti-Party group of Molotov tried to weaken our air force catastrophically. They were trying to make it vulnerable to the enemy. We must gather even closer round our Party and its leadership. Let our enemies tremble before our unity. Let them learn about our love for and loyalty to the Party. We must carry out our training and our studies in an even more efficient way. This goes for adaptations of new techniques too. There must be no place in our ranks for the undisciplined or for badly trained pilots.'

The political deputies would discuss it thoroughly with the Party and *Komsomol* organisers of their regiments. After working out and agreeing on a formula, they would call in the Party and *Komsomol* organisers of the squadrons, and then at last this great news would reach the ordinary personnel of the air force. For an important piece of news, like the decline of Molotov, the whole regiment would be assembled, and the political deputy would make a speech lasting an hour or more. Very likely the political branch of the division would send down a special agitator or propagandist to make another speech, also lasting an hour. The speeches would follow the line described above. In the course of the next week there would be two or three political lessons devoted to this orientation. It would also be discussed in the 'informative talks' held usually at the start of the day.

However, one most important condition would be faithfully observed throughout the whole process: the original meaning of the message would be preserved in the form in which it was received from General Golikov, for that is what is known as the Party line.

The Westerner may wonder how it is that so much may be made out of so small an item, but for the political officer in the armed forces this is the essence of his job. Very often a political officer will find himself in a seemingly impossible situation, like the lecturer at the Leningrad Political Academy who found himself obliged to write a scholarly study entitled: 'The great part played by Comrade Stalin in the development of the Russian language.' Since the only thing known about the relationship between the Russian language and Comrade Stalin is that he spoke it very ungrammatically and with a strong Caucasian accent, this was obviously not an easy task, but it was in fact performed, and the resulting substantial volume provoked much discussion.

In the case of items such as that concerning the decline and fall of the Molotov group, discussions will touch on many apparently unrelated subjects, such as the American monopolists, a lieutenant's visit to his girl-friend and subsequent lateness on parade, the latest developments in the Middle East, Captain of the Technical Service Ivanov's theft of two litres of service spirit (intended for technical use) and quiet consumption of the same among a small circle of his friends. Finally, Major Rogov's squadron, the best in the air army, will be mentioned.

All this has a carefully thought-out purpose behind it. Personnel have hammered into them once again what they must and must not do, and they hear once again the glorification of the Party.

Air force personnel are always encouraged to take part in discussions on every kind of political matter, and especially to ask as many questions as possible. The political leaders of the air force judge the work of their subordinate political officers by the amount of discussion they have promoted and the number of questions they have been asked. 'The more questions, the more interest, and the greater degree of political maturity' goes the Soviet catch-phrase. Naturally, none of the air force personnel must even think of failing to attend these discussions. It is also taken for granted that no one is going to ask the wrong question, but there is virtually no risk of that, since every member of the air force has been thoroughly grounded in the political routines, and the necessity for keeping to the Party line has been well driven into him.

The people responsible for proper attendance at all political functions and for political indoctrination in general are the political deputies to the commanding officers of squadrons and regiments. The lowest grade of political officer is the political deputy to the commanding officer of a squadron, usually a captain. The next in seniority is the political deputy of a regiment, usually a major or a lieutenant-colonel, then of a division, a full colonel, occasionally a lieutenant-colonel. In a corps the position of political deputy is usually occupied by a major-general, and in an air army by a lieutenant-general, sometimes by a major-general. None of these officers is, strictly speaking, an air force officer. They received their training not in the normal air force schools but in special political schools. In many cases they have never been to a military school at all, but were simply appointed by the Party to a new position which happened to be in the air force. For example, the secretary of one of the Moscow Party districts, Asaulenko, was, in the Second World War, suddenly appointed chief of the political administration of an air army, a position which should be occupied by a general. So he was promoted from a civilian to the rank of Major-General of Aviation. The secretary of the Party Committee of a Railway College of the South-Eastern Railway in the Ukraine, Fomin, a stout middle-aged man with spectacles and a rotund unmilitary stomach, found himself after the war in the uniform of a Lieutenant-Colonel of Aviation, as political deputy to the commanding officer of a large air force hospital in Austria. It is a curious fact that the commanding officer of this hospital, a regular officer of the general army medical service, wore the distinctive insignia of that service, while Fomin, a complete civilian, wore that of the flying personnel of the air force.

Political representation in the air regiments is limited officially to the political deputy to the commanding officer, but in air divisions and corps there are political branches as well, and in air armies full political administrations. This means that beside the political deputy there are also staffs of political officers, some eight to fifteen in number, including instructors, propagandists, and editorial staff. The chiefs of political branches of divisions, usually colonels or lieutenant-colonels, are subordinate to the political deputy of the division. A similar structure exists in air armies and air corps. The political deputies of air armies are also members of the military councils of their armies, and are usually better known in that capacity. Members of military councils are possessed of great authority, in fact in some ways greater than that of Commanders-in-Chief of armies themselves, since the Commander-in-Chief cannot interfere in political work in his army, while a member of the military council can easily interfere in all aspects of the army's activities, such as routine training, maintenance of equipment, supplies, promotions, punishments, and so on. Most of the Soviet leaders have been members of military councils in their time. Stalin was a member of the military council of the front commanded by Voroshilov during the Civil War; Khrushchev, with the rank of Lieutenant-General, of the front commanded by Marshal Timoshenko, and Bulganin, with the rank of Colonel-General, of the front commanded by Marshal Rokossovsky, during the Second World War.

Members of military councils are always one or two ranks lower than the Commander-in-Chief. But it would be a great mistake to draw conclusions about their importance from that fact. A Commander-in-Chief of an air army would never risk taking a serious decision without the consent of the political member of his military council. The reason for this is very simple: the Commander-in-Chief can only speak with the authority of a military expert backed by the Air Force High Command. A member of the military council speaks, and can make decisions, in the name of the Party, the real rulers of the country, and backed by the almighty Central Committee and the Party Praesidium. In this case rank and uniform are not important.

The political member of the military council of the 2nd Air Army, Major-General Ramazanov, used to say, after the Second World War, commenting on his new air force uniform: 'If the Party ordered it, I'd put on a dunce's cap!'

Major-General Ramazanov, with his few decorations and his one general's star, cut an unimpressive figure beside the Commander-in-Chief of this army, Colonel-General of Aviation Krassovsky, with his three stars and his twenty-three orders and medals. However, it was impossible not to notice that Krassovsky took Ramazanov with him on all important occasions, and always sought his advice. This intimate relationship exists between all commanding officers of regiments, divisions, and corps, and their political deputies, and has been made closer and stronger in the last year or so.

The people on whom the political deputy relies for assistance are the Party organisers and the *Komsomol* organisers, known as *Partorgs* and *Komsorgs*. They are usually officers of the flying or technical service, appointed to these positions by the political administrations of divisions or armies. The vitally necessary qualification for these positions is an absolutely blameless record from the Party point of view. A good service record is also necessary. A politically blameless record must include 'proletarian parentage', no traceable relations who have ever been prosecuted by the Soviet government, and that the man himself must never have been suspected of the smallest political deviation.

The duties of the *Partorgs* consist mainly of watching over and controlling attendance at all political functions and meetings, recommending and distributing new Party literature, organising political circles for the study of Marxism and Leninism, and promoting 'Socialist competition' between different units, competitions in marksmanship, flying abilities, and so on. *Komsorgs* carry out similar duties among members of the *Komsomol* (the Communist Union of Youth). Because of the many young men in the air force, the number of *Komsomol* members is proportionately high. In fact, the majority of the Soviet Air Force personnel are members. At each political branch and administration there are *Komsomol* sections, consisting of instructors and propagandists. The chiefs of these sections are deputies to the chief of the political administration or branch, known as 'deputies for *Komsomol* work'. The rules of the Party and *Komsomol* state that each civilian or military organisation of the USSR having more than ten members of the Party or *Komsomol* must organise its own Party (or *Komsomol*) organisation.

The vast majority of air force personnel belong to the Party or *Komsomol*, so there is such an organisation in nearly every squadron. Members of these organisations elect a secretary from among their number, who carries out similar duties to those of the *Partorg*, and is in general a helper of the political deputy. They also arrange the procedure of admissions to the Party or *Komsomol*, i.e. they hold boards and interview candidates.

Theoretically, any Soviet citizen over the age of 18 can apply for Party membership. In fact there are many snags. A person of 'non-proletarian origin' or one from a family of 'enemies of the people', would not be allowed to join the Party, nor would someone considered to be of immoral character, or accused of some crime (even of a non-political kind). Anyone wanting to enter the Party must have guarantees given by two established Party members. After the application has been discussed at a meeting of the Party organisation of his unit, voting by a show of hands takes place. The elected man becomes a 'candidate' for Party membership, in which grade he may remain for up to five years. Then, or possibly earlier if he has done well in his work and training, he will again be summoned to a meeting of his Party organisation. Voting will again take place. If he is elected he will become a full member of the Party. Membership of the Party is very useful: Party members are more likely to get promotion, and, most important, the way to the highest rank and the top positions in the forces is open to Party members only.

Every Party member, from the moment he enters the Party, has a special personal dossier on him opened. All reprimands and commendations received in his career are noted in this dossier. When the time arrives for promotion, or for a decoration, a man's superior officers always refer to this dossier. It is not to be confused with the ordinary service dossier, kept on every officer and man, including Party members, who therefore have two dossiers.

On transfer to another air base, a Party member must immediately register with the Party secretary of his new unit. This is actually the main duty of the Party secretary. Political officers and *Partorgs* are entirely dedicated to political work, but Party secretaries are not, since they have their ordinary flying or technical duties to carry out. But the Party secretary always has a chance to turn himself into a political officer, after having received special training. Officers, and especially non-commissioned officers, who are unwilling to make flying their career, are very well aware of the possibilities of making a political career in the service. For this reason they form what is known as the Party or *Komsomol* 'active' and are called 'activists'. They always speak at political meetings and discussions, criticise the offenders against discipline and those who do not keep up with their training. Moreover they often collaborate with the counter-espionage service in the air force, which will be described later in this chapter.

Candidates selected from among the activists are regularly sent to a two years' course at a political school, after which they become political deputies to commanding officers. There are also similar activists at these schools who come from civilian occupations, factories, offices, collective farms and colleges.

Personnel of the air force are never free from political influence, even in their family life or on leave. They have to study the 'classics of Marxism', to write essays on them, to join the 'evening circles' for political study, which usually take place in the home of one of their colleagues. In short, as the Soviet saying goes, the Soviet airman must 'constantly raise his political level'.

The air force, like the other Soviet armed services, has a system of political counter-espionage. This system dates back to the very beginnings of the air force in the early 'twenties. The purpose of this system is the maintenance of the strictest possible control, and the preservation of the security of the State from foreign espionage and 'diversions' and also from any kind of inside activities directed against the Soviet power. This system is known as the organisation of State Security.

However, the Soviet Government has another purpose in operating this system. Through it, it maintains its citizens, civilian and military, in a permanent state of fear and unconditional obedience. The political counter-espionage of the air force is a part of the giant security organisation, the KGB (Committee of State Security, previously known as the VChK, the GPU, OGPU, NKVD, MVD, and MGB, but in spite of these many changes of name, the original system and its purpose remain unchanged).[1] At the present moment the KGB is led by Alexander Shelepin, former head of a department in the Central Committee of the Communist Party, thus a man 'in the know' about all the intrigues and secret acts of the highest Soviet heirarchy. Directly under his control are several especially

---

[1] An indication of this is that the name of a secret police official is still 'Chekist' from the initials VChK.

important branches known as Central Administrations of the KGB. The Third Central Administration carries out political counter-espionage in all the Soviet armed forces.

This administration is the successor to the famous and powerful secret police organisation created by Stalin in 1942, SMERSH.[1] Up to 1942 this counter-intelligence work had been carried out by special cadres attached to all military units. After five years SMERSH was replaced in 1947 by the Third Administration of the KGB. It was then given a façade of legalism by attaching to it a system of tribunals (previously death sentences could be carried out without any legal processes), but it still remains the most tyrannical and arbitrary organisation within the Soviet Union. The importance of this administration can be seen from the fact that of the eight leaders of the whole secret police system since its inception, three were previously leaders of the administration, Menzhinsky, Yagoda, and Abakumov. The latest known leader of the Third Administration is Lieutenant-General Koroliev. He is one of the very few lucky survivors of the constant purges and 'liquidations' among the chiefs of the secret police. (Out of eight heads of the secret police, five have been executed, and their fate was shared by some 90 per cent of departmental chiefs.)

The Third Administration, which deals with army, navy and air force matters, has its headquarters in one of the most beautiful groups of buildings in Moscow, in Dzerzhinsky Square, a short walk from the Kremlin. Though this square is now named after the first chief of the secret police, the Soviet people still call it by its pre-revolutionary name of Lubianka. The buildings are faced to a height of one story with rosy marble, and form an arcade before which stands a bas-relief of Karl Marx, surrounded by beds of petunias and tobacco flowers. This administration, as the Russian saying goes, never sleeps. It works round the clock, controlling all its subordinate administrations in military regions, fleets, the independent armies, and the air administrations.

Below these administrations are those of the armies and the independent corps. They have the following five departments: the first, for work among service personnel; the second, operational; the third, secret; the fourth, interrogational; and the fifth, for tribunals.

The first department consists of five or six senior 'operational

[1] 'SMERSH' is an abbreviation of the Russian *smert shpionam*, 'Death to Spies'.

authorised representatives' (their official title), with the rank of major or lieutenant-colonel. The head of this department is usually a lieutenant-colonel, sometimes a colonel. The duties of this department is to control the network of its official representatives placed in all corps, divisions, regiments, and squadrons.

The second department consists of eight to ten representatives, usually majors, sometimes lieutenant-colonels. Its head will be a lieutenant-colonel or colonel. A squad of soldiers, known as the 'Commandant's squad', is attached to it. This department carries out all arrests, the guarding of prisoners, and guard duties in general.

The third or secret department consists of four or five officers with ranks from captain to lieutenant-colonel, the chief of the branch usually being a lieutenant-colonel. It receives all instructions from the Central Administration, and passes them on through the appropriate channels. It also gathers information from other branches and passes it on to the superior administration.

The fourth or interrogational department consists of five or six interrogators and senior interrogators, with ranks from captain to lieutenant-colonel, the chief usually being a lieutenant-colonel. This department carries out all investigations concerning members of the forces accused of anti-Soviet activities. It prepares what is known as 'cases' based on interrogations, and passes them to the fifth or tribunals department.

The tribunals which judge the political crimes of air force personnel consist of three permanent members, with ranks of major or lieutenant-colonel. The chairman of the tribunal is usually a lieutenant-colonel. It also has a special secretary attached to it. Because all the paperwork of this administration is considered highly secret, it has special clerical staffs of typists and secretaries, including some women, all of them of officer rank.

At the head of an air army's counter-espionage administration usually stands a major-general, sometimes a colonel. Below the army's administration is the counter-espionage branch of the air corps, consisting of a major or lieutenant-colonel as chief; his deputy, known as 'senior authorised representative', is usually a major; two or three authorised representatives, who also act as interrogators, with the rank of senior lieutenant or captain, and a secretary, usually a lieutenant. In the air division there will be a chief of counter-espionage, a major or captain, and one or two operational authorised representatives, captains or senior lieutenants. Each air regiment has one authorised representative, usually a captain. In addition to that there is sometimes one representative for every two air squadrons. During the war this was the normal practice.

Each authorised representative of a regiment or squadron organises his own network of secret informers among the personnel of his unit. There are various methods of recruiting members of this network. In some cases threats are used, in some cases an appeal is made to love of country or perhaps to Party loyalty, and in others promises of promotion are given. The Party and *Komsomol* organisations, especially the activists, are the best material for recruitment. It is an established, though unofficial, practice that every *Partorg* and *Komsorg* of the unit is an informer. This is in accordance with the words of Lenin, spoken in December 1917, that 'every Communist must be a Chekist'.

Representatives of the KGB in the air force are strictly isolated from the life of the other personnel. The place where they work can be easily picked out from the other buildings of an air army or division. It is usually surrounded by barbed wire and road blocks, and it is constantly patrolled by armed guards.

They have their own canteens and dining and rest rooms, and even off duty are kept away from the other officers of their unit. They are absolutely independent of the command of the units to which they are attached. In fact they are not service personnel at all, but regular employees of the secret police dressed in air force uniform for camouflage. For example, when Colonel Chugunov was recently appointed as chief of the KGB of an air army stationed in eastern Europe, he arrived in full KGB uniform, with sky-blue topped cap with a scarlet band, and secret police insignia on his sleeve. After two days he appeared in a beautifully tailored uniform of an air force colonel, making witticisms about his magic transformation.

The chief of the KGB of an air army is also a member of the military council of this army, together with the C-in-C of the army, his political deputy, and his *zam. po tuilu* (deputy for the rear) in charge of equipment, all kinds of supplies, and medical and technical services.

It has been mentioned above that the political member of the military council is a person of very great importance, more important than the Commander-in-Chief himself, but the counter-espionage member is more important yet. The political member derives his importance from the fact that he speaks in the name of the Party, but the counter-espionage member speaks in the name of the 'guardians of the Party', that is, the most carefully chosen and most reliable 'upper crust' of the Party. Orwell's observation, 'everyone is equal but some are more equal than others', embodies a principle that is carefully observed in the organisation of the Soviet Communist Party and its activities in the Soviet Air Force.'

Another reason for the great importance of the KGB representatives in the air force is that according to the official principles of the KGB, no one who falls into their hands receives any different treatment because of his rank, decorations, honourable service, or any other reason. The Soviet official slogan goes like this: 'The members of the KGB are guardians of the Revolution's conquests, and they are the drawn sword of the Revolution.'

In the air force units, the KGB representative will never consult the commanding officer about any action that he intends to take. For example, in the 6th Bomber Corps, in the spring of 1948, a whole day's training for one division was upset because a group of five members of the KGB arrived and began to examine all the aircraft without any explanation to anyone. The reason was that the day before one of the aircraft had developed a slight defect in the landing gear, and some Party activist had obviously reported this to the KGB representative. The KGB representative refused to accept the technical explanation that this was a normal, unavoidable defect, and was plainly determined to make out of it an act of sabotage, known in the official Soviet terminology as 'wrecking'. The sniffing out of sabotage is the favourite occupation of KGB representatives, and it has cost air force officers much nerve strain and not infrequently their careers. The range of supposed sabotage is extremely wide, from the late arrival on manœuvres of a field kitchen because of a burst tyre, to the discovery of a box of ammunition of the wrong size found among others. But the chief bugbear of the pilot is the fear that he may have one day to bale out in the course of his training. In such cases numbers of KGB groups will descend on the unit, and the pilot concerned will undergo endless interrogations. His fate will be entirely in the hands of the KGB, and neither the most reasonable explanation, nor a blameless record, nor any recommendation in his favour by his commanding officer, will have any effect. All depends on the decision of the superior officers of the KGB to whom the results of the interrogation will be passed. It is small wonder that relations between the air force personnel and KGB representatives are very much strained. The fear and hatred are impossible to conceal, and during the war when there were opportunities and control was relaxed there were many cases in which the KGB representatives were murdered.

The KGB system, together with the political system described in the earlier part of the chapter, provides an absolute control over the air force. Whether this control is good or bad can only be discussed in relation to the whole Soviet system. Certainly in any country with a government elected under a genuinely democratic system such control would not be necessary. But the Soviet leaders, illegally risen to power after forty years of ceaseless struggle and intrigue, cannot afford to abolish control over this most vital section of their people, the air force. In existing conditions this control certainly has many advantages. Every aspect of life in any unit, however small or remote, could be known within hours to the leaders in Moscow. They could be informed of the actions of every officer in the service. In these conditions with the inevitable atmosphere of mistrust and suspicion, the growth of real friendships, always unpopular with the Soviet power, is extremely difficult. The personnel of the air force, overburdened with political studies and activities, simply have no time for a private life, which also corresponds entirely with the wishes of the Soviet State.

There are also many disadvantages, some of them serious. One of the most serious, which can take on the aspect of a major problem, is that the personnel of the air force, especially those in responsible positions, can lose the ability to use initiative and take responsibility, because of the fear of being accused of sabotage or political deviations. In the first stages of the last war this attitude cost hundreds of thousands of lives and large quantities of military equipment, for many of the large units surrounded by the Germans could have been saved if their commanding officers had given orders to their men to disperse and attempt to break through the German lines singly or in small groups. But this was impossible because the commanding officers were tied hand and foot by strict political instructions to the effect that no units must ever be dispersed.

The second major disadvantage, which would cripple any ordinary state, is the vast cost of this system of political officers and KGB officials.

Another disadvantage is the amount of time wasted on talks, discussions, lectures.

But these disadvantages are not confined to the air force. They are a characteristic part of every aspect of Soviet military affairs. Nothing can be done to change this system without a radical alteration in the nature of Soviet power itself.

Despite the disadvantages and inconveniences of the Communist Party and counter-intelligence intrusions in the life of the Soviet Air Force, the high standard of aircraft production and flying training, etc. does not seem to be seriously affected. Politics and the secret police are by no means a crippling factor. On the whole they may stimulate the laggard more than they handicap initiative and leadership. Perhaps airmen as a race are fairly immune to politics of all kinds.

CHAPTER 14

DAILY LIFE IN THE SOVIET AIR FORCE

Boris Kuban

THE PATTERN OF daily life in the Soviet Air Force varies very greatly. It depends on the service and unit concerned. Numerically the largest part of the air force are the flying units, therefore their daily routine is the most characteristic, and also the most interesting.

Air force units scattered throughout the Soviet Union are usually strictly isolated. The air units are very often stationed together with those of other branches of the services in 'little military towns' (*voennui gorodok*), which are usually situated in a suburb or right outside a town, sometimes in barracks formerly used by the Tsarist army. During the Second World War many of these barracks were destroyed or damaged, but after the war, in spite of the severe shortage of housing and the slowness of civilian rebuilding, a special military building organisation was set up and given top priority, and a labour force of slave labourers and German prisoners of war was made available to it, so that by now these military quarters are restored and rebuilt in their original form.

As a typical example of quarters used by an air garrison those in Voronezh could be described. The air garrison in this town is one of the oldest established in Russia. In the post-war years a bomber division was stationed here. The main part of the quarters consisted of several four-storied buildings; one of them, with a striking high tower, is an officers' club and restaurant. In this group of buildings the divisional headquarters and two regiments are located. Across the nearby airfield there are two more buildings in the pre-revolutionary Tsarist style, housing the third regiment of the division. In neighbouring buildings, bordering on the territory of infantry units of the Voronezh garrison, there is an air-technical regiment, attached to this air division. An air-technical regiment is part of the usual structure pattern of the air force, in which each regiment has an air-technical battalion attached to it, each division a regiment, each corps a division, and each army a corps. These technical units carry out various servicing and supply duties such as the maintenance of airfields, catering, medical service, fuelling, munitioning, signals, transport, and repair work of various kinds.

The day usually begins at 6 am in summer and 7 am in winter in peacetime. A bugle is sounded, and the duty officer, with the bugler, walks through the quarters. The aircrews hurry from their quarters. The nature of their day's duties has been laid down on the previous evening, so they are dressed accordingly and they know exactly where to go. Most of the crews are officers; with a few non-commissioned officers on voluntary extended service which brings them various privileges and raises their position almost to the level of the officers.

Almost all of the crews live in the divisional quarters, though they are not obliged to; the practice of living outside is not encouraged by their superiors. In any case the exigencies of Soviet life solve this problem more or less automatically, since in Voronezh, as in many other Russian towns almost entirely destroyed during the war, finding decent living accommodation is practically impossible.

The officers and men usually begin their day in Russian fashion with a cup of tea taken at home. After the bugle has sounded, each unit has a short period for exercises, and then the working day starts, usually with a spell of indoor work, starting regularly with half an hour of political information, read by the political officer of the unit.

After that, there may be training in subjects like map reading, or a study of the internal regulations and orders of the air force. Breakfast starts at 8 am. Flying personnel have their own dining-room, one for each regiment. If the man is married, his family is entitled to army rations, though not of the same kind as his. Officers are obliged to contribute to their food out of their pay, but the amount is modest.

All flying personnel receive food ration number five. This is the best food ration of the Soviet armed forces, and can be compared only with that given to submarine crews.

This ration includes a pound (400 grammes) of meat per day, and roughly three ounces of butter besides other fats. Bread is a staple food in Russia, and this ration gives unlimited quantities of white and rye bread.

Though this ration is meant only for the flying personnel, it is

H

often enjoyed by senior political officers and personnel of counter-intelligence attached to air units.

Non-flying personnel of air regiments are entitled to food ration number six, known as the 'technical' one. This ration is not much different from number five, except for a smaller quantity of meat and butter. There are other food rations in the air force: number nine, in training schools, which includes extra fruit and vegetables; number eleven, for hospitals, and number twelve for air force sanatoriums and rest homes. These last two include extra quantities of milk products and eggs.

Air-technical units have the number two food ration, like the other Soviet military ground services. The food on this ration is coarser, and contains more bread and cereals, and the meat ration is only 120 grammes a day.

Breakfast for flying personnel usually consists of one hot dish, meat with potatoes, rice or vegetables, tea or coffee, and bread and butter. After breakfast, the main work of the day begins. Crews engage in various kinds of drill and training, with the main emphasis on actual flying. Squadrons usually carry out their own flying training separately. Squadrons are divided into the smallest unit of the Soviet Air Force, the *zveno* of three planes. There are days arranged on which flying exercises are carried out on a regimental or even divisional scale. Flights go on until dinner-time at one or two o'clock. Dinner is the main meal of the day. It consists of three courses for the flying personnel, a thick soup or bortsch, meat with vegetables, or rice, and fruit or pie. Two hours are set aside for dinner and a rest period.

Then training and studies are resumed, mostly of a technical character, such as the study of new forms of equipment, detailed analysis of previous flights, work on the aircraft armoury and also the personal small arms (for officers). With this the regular working day concludes, but official activities are by no means at an end: various lectures, Party and *Komsomol* meetings, and the 'Circles for Political Study' (described in the preceding chapter) begin. It is unusual for the personnel of an air regiment, on a normal working day, to have time to themselves before eight or nine o'clock in the evening, even though they may have been officially off duty since six.

Supper usually takes place between eight and nine, and resembles breakfast: one hot dish, tea or coffee, and plenty of bread and butter.

Certain days every week are set aside for 'Officers' Seminars' and officers' pistol practice on the range. Attendance is compulsory. Officers' seminars are conducted by high-ranking officers, usually a general, and are devoted to a thorough analysis and study of the latest developments in the Soviet Air Force of a strategical and tactical character.

Pistol practice too is regarded as very important. The experience of the war and the post-war period showed that most officers neglected their personal arms completely. In some cases they hardly knew how to use them, and seemed to think of them merely as an adornment. For this reason the regular weekly practice is always carried out in the presence of the commanding officer of the regiment or one of his deputies. Strict inspections are also carried out, and the arms must be maintained in perfect condition.

The daily routine of non-flying personnel is kept to roughly the same hours as that of the aircrews. Technical units have a daily routine similar to that of the infantry, with maintenance of airfields, technical work, mounting guard, taking the place of ordinary infantry drill and exercises.

Normal air force routine is often interrupted by inspections and large-scale tactical training. Inspections are usually carried out by representatives of the Defence Ministry or of the High Command of the air force. Commanding officers are usually warned beforehand of the coming inspection. Preparations are made for several days before the inspection, and on the actual day normal routine is suspended, and training and practice are carried on under the direction of the inspecting officer.

Air force units take part in spring and autumn manœuvres. It is not uncommon during these manœuvres for large air units to be moved a thousand or more miles from their base. Normal routine is suspended and replaced by as near as possible wartime conditions.

However, officers and men of the air force regard the great annual parades on the 1st May and the 7th November, and Aviation Day (usually about 29th June) as their principal curse. Units selected to take part in the display over the Red Square are considered the most unfortunate of all because of the abnormal precision introduced into these parades by Stalin and still carried on. The selected units may be stationed at any distance from Moscow. Several weeks before the parade they are transferred to what is known as the meeting base, a hundred or two hundred miles from Moscow. On the day of the parade the various units have to rendezvous in the air with split-second timing, and they have to arrive over the Red Square exactly simultaneously with the arrival of the first tank of the ground forces into the square. Deviations of even half a second are frowned on. This highly dramatic moment of the parade was a source of great pleasure to Stalin, who never failed to draw the attention of foreign observers to the fine effect produced by the neck-and-neck arrival of the first tank on the ground and the first aircraft in the air, but it was no pleasure to the air force generals in attendance, who spent the minutes beforehand looking frantically at their watches and those afterwards almost hysterical with relief.

In normal circumstances personnel are on duty five and a half days a week, since they are free from midday on Saturday. In their free time officers are permitted to wear civilian clothes, but they seldom do so, for three good reasons: a suit at 2,500–3,000 roubles is rather too expensive even for the comparatively well-paid officer; the air force officer is one of the aristocrats of Soviet society, and he is conscious of his standing and likes others to know about it (this is especially true of young, unmarried officers, for they know that they rate particularly high with the girls); and the uniform is smart and of very good quality.

Several different outfits are issued to air force personnel. Everyday or working dress consists of dark blue breeches or long trousers, with a narrow sky blue stripe, with a khaki or dark blue tunic, steel-grey or light khaki shirt and a black tie. For evening a white shirt is worn. The parade uniform includes a tunic with round collar with gold embroidery, white gloves and white belt. The caps, somewhat on the German pattern, do not bear 'scrambled eggs' as in Britain, but 'cabbage'.

It is not unknown for young officers to introduce extras. Among these are extraordinarily baggy breeches, soft leather boots put on in the so-called harmonica fashion, with many wrinkles, cap very much on the side of the head, and pistol, instead of on the right side, worn right at the back. The Soviet military police are engaged in a constant hopeless struggle against these innovations.

The air force is well equipped with special dress for flying duties or ground technical work. There is an adequate range of winter clothing, from short leather jackets with imitation fur linings to long lined overcoats, dark blue or steel grey, and hats with ear-flaps of imitation caracul; real caracul for ranks from Colonel upwards.

The officer pays for his everyday uniform, not for special dress. In relation to ordinary prices what he pays is ludicrously little, and would hardly buy him a shirt in a civilian shop.

In all garrisons there are special shops maintained by *Voentorg* (military trade), under the Ministry of Defence. Here there are clothing, food, and many other goods on sale, including even toys for children, at reduced prices, and often including articles that are unobtainable outside. Families of air force officers and men are permitted to shop here.

There are very definite distinctions between ranks, though these distinctions are not very noticeable among junior officers up to the rank of major, including non-commissioned officers on flying-officers' duties. The scale of pay rises slowly, by 200 to 400 roubles a month with each rank. But the lieutenant-colonel receives not only a substantial increase in pay but also many other privileges, not so much because of his rank but because of his position, since he is likely to be at least deputy to the commanding officer of the regiment. He will have large and comfortable quarters, unrestricted use of a car, and, unofficially, all the best that the unit can provide: the best food at the canteen and the shop, and the best and most difficult to come by goods at the shop, for him and his family. His driver and batman will be personal servants to his family. The general will have more extensive privileges. A general commanding a division or corps will automatically share in the comforts enjoyed by local Party and government officials in his area. He will be able to make use of the shops for high officials, which are completely closed to the rest of the population, where everything, including foreign made goods, can be bought at greatly reduced prices. Besides the car or two provided by the service, he might well have his own, and might also provide one for his children. He and his family would have one of the best homes in the town, not necessarily at the base. Marshals of Aviation lead the life of the highest Party officials, the most favoured authors and scientists, ballerinas and film stars.

This includes villas by the Black Sea, small fleets of cars, country houses, hunting lodges, large staffs of indoor and outdoor servants, and diamond-decked wives and mistresses. Their actual pay is not so fantastically high, the highest is from 10,000 to 12,000 roubles a month, but they have so many other privileges, such as buying at very greatly reduced prices in the special shops, servants' wages and maintenance of cars provided by the State and food from special farms exclusively for the use of the privileged. The building and maintenance of their houses and villas cost them nothing, for they are done by the military building administration free of charge. Obviously the differences between their lives and that of the average air force officer with 900 to 1,200 roubles a month (not to mention the private in the army with eight to twelve roubles a month) put them in another world.

Promotions tend not to follow the official scheme. According to this scheme, an officer should be promoted every three to six years, the interval increasing as he rises in rank. All officers graduate from the air force schools with the rank of lieutenant (the wartime shortened course produced junior lieutenants). It is not uncommon that of two lieutenants who enter the air force at the same time one is in four years' time a senior lieutenant and the other a major. The main factors in promotion are personal qualities and initiative. Any officer who has shown himself to be exceptionally able will find the road open to the highest rank, but this healthy and sound practice is sadly marred by political considerations. The case of Stalin's son was not unique, though it was indeed the worst of them. In the normal course of events Vassily Stalin might have reached the rank of major; he was in fact a lieutenant-general.

But perhaps even worse than open nepotism is the standing unwritten rule that an officer who is not a Party member has no chance whatsoever of reaching senior rank. Officers therefore have no choice but to join the Party and thus artificially swell its ranks. It could not happen that an officer would not be permitted to join the Party, because if he was politically suspect to such an extent he would not have been allowed to enter officers' school as he would be 'socially unsuitable', as the Soviet phrase has it.

At the first meetings between the Soviet forces and their Western Allies, Soviet officers were always surprised by the age of their Western counterparts, who always seemed to them rather old, especially in the air force. In the Soviet Union it is not at all uncommon to find a Colonel-General of Aviation (equivalent to a

British Air Marshal) who is still in his thirties, and it is not impossible to find a Marshal of Aviation who is under forty. On the whole these men have all been promoted on their merits. General Smooshkevich and General Proskurov, who were both round about 35 years old, were executed in the great purge of the 1930s, when the former was Commander-in-Chief of the Air Force and the latter C-in-C Fighter Command.

The Soviet Air Force is certainly the most decorated service in the world. Air force 'Heroes of the Soviet Union', the highest Soviet award, increased to an unnatural number during the war. Further decoration of those who had already become Heroes became a problem, and it was decreed that they could become Heroes twice, thrice, or even four times. The first men who received the third golden star of the Hero were both fighter pilots; the 25-year-old Major Ivan Kozhedub, and 32-year-old Colonel Alexander Pokruishkin. The only four times Hero is in fact Marshal Zhukov, who received his fourth star just before his dismissal.

Almost all commanders of air armies and corps have once or twice become Heroes of the Soviet Union, but the decorations have fallen thickest on ordinary air force officers, especially those in fighters. Before the war it had been extremely unusual to see a junior officer wearing the Order of the Red Banner, not to mention the Order of Lenin; it is now not uncommon to see six of these orders on the breast of a young captain.

Before the war, each decoration was accompanied by a small grant of money. After the war this practice was abolished, because, as the current witticism had it, 'the Soviet bank would have been emptied' if all the grants had been paid.

Decorations, particularly in the air force, had lost their meaning, except for that of the Hero of the Soviet Union or the Order of Lenin, and possibly the Red Banner. The end of the war checked this flood of medals. Orders such as those of Kutusov or Suvorov cannot be given in peacetime, and in wartime only to officers in charge of strategic units. This also applies to the Order of Alexander Nevsky and the Patriotic War, except that they had a wider range of recipients.

In peacetime there is a standing regulation on decorations, according to which any member of the forces, regardless of his rank, who has completed 25 years service, receives the Order of Lenin, after 20 years, the Red Banner, after 15 years the Red Star, and other medals for shorter terms of service.

Many decorations are given to those who have seen no active service except in staffs and political administrations. Members of political counter-espionage attached to air force units also received many high decorations for no obvious reason.

Air force personnel are recruited from the yearly intake of conscripts. The main requirement is health. There are usually more men anxious to join than there are places for them, but when they have been sifted the position is reversed.

Most personnel, especially officers, are very reluctant to retire. The main reason for retirement, apart from age, is health. The reluctance is easily explained: on retirement the standard of living drops sharply, especially in the case of high-ranking officers. It is not only that pensions tend to be insufficient, but the high-ranking officer will find himself stripped of all his luxuries and privileges.

Before the war, retirement meant complete severance of all ties with the service, but after the war the Government made certain concessions on this point. Officers are permitted to wear their uniforms (with a special stripe on the epaulette). They are known as 'Colonel or General So-and-So, in retirement'. They may enter officers' clubs and restaurants, and are entitled to salutes.

Promotion in the air force is easy and quick; so is demotion. Any general or marshal of the air force could lose his rank and all that went with it without much warning. If he was lucky he could merely be relieved of his rank and sent to some insignificant post, as happened, for example, to General Musienko, Deputy to the Commanding Officer of the 2nd Air Army, who suddenly found himself chairman of a large State agricultural undertaking (*Sovkhoz*) in the Ukraine, to which he was sent on the order of the Central Committee of the Party. If the worst happens, and he falls into political disgrace, the question of rank will hardly arise, since he will be lucky to escape with his life.

In wartime ordinary officers could be demoted in large numbers for such offences as abandoning their equipment or for suffering too many casualties among their men. Many air force officers had a very anxious time trying to convince counter-intelligence that they had been obliged to parachute and abandon their aircraft. Ultimately pilots became terrified of surviving themselves without their aircraft, since the punishment for what was judged to be the very serious offence of abandoning equipment without sufficient reason was demotion to the ranks, loss of all decorations, and service of from three to eight months in a punishment battalion. The actual term to be served in such a battalion mattered little, since it was very unlikely that anyone would survive for more than a few days.

In peacetime, too, strict disciplinary courts are maintained. The worst offences are treason, and defection to the West. Sentence for these offences is death, or at the very least 15 years slave labour, in the latter case, of course, passed *in absentia*.

All offences are strictly divided into political and non-political. Anything that the Secret Police and the political authorities choose to regard as an anti-Soviet activity would automatically mean the ruin of a man's entire career, expulsion from the service, and almost certainly a long term of imprisonment. There is no limit to the imagination of the authorities as far as anti-Soviet activities are concerned, and they may range from the plotting of a revolution to the relation of funny stories about the Soviet leaders.

Non-political offences are mostly of two kinds: theft of Government property, and offences against morals. The first is again of very wide range: the supply officer of an air division or corps may make a few million roubles by manipulating the property and funds in his charge; or a technician may take away a few pints of a spirit designed for technical purposes, and drink it with his friends. This last is a traditional offence in the air force.

Punishment in the first case depends on the political standing and the political contacts of the officer. In 1947 Major Lozovsky, in charge of supply in an air army, took home to Russia from occupied Austria two railway carriages full of valuable goods and several million roubles in cash. An investigation was carried out, and a considerable scandal was caused; a few months later Major Lozovksy was observed walking peacefully down a street in Moscow, wearing civilian clothes, and it was discovered that he was a high executive in the Moscow Restaurant Trust. He was the nephew of the Deputy Foreign Minister Lozovsky, otherwise he might well have got up to ten years' imprisonment.

Lesser offences of a non-political kind may be punished by demotion and imprisonment of up to five years. But there is always a chance that even without political standing and contacts an offender may be let off scot-free, for the Secret Police tend to turn a blind eye to non-political offences.

Offences against morals include rape, exceptionally stormy married lives which disturb the peace of the garrison, and venereal diseases. Rape is taken very seriously as a rule. In one instance an Engineer General of the Technical Air Service, who raped a girl of thirteen, was relieved of his rank and decorations and demoted to a building technician on an airfield. The second offence is usually dealt with by the local political authorities without calling in the military tribunal, and the man may lose his seniority and might even be demoted one or two ranks. Venereal disease became an offence, particularly serious in the air force, towards the end of the war. At first victims of venereal disease were regarded with sympathy and understanding by their superiors, and to get syphilis was affectionately known as 'to become a general' and gonorrhea as 'to become a colonel'.

Later, when the number of cases in the air force had increased catastrophically in the units stationed in the occupied countries, contraction of the disease became an offence, and an officer or man would be sent home with a black mark in his dossier: for an officer this meant the ruin of his career.

An officer or man contracting a normal illness while serving receives first-class treatment, in special air force hospitals. There is a central air force hospital in Moscow, with the latest modern equipment and research laboratories. Each air army also has its own similar hospital on a smaller scale; corps and divisions have medical battalions that also have a certain number of beds available. Regiments have medical companies that can give first aid and clinical treatment, but have no beds. All air force hospitals are under the control of a special medical administration under the air force high command. This administration also maintains rest homes for air force personnel, including some in the most beautiful parts of Russia, the Crimea and the Caucasus.

The high command is very reluctant to invalid personnel out of the air force, and very prolonged treatment is often given to restore a man to health rather than lose him from the service.

Since the war the system of annual leaves has been restored. The length of the leave depends on various circumstances: the personal record of the man concerned, his distance from his home (this is a big factor in Russia). According to these circumstances, his leave may be from two to five weeks. In peacetime there are also one day and week-end leaves. Leave on a working day is usually granted only under special circumstances. At the week-end all personnel off duty are entitled to go where they please, providing their behaviour in the past week has been satisfactory. There is always a certain number confined to barracks.

On the whole the facilities for sport are not good. There are some excellent football teams, such as the ZDSA, the Central House of the Soviet Army, in which air force officers are included, or *Kruilya Sovetov* (Wings of the Soviets), but the players in these teams could hardly be described as regular air force officers, because they are really professional sportsmen and their air force commissions are merely formalities.

Air garrisons usually have sportsgrounds with various facilities, but attendance, unless compulsory, is very poor. Air force personnel have very little free time, and what they do have they want to spend on their own pursuits.

Every air garrison has its own officers' club, besides the officers' clubs for all services, in which are restaurants and bars where drinks can be bought. But serious drinking is usually done outside these establishments, away from superior officers. Of the Soviet services, the air force is the most hard-drinking, since they are the best paid, and have the highest proportion of young unmarried officers. The usual drinks are various kinds of vodka, and the traditional drink, 'technical spirit', which is highly thought of as being stronger than ordinary liquor, pure, and above all costing nothing, apart from the slight risk of being caught stealing it. People say it is: 'Clear as the tears of the Mother of God, and strong as Soviet power.'

Slang in the Soviet forces is usually too indecent to be repeated; there are one or two sayings, however, such as 'Where discipline ends, the air force begins'.

Air force songs are also extremely indecent, on the whole, and very popular. There are also songs written by Soviet composers glorifying the air force, and one of these has been declared to be virtually the anthem of the air force.

> We are born to turn myth into reality
> To overcome distance and height
> Intellect has given us steel hands—wings,
> And instead of a heart, a burning engine.

Each air regiment has its own brass band. Regimental clubs have musical instruments, the most popular of which are accordions.

Women played a fairly important part in the air force during the war. There were whole regiments of women. The most famous was that of Colonel Valentina Grizodubova, which fought successfully on the south Caucasian front. Many women became Heroes of the Soviet Union and received other decorations. After the war, these units were disbanded, and there are very few women in the air force. Most of the ones who remain are employed in the medical service. Clubs, canteens and laundries also employ women, but they do not belong to the regular serving personnel. These girls usually have boy-friends among the officers but their popularity tends to depend on the position of the garrison and the number of girls in the surrounding district.

It is often possible to locate an air garrison in a town by the number of girls patrolling outside. The military police often have to chase them off. 'There is no prostitution in the Soviet Union.'

Much of this may not seem very different from other air forces; it is in the realm of political indoctrination and control that the differences become remarkable: the subject was dealt with in the last chapter.

CHAPTER 15

THE GERMAN LEGACY

Richard E. Stockwell

BOTH WORLD WARS left Russia with an acute awareness of its shortcomings as a military power. Both times this led the USSR to seek German science and engineering as a means for catching up with the rest of the world.

The Versailles Treaty, with its restrictions on German aviation, fostered an era of co-operation between Germany and Russia after the First World War. At that time, hundreds of Germans wanted to continue to fly and there were German firms with ideas for new aircraft. Russia, on the other hand, was concerned with the development of an aviation industry of its own, the need to train mechanics, designers, and pilots. Quite naturally, the two countries got together.

In 1921–2 a secret agreement was signed between the Red Army and the German *Reichswehr*. Under its terms, Russian officers were trained in Germany and a German military mission was sent to Moscow. An aircraft factory was built at Fili, near Moscow, with German money, and many German pilots went to Russia to train Russians in the art of flying, for instance at bases near Kiev and Leningrad.

The German Junkers firm, which built the factory near Moscow, soon found itself in the air transportation business in many different countries, including Russia, where it helped establish one of the first Russian airlines DERULUFT.

Russo-German co-operation continued until 1935, when Hitler called a halt to it. However, by then the die was cast. German ideas about air power had been sown deep in the Soviet Air Forces. The purging of strategic air power advocates in 1936–8, together with experience gained in the Spanish Civil War and with the Japanese in Mongolia, pretty well ended Russian ideas about long range bombing in the pre-war period. Instead, the Russians developed their air power along German lines as an instrument of the ground forces.

When the Second World War came it showed the Russians their mistakes and shortcomings. The experience was a crucible from which came a new appreciation and a determination to catch up and surpass the West in aviation. The Second World War experience against the Germans showed the Russians lacked piloting skill and discipline; their concepts of air power were too limited; their long range aircraft performance was poor. Flexibility and mobility of their tactics and facilities left much to be desired. In a phrase, they simply were not as professional as the Germans. This forced the Russians to review, examine and restudy their airpower concepts, technology, and training after the Second World War.

Long before the Communists took over in 1917, Russian scientists had shown an interest in such things as jet propulsion and rocket development. However, like so many things in Russia, little effort was put into their practical application. The need to apply science and engineering more intensively to their military problems was another lesson driven home to the Communist hierarchy by the Second World War.

To catch up with the West meant that they would have to copy its technology; and nearby, in defeated Germany, was one of the largest pools of scientific-engineering skill and manpower in the world. In Silesia, over which the Red Army swarmed on its way to Berlin in 1944–5, the Soviets got fully 80 per cent of the German aircraft industry: it had been concentrated there because of Allied bombing attacks along Germany's western approaches.

Similarly, the remarkable rocket test facilities at Peenemunde fell into the Soviet hands, along with some of the production facilities for *V2s* at Nordhausen and Magdeburg in East Germany. Apparently the Russians did not immediately appreciate what was in their grasp, for they wantonly destroyed many facilities which they tried to rebuild for their own use a few months later. Similarly, the Germans themselves destroyed some things and even more important, carted off special tools and designs, to hide them from the enemy.

Soon word spread back to Moscow, however, and engineers were sent scouring the German countryside to learn industrial and military secrets that could be used in the USSR. Among others, there were representatives from the Commissariat of Aviation Industry; specialists from TsAGI, the Central Aerodynamics and

Hydrodynamics Institute in Moscow, as well as from VIAM, the
All-Union Institute of Aviation Materials, and NISO, the Scientific
Research Institute for Aeroplane Equipment. Armed with special
powers, these groups did what they could to reassemble the scattered
and broken pieces of what was left of the famous German aeronautical research centre, *Deutsche Versüchsanstalt für Luftfahrt* (DVL),
the Kaiser Wilhelm Institute (where atomic research had been
under way), the *Luftwaffe* and *Heeres Versuchstelle* (rocket test
and development facilities) at Peenemunde and elsewhere. At
Schosberg they took over the latest pulse-jet test facilities; at
Warnemunde the Arado Aircraft Plant; the Zeiss Optical Works
at Jena.

Reassembling the broken bits and pieces was a difficult task and
the Russians wouldn't have done nearly so well with German
military technology if it hadn't been for Allied help. Late in the
summer of 1945, when new occupation zones were agreed upon for
Germany, the Western Allies gave up some East German territory
that had been in their hands. How this worked in favour of the
USSR is explained by a Russian eye-witness, a representative of the
Commissariat of Aviation, who was sent to the Junkers plant at
Dessau when Allied forces turned the area over to the Red Army:

'Individual dismantlers who were sent on a reconnaissance of
the district encountered pleasant surprises everywhere. There were
small factories, branches of Junkers and other firms, which had not
been dismantled by the Americans and which were still working. In
one small place on the banks of the Mulde, they discovered a
former paper factory which was still engaged on the assembly of
BMW aeroplane turbines (*BMW 003*), one of the latest jet engines
at that time. Two storeys of the factory building were filled with
crates containing new turbines in perfect order.

'In Dessau the first Soviet truck with a group of dismantlers drove
through empty streets. The town seemed dead. It was just the same
in the Junkers factory. Except for the two German guards, there
wasn't a soul in sight. The American unit previously stationed at
the factory had left the rooms spotlessly clean and had swept up the
entire factory area before its departure. All the equipment, with the
exception of a few precision tools and instruments, were in the right
places. It was possible to start work. The dismantlers made a dash
for the construction office. But all the shelves had been cleanly

tidied up, just as had the factory area. Not a single diagram, not a single scrap of paper remained.

'The next day the news spread through the town that the Russians were starting up the factory again. The German workmen and engineers began to come in. The next piece of news astounded the Germans: the Russians also were giving jobs to leading specialists, notwithstanding their long record of membership in the National Socialist Party. One after the other, people "with a name" began to turn up, happy that they were not looked at askance for having a party card.

'The same thing happened in the Siebel plant in Halle, the Junkers engine factory at Bernburg, and the Heinkel factory at Oranienburg.'[1]

As fast as they developed a trust in the Russians, the Germans returned to work at the aircraft, missile and electronics factories that were now of such interest to the USSR. They returned the precision equipment they had carried home to hide in attics and basements; they told of past experimental and developmental progress; they helped the Russians find one or two advanced proto-type engines hidden in barns; they came up with the drawings for even more advanced engines and aircraft and they pointed out key areas where there was need for more developmental effort.

In all aviation history this was perhaps the most valuable loot one nation ever got from another as a result of a war. The list reads like a Who's Who and What's What of some of the world's most advanced military technology which the Germans, late in the war, had begun to unfold. They had pointed the way, but had failed to get the new technology out of its development phase and into truly volume production in time to turn the course of the war.

The leaders of the USSR clearly understood this. They quickly took over the new technology where the Germans had left off, and sought to advance it with all possible speed.

They got prototypes of the *JU 287 K*, a Junkers jet bomber that was being developed for long-range operations. Also from Junkers they got the *JUMO 004* turbo-jet engine as well as a prototype of a more advanced turbo-jet engine, and drawings and plans for large turbo-jet and turbo-prop engines. At BMW they got the *BMW 003*

[1] V. L. Sokolov, *Soviet Use of German Science and Technology, 1945–46*, Research Program on the USSR, New York, 1955, pp. 8–10.

turbo-jet engine, and more drawings of advanced turbo-jet and turbo-prop engines, as well as a *BMW 718* rocket booster engine.

In Prague, where the Walter firm had sought shelter from Allied bombing, they picked up the *HWK 109 509* rocket engine which then delivered 4,400 lbs thrust and would keep the *Messerschmitt ME 163 B* rocket interceptor aloft for about twenty minutes. They also picked up other Walter-developed rocket engines, including the larger *HWK 11/211* which is believed to have since achieved 7,500 lb thrust.

In addition to the *Messerschmitt ME 163 B* rocket interceptor, they picked up from the same firm the latest version of the *ME 262* jet-powered interceptor which the Germans had been using with good effect against Allied daylight bombers.

At the Heinkel plant at Warnemunde they found in production a light, inexpensive jet fighter, the *HE 162*. And, of course, they got the *V1* and *V2* missiles as well as the *Rheintochter, Wasserfall Feuerlillie, Taifun,* and a whole host of lesser missiles as well as guided, glide and rocket bombs such as the *Henschel 293* and the *FX 1400*.

There were paper plans to be had everywhere. One of the most important was Professor Kurt Tank's *TA 183* jet interceptor at the Focke Wulf plant. But they also got sketches of Tank's *TA 283*, an advanced craft to be powered by two ram-jets. They found drawings of the Blohm & Voss flying wing design for an interceptor; the rocket-powered *Heinkel P 1077* and the *Messerschmitt P 1111*.

In addition to all of the equipment and advanced paper work, the Russians reaped a harvest of skilled German production workers and key technicians who were taken over with the factories. Still others were sought by the Secret Police, the NKVD, which proffered high salaries and other inducements to bring top men out of hiding or to get them to return from the West. NKVD informers were hired and turned up others.

Often it is claimed that the best brains in German science and technology came to the West at the end of the Second World War. However, it is not clear how significant the claim really is, for those who were brought to the West were not employed as efficiently as those in Russian hands. Some of the best talent that came to the West was put on work that was beneath its ability.

I am of the opinion that whatever the Russians did not get in quality, they made up for in numbers and intensive application. One who fell into Russian hands was Professor Gunther Bock, chief of research for the experimental aeronautics institute, *Deutsche Versüchsanstalt für Luftfahrt* at Berlin-Aldershof. Through him the Russians got the research secrets of the *Luftwaffe*. Professor Bock was taken to Moscow in 1945 and is credited with helping the Russians recruit a large number of technicians who had worked at Peenemunde.

Professor Vollmer and Professor Hertz of the Technical University in Berlin and some specialists from their electronics laboratory were transferred to the Crimea where they have done work in nuclear physics. They are still in Russia. Such men as Messerschmitt's Rudolph Rental, project engineer for the *ME 163* and *ME 263* rocket-powered interceptors developed by the Germans, came into Soviet hands. Doctor Adolph Betz, an authority on swept-wing aircraft, fell into the net. Siegfried Gunther, a senior German designer from Heinkel, who tried first to give his services to the Western Allies, only to be suspected of duplicity, was found by the Russians working in a garage in the French Zone and eventually was persuaded to join them.

At Stendal they took over an entire school the Germans had established for parachute jumpers; at Wittstock they got all of the latest paratrooper equipment. However, airborne forces were not new to the Russians, and it is doubtful whether there they had much to learn from the Germans in this field.

Among the loot they also got two of the world's largest hydraulic die-forging presses, one with a capacity of 33,000 tons and the other of 15,000 tons. These had been used to turn out spars for the *Junker JU 88* in one operation. Though it took the Russians some time, by the early 1950s they had plans for building and installing thirty such presses in the USSR. In 1957 a model of one of the presses, of 30,000 tons capacity, was on display in Moscow at the Agricultural and Industrial Exhibition.

At the Siebel plant in Leipzig, they got plans and samples of floating anti-aircraft platforms the Germans had developed for cross-channel invasion of Britain. The same plant also had in production a device which made it possible to land on exceptionally short runways.

In or near Leipzig, they got tremendous supplies of German

scientific texts, for the city was a printing centre. A synthetic fuel plant had also been established at Leipzig and some of its personnel and the entire plant were moved to Irkutsk. When the East Germans replaced it with a second, it too was taken over by the Russians. At Wurzburg they picked up several different kinds of systems for guiding missiles, including shortwave radio, optical controls, and infra-red detection.

At first the Russians set up Special Construction Bureaux in East Germany and attached the skilled German talent they had netted to these to work on special projects, including such things as electronic controls, engine and airframe designs or chemical fuels for rockets. The Germans assigned to this work received very good pay, were well housed and got other special considerations. This method did not work too well, however, and there was disagreement among the Russians in Germany as to whether this was the best way to get things done.

By 1946 there was evidently a feeling in Moscow that a greater effort must be put into the race to catch up with the West in the air. Purely Russian aircraft, even those with German jet engines, like the new *YAK 15* and *MIG 9*, simply did not have the requisite performance. Then, too, the technological lessons from the Second World War were being driven home more and more to the Russian leaders.

In October 1946, the Russians swooped upon the hapless German technicians and specialists, put them aboard trains and shipped them off to Russia. The plans had been carefully and secretly laid, and entire German families were packed off as a unit, including anyone so unlucky as to be visiting them at the time.

No accurate count is available of how many key people were taken to Russia, though some German estimates have run as high as 300,000, including production workers. It is fairly well established, however, that about 3,000 airframe and engine workers, and design, research, and development people were moved to the USSR.

Skeleton German production crews were left behind and the plants in East Germany continued their work as before, turning out *V2s*, *BMW 003* and *JUMO 004* turbo-jet engines. While work continued at Peenemunde, some groups of German technicians and engineers were set up in Khimki just outside Moscow, and they also worked on missiles. Chemists who had worked on rocket fuels in Germany suddenly found themselves working on rocket fuels at an Institute in Moscow or at the Academy of Sciences in Leningrad. Several German airframe design groups were scattered in small communities not far from Moscow where they worked with Russian design bureaux headed by such men as Yakovlev, Mikoyan and Lavochkin.

Design groups from these units that had been established in East Germany were split up into small operating groups and assigned special projects by the Russians. As they completed each design study on paper, it would be submitted to the Russians, who apparently compared it with similar work done elsewhere. Sometimes the German design group would be asked to do certain aspects of a design again, or the Russians would do this themselves, to fit the work to over-all Russian requirements.

Siegfried Gunther, for example, was given the job of reviewing the *TA 183* design by Doctor Kurt Tank, and later this work was carried forward by a Russian design bureau headed by Mikoyan. This design became the *MIG 15*.

In 1945, the Russians used turbo-jet engines as they came from German production lines, hastily reworking some of their then existing aircraft into jet types. Yakovlev, for instance, one of the USSR's best designers, quickly converted his *YAK 9* of Second World War fame, into a jet, the *YAK 15*. Mikoyan went ahead with a reworked design to produce the *MIG 9*, powered by two *JUMO 004s*, whereas the *YAK 15* had only one.

These were makeshift methods and produced makeshift aeroplanes capable of only 500 mph and lacking range and altitude performance. The Russians clearly needed better turbo-jets to get the performance they would need for interceptors capable of shooting down USAF jet bombers, for example.

With German help, in East Germany and, by 1947, in Russia, they went ahead improving German axial-flow turbo-jet engines, trying to get more thrust out of them. Progress was slow, even though they carried the Junkers basic *JUMO 004* to what the Soviets chose to designate the *RD 10*.

Meanwhile, the top German engine designers who had been swept up by the Russians were hard at work at Kuibischev. Under the direction of a general engine designer named N. D. Kuznetsov one group worked on turbo-props. Their first engine model produced 5,000 equivalent shaft horsepower, but no sooner was the engine run than the Russians decided they also wanted something larger and set the Germans to work on a design for a 12,500 eshp turbo-prop. This engine was first tested in 1948, and today it is basic powerplant in the NATO-designated *Bear*, the huge Russian bomber grossing over 300 tons, and the *TU 114* transport capable of carrying as many as 220 people tourist class. Today Kuznetsov, and his principal assistant, chief designer Ivchenko, are credited with most of the turbo-prop engines in the USSR, even though it is quite clear that the Germans did much of the critical design work.

Other Germans worked on new turbo-jet engines, one of which, the *AM 3*, was produced under the direction of Mikulin, one of Russia's best engine designers, and today powers the *TU 104* jet transport. This is a huge engine, of some 48–49 inches in diameter, and in general outline resembles the original *BMW 018*, a paper design of the Germans, or the *J 53* design of the General Electric Company in the United States. It produces about 15,000 lb thrust.

Junker's B. C. Baade, an airframe designer, was put to work by the Russians on a satisfactory bomber design. A series of prototypes resulted, the most promising of which was the *EF 150*, a twin-jet affair, with large single engine pods under each wing. This aircraft, while test flown, was not put into production, though many of the principles demonstrated and discovered in its development were later applied to *Badger* and *Bison*, Russian medium and long range jet bombers. No doubt they also found their way into the *TU* series of jet transports, the *TU 104, 104A, 110* and *114*.

The *ME 262* came through Russian design bureaux practically unchanged to become a night fighter, credited to designer Lavochkin. However, it never was built in large numbers.

In the missile and electronics field the trail from German ideas to Russian production is much harder to trace. For one thing, many German scientists and technicians in the rocket missile and allied fields have not yet returned from Russia.

Some 200 Peenemunde specialists were taken to the USSR in October 1946, along with production and fuels experts from manufacturing plants contributing to the *V2* missile. The entire rocket test station at Lehesten was packed and shipped about this time.

Experts from Askania, a German firm making theodolites used to track missiles visually were caught up in the same net, along with electronics people from Lorenz, Siemens, and Telefunken, where radar work was also in progress.

Those people familiar with the work at Peenemunde were taken to Ostashkov, north-west of Moscow, and worked on missile designs. After 1952 this group was disbanded, apparently because it was no longer useful, and for the most part the Germans were allowed to return home.

Other missile experts at Khimki worked on a programme to improve the *V2* and otherwise advance the state of Soviet long-ranged rockets. They were under the over-all direction of Professor Artakianov of the Soviet Academy of Sciences, and apparently made significant contributions to Russian engineering in the missile field. Rocket engine work was carried on both at and near Kuibischev, where Kostikov, a Soviet missiles expert and one of his chief collaborators, Ivan Gvai, were at work. It is here that Russia's major rocket power-plants have been developed.

In addition to the *V2* as a starting point, and the design for a two-stage missile based on the *V2* on which the Germans had done some work, the Russians took over the following missiles: For air-to air use and installation aboard such aircraft as the *YAK 25*, they got the German *R4/M*, a 55 mm rocket carrying about a pound of explosives. In addition, they got a German missile called *Sokol* with small swept-back wings and a canard-type nose, and a series of experimental missiles carrying such designations as *R 10*, *R 12*, and so on.

At least three air to surface missiles went to Russia. The *RS 82*, a small missile fired against ground targets, was obsolete when the Soviets got it, but such German-designed flying bombs as the *HS 293* and *FX 1400* and the so-called *V1* flying bomb represented basic research and operational advances in this field. It is known that the Soviets have done work to develop air to surface missiles of large size, and the early German work made its contribution here. A German design group sent to Podberezhye, again not far from Moscow, worked on the design for such a missile. Both straight-wing and delta designs were tested and some of the test data are believed to have been applied to Soviet rocket-powered interceptors, such as the *YAK 21*.

Many of Russia's surface to air missiles can be traced directly to German origins. One called *Rheintochter* was in production at Rheinmetall-Borsigg A.G. It was a two-stage affair, with large fins and a span over six feet. It weighed a ton and a half. The Germans directed it by radio impulses, and two radars, one focused on the missile and the other on enemy bombers overhead. The Russians are known to have taken this missile over and to have developed it further.

The German *Wasserfall* had not been flight-tested when taken over by the Soviets. German designers worked on it in Russia, trying to cut its weight from 8,400 lb to something like 7,500 lb. The Soviets developed the missile along the lines previously set out by the Germans and designated it their *C 2* missile.

A whole series of *Henschel* missiles went to Russia. Among them was the *HS 117*, called *Butterfly* by the Germans. It got off the ground with the aid of two booster rockets, and was then powered the rest of the way by a rocket engine. Both the *BMW 109-558* and the Walter *HWK 109-729* engines were used in this missile, and of course went to Russia, as well as some ramjet powerplants that also were tried in *Butterfly*.

The German *Taifun* that was being built by the Elektromechanische Werke and designed for high altitude interception went the way of the others, on the long road to the USSR. It had a trajectory of seven and a half miles as the Germans had developed it, and could reach an altitude of 50,000 feet. There have been reports that *Taifuns* have been installed on some Soviet Navy cruisers, such as the *Sverdlov* which visited Great Britain for the crowning of Queen Elizabeth.

The Germans had developed a missile that could be fired from under water. Tests were run on it in the Baltic Sea and several successful firings had been carried out. This work also was taken over by Russia with the idea of developing missiles that could be launched from under water a hundred or more miles from a land target.

To this day, large amounts of fuel for Russian missiles are produced in East Germany, along with electronic equipment having to do with guidance, control and testing. Radar tubes, measuring and control instruments for the USSR are produced by Radio-Werke No 1 plant in Erfurt and the RAFT-Werke plants in Leipzig and Zwichau.

Apart from purely military equipment and ideas, the Russians took from East Germany a tremendous amount of production technique and equipment. Before the Second World War, Russian machine tools were notoriously poor, and would turn out only a fifth to a third as much work as a similar purpose machine built in Germany, England, or the US; lathes, for example, turned at 600 instead of 3,000 rpm. Cutting tools were of poor quality and the Russians hadn't developed very much equipment of their own suited to the fine tolerances required for some of today's important military weapons. This has now changed, thanks, in part, to machine tools and skills taken over from the Germans. The change has come to both Soviet defence and consumer industries, thereby improving Russia's industrial base. To this day Russia gets much help from East Germany in the form of special machines that help bolster Soviet production.

Had it not been for the loot they got from Germany, Czechoslovakia and elsewhere, would the Russians be where they are today? The answer is no, of course, without in any way meaning to detract from what they have done by themselves. Undoubtedly the Russians have the science and could have learned the skills to do the things they have done without German and other help. But, just as clearly, they would not have achieved their present position as a world power as soon, if it hadn't been for the help they received.

CHAPTER 16

SOVIET AIRCRAFT PRODUCTION

Richard E. Stockwell

IT HAS TAKEN Russia little more than a generation, under Communism, to move from the two-wheeled peasant cart to the modern jet aeroplane, space vehicles and rocket-powered intercontinental ballistic missiles. This is one of the most remarkable transformations the world has ever seen.

Today Russia produces about as much coal as the US, more steel than England and West Germany combined. However, it turns out only one-sixtieth as many automobiles in a year as the US. In those two contrasting, seemingly contradictory facts, are the essential features of Russian progress and purpose in the middle of the twentieth century.

Far, far more industrial emphasis has been put on heavy industry, the means of production, than on consumer goods. And even though industrial production has shown a phenomenal rise in the USSR over the years, most of the increase has gone into armaments, to give the USSR the largest, most modern land army; the largest air force in the world, and a navy second only to the US and ahead of the latter in submarines.

Not only has sheer volume of heavy industry gone up since the revolution of 1917, but the quality has shown an equally phenomenal rise. There is no better place to see this than in their successful aircraft and missile production, for which more exacting skills are required and into which only materials of the highest quality can go.

There is a vast difference between the steel that is acceptable for building steam locomotives and that required for the turbine wheel and buckets of a modern jet engine. Aluminium for pots and pans is not nearly good enough for the wing-spar of a supersonic fighter. Machine tolerances of the Second World War have long since been surpassed in today's Soviet war equipment.

As the Russians have increased the volume of their military production, they also have greatly improved the quality.

That the Soviets should develop a large air force with its attendant 'cost' in terms of skilled labour, materials and technology is not as surprising as the 'Russia is a land power' advocates would have one believe. Before the Bolsheviks, Russia was interested in both aviation and rocketry. Under the Tsars she turned out a surprising number of interesting aircraft designs.

Though they are usually laughed at for their claim to have flown the first aeroplane in 1882 (driven by two English-built steam engines), it is clear that the Russians were early in aviation, if not necessarily the first. They were designing, building and flying aeroplanes of their own design as early as 1908. One of the early men in Russian aviation was Igor Sikorsky, who later came to the US. His headquarters were at the Baltic Car Factory's aviation plant in St Petersburg, now Leningrad. Working there was a young man named Andrei Tupolev, today Russia's doyen of aircraft design.

During the First World War, Sikorsky designed and built seventy-five large, four-engined bombers for the Tsar's armies. By the time of the Revolution in 1917, Russia was building about a thousand planes a year. They were of many different types; few were outstanding aircraft. The Government supplemented the country's aircraft production by purchases from the Allied Powers, especially France and Italy.

After the Revolution, the aircraft industry in Russia fell apart, like most other industries. People left the factories for the country, where at least there was enough to eat. Some of the best designers and others who felt that they had been too closely identified with the Tsar's regime, feared the Bolsheviks and fled the country.

In 1918, Professor N. E. Zhukovski, the father of Russian aviation, and Tupolev, the young designer, went to Lenin and persuaded him that the Communist Government should get behind aviation in the country. Zhukovski had built the first wind tunnel in the USSR in 1910 and with Lenin's support he founded the Central Aerodynamics and Hydrodynamics Institute (TsAGI), where research and advanced training were carried out. TsAGI today is one of the key institutes in the Soviet aviation industry, with elaborate wind tunnel installations, experimental hydrodynamic facilities, and design teams. Like all institutes in Russia, it works closely with higher educational establishments to give advanced and practical training to specialists.

French firms and capital can best be credited with giving the Soviet aircraft industry its start. Beginning in 1908, the French began to make investments in aviation in Russia and during the First World War the number of plants got up to sixteen, with some 10,000 workers.[1] Except for designs done at the Baltic Car Factory plant, all production was of copies of foreign designs.

By the time the Revolution and the Civil War were over, there were only five plants left in the USSR.[2] The industry remained in the doldrums for several years, despite efforts to aid it by introducing foreign help. The German firm of Junkers was invited to establish a plant at Fili, outside Moscow. The German firm of Heinkel also built aircraft plants in Russia during the 1920s, and German designs found their way into Soviet production channels. Engines were bought from France, Britain, Germany and Italy. Russian airframes were designed to fit them.

In 1928 the Russians launched their first Five Year Plan, and this gave the aircraft industry a much-needed incentive. When the first plan was completed in 1932, the aviation industry's labour force was 7·5 times greater than it had been in 1928 and the number of engineers and other technical personnel had undergone a ten-fold increase, according to Soviet figures.[3] The best estimate available indicated the Soviets then had six major airframe plants and twelve plants turning out aircraft engines, the latter mostly from parts shipped in from abroad.[4]

By 1932 production was nearly 2,000 aircraft a year, but it was a strange collection of odds and ends. Designers, a whole new generation of whom were then getting under way, were apparently allowed to follow their whims, which left the Soviet Air Forces disproportionately weighted with float-planes, of all things.

It was during the second Five Year Plan that Hitler came to

[1] Tupolev, A. N., 'Sovetskaia aviapromyshlennost' (The Soviet Aircraft Industry), in *Kryl'ia Rodiny*, 1953, p. 3. Also see *Bol'shaia Sovetskaia Entsiklopedia* (The Large Soviet Encyclopedia), 1949, Vol. I, p. 77, which says there were ten aircraft plants during the First World War. Number of plants used in text includes both airframe and engine plants.

[2] Tupolev, as above, p. 3.

[3] *Aviastroitel* (The Aircraft Builder). Published in Moscow by the Chief Administration of the Aircraft Industry. 1933. Number 6, pp. 1–2.

[4] Lee, Asher, *The Soviet Air Force*. Published in London by Gerald Duckworth & Co. Ltd. Second edition, 1952, p. 75.

power in Germany, and soon after came the *Reichstag* fire, and the Japanese attack on Manchuria. The men in the Kremlin apparently saw the threat better than most in those years, and so aircraft, and military production generally, were pushed even harder during the second Five Year Plan.

Technical education had already been expanded, and the effects began to be felt. More airframe and engine plants were built, most of them in the east, behind the Urals, and production was rationalised by concentrating on fewer designs, with greater emphasis on military types. Foreign assistance was sought, and the US Department of State approved the building of Wright *Cyclone* engines at Perm in the Ural Mountains. Russian engineers visited aircraft plants in the US where the industry was also expanding in the 1930s.

By 1938 aircraft production was up to 4,400 planes a year, putting the USSR on a par, in numbers of planes produced, with Germany, Great Britain and the United States. That year, according to the always mysterious Soviet percentages, the industry's output was 550 per cent over 1932.[1] The industry had about twenty airframe and ten engine plants, and the largest employed 15,000 workers.[2]

It was during the second Five Year Plan that the great purge got under way, and this was to have a marked effect on the Soviet aircraft industry. Several designers disappeared from public life, among them Andrei N. Tupolev, whose movements were restricted, but who continued to work on airframe designs. Tupolev had long been an advocate of bombers and strategic bombing. In the armed forces there were a few officers who thought the same, but most of them thought along more traditional lines, and saw airpower as a supporting arm for the ground forces.

Experiences in the Spanish Civil War had seemed to bear out the idea that bombers were not as important as ground support and fighter aircraft that could work closely with the troops. Experience in Mongolia, where armed forces under Georgi Zhukov had successfully staved off the Japanese, was confirmatory.

The net result seems to have been that those who advocated strategic air power in Russia got swept up in the purge, and for the

[1] *Bol'shaia Sovetskaia Entsiklopedia* (The Large Soviet Encyclopedia). Moscow, 1949. Vol. I, p. 77.
[2] Lee, Asher, *The Soviet Air Force*. Published in London by Gerald Duckworth & Co. Ltd. Second edition, 1952, p. 84.

most part disappeared from the scene. Production of large bombers all but stopped in the years immediately before the Second World War, and fighters and ground support types appeared in greater numbers.

This was reflected in the third Five Year Plan, which got under way in 1938. Great effort went into the programme, and to compensate for the designers who had been jailed or had 'disappeared'. New design teams were formed. Mikoyan was brought back from a plant in Kazan and teamed with Gurevich to turn out the first of the famous *MIG* series of fighters. Lavochkin was teamed with Gorbunov and Gudkov to begin the *LAGG* series. The dour Ilyushin came up with the famous *Stormovik*. By 1939 about thirty-seven airframe, engine and component plants are thought to have existed in Russia.[1] By the time the Second World War broke out in September of 1939, the Soviet Air Forces were second only to Germany in number of aircraft.[2]

But when the Germans struck, the Russian Air Forces were short on experience and aircraft performance. The main part of Russia's tactical air force, numbering 5,000 planes, was met by about 3,000 German planes, or roughly two-thirds of the Germans' operational strength.[3]

The *IL 2 Stormovik* was relatively the best performing aeroplane the Russians had against the Germans in 1941. Not only did it show up well against the German *Junkers JU 87*, but it was an excellent support aircraft for ground forces, with two forward-firing machine-guns and two cannon. The aircraft could also carry bombs and later in the war it was adapted to fire rockets.

Another successful aeroplane was the *PE 2*, a twin-engine fighter, But the *LAGGs*, early *MIGs* and others were much less satisfactory against the German competition for control of the air.

As the Germans blitzed their way across the broad Russian plains up to the outskirts of Leningrad and swept across the Ukraine, they

[1] The Russian publication, *Mashinostroenie* (Machine Building), put out by the People's Commissariats of the Machine Building and Defence Industries, in issues from 5th October 1937, through 31st December 1939, identified thirty-seven different aviation industry plant directors by name.

[2] *World Aviation Annual*, published jointly by the Aviation Research Institute, Washington, D.C., and the James Jackson Cabot Professorship of Air Transportation of Norwich University, Northfield, Vermont, 1948, p. 499.

[3] Lee, Asher, *The Soviet Air Force*. Published in London by Gerald Duckworth & Co. Ltd. Second edition, 1952, p. 118.

threatened the very existence of the Soviet aircraft industry, most of which was concentrated in European Russia. When the cold weather brought the German advance to a halt in the winter of 1941, the Russians hastily packed up the movables in their war factories and shifted them to the Volga, the Urals and Siberia. Some 600 machine-building and other types of plants and research institutes were moved in one of the greatest industrial treks of all time. Aircraft factories from Smolensk, Moscow, Kharkov, Voronezh, Zaporozhe, Kiev, Kuibischev and Leningrad, to name but a few, were moved to Novosibirsk, Komsomolsk, Molotov, Sverdlovsk, Magnitogorsk, Tashkent, and other cities. By the end of 1941, aircraft production in Russia was down to 500 planes a month, or 6,000 a year.

That was the low point, and from then on Russian production steadily increased until near the end of the Second World War the Russians were turning out about 40,000 planes a year, according to their own claims. Most were fighters and tactical types.

Following the Second World War, the Soviets set out to apply the lessons they had learned. Though the country was badly shaken by the war and greatly needed to rebuild its civilian industry and facilities, the prime emphasis was on heavy industry for the military. The Kremlin decided on a rough sort of priority for aircraft development. It all amounted to 'Catch up with the West'.

The programme was a four-part affair, and in a general way it has been kept intact through the years. The first emphasis was on defensive aircraft: interceptors that would protect Russian air frontiers. This meant they had to move from piston-engined, fabric-covered interceptor aircraft that would do an honest 400 miles an hour to jet fighters that would do 600 miles an hour. The first efforts, in the *MIG 9* and the *YAK 15*, appeared in 1945, with German *JUMO 004* power-plants designed by Junkers. They were not satisfactory, and so the effort was redoubled and resulted, by 1947, in the *MIG 15* and the *LA 17*, both powered by Russian copies of the British *Nene 1* engine, purchased in 1947.

The second major emphasis in the development of Russian air power after the Second World War was on tactical air power. For this purpose, the *IL 28* and *TU 10* bombers were put into production in sizeable quantities, and more and more *MIG 15s* were assigned to tactical work with the ground forces. The *YAK 23* ground support aircraft also was designed and built for this purpose.

By 1949 or 1950 the Russians were ready to undertake the third step in their post-war efforts to develop air power. That was to build a modern bomber fleet, now represented by the NATO-designated *Badger*, *Bison* and *Bear*.

Finally, as their fourth step, the Russians have sought to develop a modern transport fleet, a programme which now is under way.

The Russians have taken what is for them a very practical view of aircraft production in the post-war period by seeking quantity at some slight cost in quality. The *MIG 15*, for example, was designed simply, with few of the extra gadgets that so often characterise aircraft in the West. It does not have pilot safety features such as dual hydraulic systems and other devices which add weight and cut into over-all performance. Similarly, designs have been standardised in Russia to a greater degree than in other countries. Aircraft that finally go into production are usually turned out in large quantities, and the production line is rarely halted (as it so often is in the West) for minor changes in design.

Necessity was partly the mother of simplicity and standardisation in Russian post-war aircraft output. The Russians lacked both trained, skilled labour and elaborate machine tools to do unconventional work. In the late 1940s, machine tool building was greatly increased in the USSR, but the emphasis was mostly on general machine tools, and upon improving their operating speeds, rather than on machines suited only to special, highly sophisticated aircraft and engine work.

Between 1940 and 1951, machine tool output in the USSR increased about 60 per cent from 50,000 a year to 82,000. In the same period the speed of metal-turning lathes, for example, increased from 600 revolutions per minute to 3,000. Many of the machine tools were copies of German, British and American designs which had been taken as loot, or had been purchased or lend-leased. A whole production line from the Heinkel plant in East Germany was moved to Russia where it served as a model for the rest of the plants under the Ministry of Aircraft Production.

Of course there were many other examples of German assistance, given willingly or unwillingly, following the Second World War. (See Chapter 15.)

In the late 1940s, the top air force command was changed in Russia, and ministers and plant directors lost their jobs as output failed to reach Stalin's target totals. The aircraft industry went through a long shakedown in those years. Rejection rates for parts in some factories sometimes got as high as 50 per cent, and all too frequently new planes crashed on take-off.

However, since 1950 the industry has made giant strides. Production of the *MIG 15*, believed to have totalled 15,000, represented the first post-war jet aircraft production order of real size. Shortcomings in production facilities and equipment brought out by experience with the *MIG 15* were alleviated quite rapidly in 1948, 1949, and 1950.

At the same time, the many new plants that had been set up immediately after the war were in full operation by 1950 and had been integrated successfully into the over-all aircraft industry pattern. Not all of the plants that had moved east during the first winter of the war with Germany were returned to European Russia after the war, and most of the new facilities were built in the Urals or to the east of that mountain range. Kubischev, however, remains the main production centre of aircraft engines.

Perm, in the Urals, where the first plant in Russia to produce Wright engines is located, today is a major aircraft centre with vast additional 'construction halls' for building bombers. It is believed that *Badgers*, the twin-jet medium range aircraft somewhat similar to USAF's *B 47*, are produced in Perm. Other centres that have grown since the Second World War, or have been expanded, include: Tashkent, Omsk, Novosibirsk (to which an important section of the Academy of Sciences is now being moved), Semipalatinsk, Tomsk, Belovo, Krasnoyarsk, Irkutsk, Komsomolsk and Magadan. Before the Second World War, about 75 per cent of Russia's aircraft output was west of the Urals. While moves to the east have been significant and the industry's new expansion has been limited almost entirely to the Urals and east of there, it is still true that about half of Russia's aircraft output is in the European part of the country.

Two considerations have caused the Soviets to spread their aircraft industry. The first has been a general policy of industrial decentralisation, which reached its zenith in 1957 with the creation of 105 separate industry-administrative areas in the country. Secondly, by scattering its defence industry, and especially its aircraft factories, the Kremlin has sought the most practical kind of protection from enemy bombing. No longer does the Soviet aircraft industry present a dozen concentrated targets as it did, more or less, before the Second World War.

Decentralisation means that no one or two plants become a country's sole source of supply for a given aircraft or part. Production is now geared more directly to regional needs in the event of an all-out war. Thus, armies can be semi-autonomous, with their own production facilities in the general area in which they are located and which they may be called upon to defend. Today fighter aircraft are produced in European Russia, in Central Siberia and the Far East in quantities which suggest that these three regions are separate and autonomous in the production of these aircraft.

Decentralisation has been brought about in a second important way. It is one of Russia's pieces of good fortune that many key raw materials, such as coal, iron ore, aluminium and other metals are spread across the USSR and do not have to be hauled the length of the country to processing facilities. For the most part, the three general areas, European Russia, Central Asia and the Far Eastern part of Siberia, are self-sufficient in the basic material products required for aircraft production. To help reduce transportation costs, the Russians have located much of their industry near to the appropriate raw material. Because it depends on so many other heavy industries for semi-finished products, the aircraft industry has followed the general pattern. Even this has not been enough to assure the Russians that their key defence industry is safe from bombing, and so some plants have been moved underground. This is particularly true at Kuibischev, where two large engine plants and some key instrument-producing facilities are underground, according to German sources.

The Russian aircraft industry employs about 500,000 people, nearly half of whom are women. Women are hard workers in Russia and are inclined to stay on the job and perform their tasks well and uniformly. Men, on the other hand, are addicted to prestige work, such as running machines or supervisory posts.

Estimates vary a great deal on the quantities they actually produce, and I do not believe that any of the published figures is reliable. A figure of 10,000 per year strikes a rather good average among the various estimates, with about half of them single-engine, non-military aircraft. The other half consists of various military types and transport planes.

I

The Russians are able to produce that number of aircraft with fewer people for a variety of reasons. For one, a higher proportion of those employed by the industry in Russia are in fact production workers. Elaborate sales, promotion and advertising departments, for example, simply are not a part of the Soviet aircraft industry, and it is doubtful whether the thoroughgoing bureaucracy the Communist system creates in such areas as book-keeping consumes any more manpower than government contracting elsewhere in the world. Thus, one does not find as many ancillary employees in a Soviet factory as there are in a similar factory in the US.

Simplicity of design and careful attention to ease of production are other features of the Soviet aircraft industry to foster volume production. The extra refinements put into aircraft produced in the West simply are not found in Russia. In some instances, this makes for weight saving and higher aircraft performance, as well as ease of production. Finally, until 1957, the 48-hour week prevailed in Russia and in the aircraft industry overtime work was fairly common. All these things had the effect of making 500,000 people perform like 600,000 or even 700,000 in Western countries.

Incentives are great in Russia to get people to perform at levels that will afford them more than subsistence. Even so, the response has not been good from the vast majority of the people. Those employed in industry represent the most ambitious elements of the population: those who are most anxious to improve their lot through increased earnings. In effect, there has been a very big carrot in front and a very big stick behind the workers and the individual plants. Each plant has been assigned work quotas, which are computed as work 'norms' for individual workers, who must meet and surpass the quota to win the carrot in the form of a bonus. Bonus payments rise steeply for work over and above the norm. The average industrial wage in Russia is about 800 roubles per month, of which 40 per cent is spent on food, about 10 per cent on rent, and the remainder on clothing (which is very expensive) and the other requisites of Russian living.

In terms of its success in turning out good aircraft and aircraft engines, the Soviet aircraft industry presents a rather spotty picture. It appears to have done its best work in the creation and production of fighter and ground support aircraft. With bombers it has been somewhat less successful; in helicopter design and production it may be ahead of the West in some respects. In transports, while its *TU 104* has clearly given it the lead in having the first successful turbo-jet passenger plane, the aircraft leaves something to be desired in terms of competitive performance. The *TU 114* turbo-prop transport would however appear to be the most successful machine of its kind in the world.

The *MIG 15* was clearly a great achievement, for its time, though much of the credit must go to Great Britain for the design of the engine. The *MIG 15*'s reputation is tarnished only by inadequate pilotage, by its relatively poor gun-sight, some unfortunate flight characteristics when in a tight turn, and its short range. The aeroplane was fast for its time; it was quite capable of 650 mph at its optimum altitude. It was light in weight, readily maintainable (an engine change was a simple matter, and engines required very little field tinkering between prescribed changes), and had superior altitude capability.

The Mikoyan-Gurevich team produced the *MIG 17* after the *MIG 15*, and this aircraft, while a little faster and a little larger, affords more range and a little better performance in terms of speed and altitude.

After the *MIG 17*, the trail of progress is obscured by a sequence of less conclusive developments. There has been a *MIG 19*, a *MIG 21*, and in the summer of 1957 a *MIG 23* was spoken of in the writer's presence. In addition, there has been a family of delta designs credited to Sukhoi, and a series of *YAK 25* types.

The general parameters of performance of these aircraft, and the rapidity with which one design has followed another, give one good reason to believe that the Soviets have not been satisfied with any of their interceptor designs since the *MIG 17* to a degree that major production was warranted. Both the *MIG 19* and *MIG 21* have been put into small series production, and so has the bulb-nosed *YAK 25*, the all-weather interceptor. Reportedly, *MIG 19s* were sold to the United Arab Republic late in 1957, along with some *MIG 17s*.

What shortcomings the Russians may have encountered in the performance of these interceptors isn't known, but it is fairly evident on the surface of things that they have not had engines that would give them what they need. Russian turbo-jet engine design has lagged somewhat behind that of the West, from all indications, though this is certainly not true of turbo-props. The *AM 3* engine, which I saw on display in the Air Museum in Moscow in 1957, and which is officially credited as the powerplant in the *TU 104* jet transport, does not represent a very advanced state of the art. This engine, which may have been in series production for several years as the powerplant for the *Badger* bomber, had thick chord blades of conventional design, both in the compressor and turbine, and despite its large diameter of nearly 49 inches, the engine puts out only about 15,000 lb thrust. It has a simple eight-stage compressor. Fuel consumption is high, in excess of 0·9 lb of fuel per pound of thrust per hour. On take-off the engine is handled with some care and the aircraft makes a rather slow climb, presumably because of engine limits.

The *AM 3* may represent the 1954 state of the art, when the first *Badger* bomber appeared, or it may represent the 1956 state of the art when the *TU 104* was unveiled. Whichever year it represents, it indicates that the Russians were more or less behind the state of the art in the West. Of course the Russians have made significant strides in jet engine development since the *AM 3*. But so has the West, and in this single instance it is more than likely that progress in the West has been faster than in Russia. Today the United States Air Force *B 58* bomber, equipped with the General Electric *J 79* turbo-jet, can outrun any Russian interceptor, in so far as performance of any of the latter is known.

Russian appreciation of this fact may very well be causing them to push hard to improve the capabilities of their interceptors. While little is known of the *MIG 23* and its performance, the *MIG 21* and the *Sukhoi* deltas still leave something to be desired. Evidence that the Russians have installed a rocket-booster engine in the *MIG 21* to supplement its speed and altitude performance for short bursts would appear to be further confirmation of this assertion. Finally, the fact that the *MIG 23* design came soon after the *MIG 21* is a further straw in the wind indicating that the Soviet air defence force is not satisfied with its interceptor performance.

The all-weather interceptor picture parallels that of the *MIG* series. The *YAK 25*, which has been in production for several years in various forms, is not yet an aeroplane that can cope with the speeds of present-day US bombers or such long range interceptors as the *F 100*.

Russia's strategic air power is built around three aeroplanes, the

Badger and *Bison*, powered by two and four turbo-jets respectively, and the *Bear*, powered by four large turbo-prop engines. *Badger* has an operating radius of between 1,500 and 2,000 miles, and *Bison* has 6,000 miles according to some claims, though I am inclined to believe it is only 3,100 miles.

Much has been said about these two aircraft, including a claim, based on production capabilities, that fifty *Badgers* are produced each month. The same capability data indicate the production rate on *Bison* is thirty per month.[1] One cannot quarrel with claims that the Russians have the capacity to turn out these aircraft in such numbers, but there is reason to question whether they have done so. The factories, equipment and personnel used to turn out these bombers appear to have been shifted to the production of jet transports in the last two years, which would help account for the growing number of transports that have appeared in Russia. According to Communist Party Chief Khrushchev, the big bomber is out of date in today's world, because of the missile. Quite likely this represents current Soviet thinking, and seems to fit the pattern of unfolding aviation and missile events in the USSR. It is also one way of rationalising the non-intercontinental performance of these two aircraft.

The big turbo-prop bomber called *Bear* does have intercontinental performance, and lacks little in speed. It is capable of Mach 0·8 and would be a good machine for a sneak attack, coming in low, beneath radar line-of-sight. *Bear* does not suffer from the high fuel consumption problem that seems to afflict Soviet turbo-jet powered aircraft; rather, its 12,500 horsepower engines are credited with remarkably low fuel consumption, even by turbo-prop standards.

Two of Russia's large bombers have their transport counterparts. The *Badger* has become the *TU 104* and *TU 104A* transports, the *Bear* is the *TU 114*.

The *TU 104* is powered by two *AM 3* engines and a tourist version, the *TU 104A*, may have more powerful engines. Both have a range of about 1,800 miles. The *TU 110* has four turbo-jet engines and the *TU 114* has four *Kuznetsov* turbo-props, about the same engine as used in *Bear*, credited with 12,000 horsepower. The *TU 110* has a

---

[1] Estimates of *Bison* and *Badger* production based on the so-called Killian Report made to President Eisenhower in 1955 and reported by Joseph and Stewart Alsop in the *New York Herald Tribune*, 9th September 1955.

little more range than the *TU 104*, but has greater load-carrying capacity. The *TU 114* can fly non-stop from Moscow to New York, with 120 or more passengers.

Two other transports appeared in 1956 and 1957. One was the *AN 10 Ukrainia*, a medium-haul four-engine turbo-prop and the *IL 18 Moskva* of similar size. The *Moskva* closely resembles the Lockheed *Electra* developed in the US. The *Ukrainia*, or *Flying Whale* as it has been affectionately called by its designer, O. K. Antonov, while suited to passenger hauling, also appears to be well-designed for military transport work. It is capable of landing on soft ground, and can be equipped with a large drop-door in the rear.

Both the *Ukrainia* and the *Moskva* are powered by turbo-props which trace their origins to German contributions from Junkers and German design work at Kuibischev in 1946–7.

Helicopter development in Russia traces a long and laboured history from the early 1900s. Today the helicopter is coming into its own in the USSR as a valuable tool that helps gear the Soviet army to its concept of atomic warfare.

Three helicopter design teams are at work. Perhaps the most famous is headed by N. Mil, whose Sikorsky-like designs in 1957 led to the largest helicopter in the world, the *MI 6*. It is powered by turbo-jets. The *YAK 24*, a twin-rotor helicopter, designed by Yakovlev and his co-workers, can carry sixteen men, a jeep and a small field-piece. Many *YAK 24s* have been built and this machine has been used in connection with armed forces manœuvres in recent years.

Finally there is designer N. Kamov, whose small helicopters, suitable for one or two men, are used by the Soviet Navy, and by the Chief Administration of the Northern Sea Route, to scout passages through the ice.

What of the future? The Russians remain the enigma they always have been, but perhaps a few trends are indicated. First, they are now past the relatively easy, early stages of turbo-jet engine development. From now on progress will be more expensive in this field, and so they will have to put more effort into it it if they are to keep up with the West in turbo-jet engines.

And even if they do not consider the turbo-jet so important to their military weapon systems now that they have rocket engines for ICBMs, they will still have to develop turbo-jets for transports, interceptors and light bombers. With its tremendous area, Russia needs air transport. For reasons of economy, commercial travel between two points on earth will be done within the limits of the atmosphere for many years to come. This means a long period of development yet ahead for air-breathing engines, such as the turbojet. It would seem only prudent that the Russians should continue their development efforts in this field so as better to maintain their competitive position.

Second, the Russians say they are working on atomic powerplants for aircraft. This is another race to the first demonstration of performance that they have chosen to run with the West. They may win it even before this appears. Atomic aircraft would of course give them supreme range for either a bomber or a transport.

Third, they have just begun to enter the world air transport picture. Soon they will have three turbo-jet and three turbo-prop transports operable and qualified. They can be expected to introduce them on a great many of the world's air transport routes for political if for no other reasons.

Fourth, they will seek inroads into the world aircraft market by offering their jet transports at low prices. Similarly, they are now encouraging and will continue to encourage the satellites to enter the trainer and light plane markets.

Fifth, they have large reserves of partially obsolete military aircraft, and they can be expected to use them to win friends and influence people in whatever form of lend-lease will benefit Communism.

Finally, I believe Russian industry generally, and the aircraft industry and missile industry in particular, are now going through an evolutionary process that soon may be reflected in greater sophistication and refinement in all military and basic industry equipment turned out by the USSR.

CHAPTER 17

SOVIET CIVIL AVIATION

Dr Kenneth Whiting

THE SOVIET PLANNER has always had to face the hard facts of enormous distances and inadequate transport. In addition to its sheer size, almost one sixth of the world's land area, the USSR has another geographical disadvantage: her extremely northern location. The Soviet Union is like a vast amphitheatre, elevated in the south and east and dropping off to the north-west; there is nothing to stop the Arctic air masses from flooding over this huge plain. A circle of latitude through the northern edge of Edmonton includes about 200,000 people of Alaska and Canada, but about 150,000,000 people of the Soviet Union. Because of the northerly latitude and continental climate, well over 40 per cent of the USSR (three and a half million square miles) lies within the 'permafrost' zone, and this complicates the building of railways and motor roads.

The railways, which haul over four-fifths of Soviet freight, are far and away the most important form of transport in the USSR. Water transport, inland and oceanic, takes care of another 12 per cent of Soviet freight turnover, but again the northerly position of the USSR makes this a seasonal activity for the most part. There are slightly over 130,000 miles of hard-surfaced motor roads. Motor transport is little more than a lusty infant as yet. Furthermore, Soviet transport is concentrated in European Russia and the southern strip of Siberia (the Trans-Siberian Railway and its feeder lines) which means that the immense area from the Urals to the Pacific is largely without surface transport except for the seasonal use of rivers. All of this points to the Soviet Union's desperate need for means of overcoming her transport deficiencies and air transport seems made to order to fill in some of these lacunae.

The founders of the Communist State realised very early that the aeroplane was at least a partial answer to the problems presented by the vast distances in their new state. In 1918 Lenin gave government support to N. E. Zhukovsky in the establishment of a central aeronautical research institution and TsAGI (Central Aero-Hydrodynamic Institute) was founded. One of Zhukovsky's chief assistants was A. N. Tupolev, still the leading Soviet aircraft designer of bomber and transport machines.

The first regular airline operating in the Soviet Union was a joint German-Soviet endeavour, DERULUFT (*Deutsche-Russische Luft-verkehrgeschellschaft*), organised in 1921 with a capital of 300,000 marks. DERULUFT flew a regular service between Berlin and Moscow, and from 1928 from Leningrad to Berlin with stops in most of the large cities along the eastern Baltic. This joint German-Soviet line remained in business until relations between the two countries became very strained in 1937. It resumed operations again to a limited extent under the blessing of the Molotov-Ribbentrop Pact between 1939 and 1941.

The first regular Soviet airline was between Moscow and Nizhni-Novgorod (now Gorki), established by the AVIAKULTURA society in 1922, which hauled passengers and mail over the 420-kilometre route in two and a half hours. The 1920s was the era of the New Economic Policy (NEP) in which 'voluntary' organisations flourished, and civil aviation had its share of these semi-official societies. On 9th February 1923 the Council of Labour and Defence established a Council on Civil Aviation which in turn created three voluntary societies: DOBROLET (Russian Society of the Voluntary Air Fleet), UKRVOZDUKHPUT for the Ukraine, and ZAKAVIA for the Trans-Caucasus. In 1925 UKRVOZDUKHPUT swallowed up ZAKAVIA and was itself absorbed into DOBROLET in 1930. Thus from 1923 to 1930 Soviet civil aviation was organised largely by DOBROLET, which established airlines, carried out ice reconnaissance and exploratory work for the Northern Sea Route administration, and in 1929 even flew young herrings from the Caspian to stock the Sea of Aral.

However impressive the statistics and the proliferation of organisations with imposing titles, the fact cannot be concealed that Soviet civil aviation in the 1920s was pretty much of a pioneering affair. This was after all true of all airlines all over the world. One example suffices to show this. In 1929 Vodop'yanov, who later became an outstanding figure in Soviet polar aviation, was directed by DOBROLET to proceed to the Far East to set up and operate an airline between Khabarovsk and the island of Sakhalin. Vodop-'yanov at that time had been a pilot for only six months and he was given only one plane with which to operate his airline.

By 1930 the free and easy days of the NEP came to an end, and in the new planning era there was no place for 'voluntary' societies. DOBROLET was liquidated and after some experimenting a new agency emerged in 1932, the Main Administration of the Civil Air Fleet (*Glavnoe Upravlenie Grazhdanskogo Vozdushnogo Flota*), often abbreviated to GVF or else referred to as AEROFLOT. In 1935 the Air Code of the USSR defined and regulated the activities of GVF. GVF was given supervision over all aviation except that of the Red Army.

Until the industrialisation drive of the 1930s, in other words the series of Five Year Plans beginning in 1929, the Soviet Union was hardly in a position to go very far in the production of her own aircraft. DERULUFT operated entirely on foreign aircraft during the first few years of its existence and DOBROLET had a very motley inventory of foreign aircraft, some models with Soviet-built airframes and foreign (mainly British and German) engines; even those of its planes completely built in the Soviet Union had engines manufactured under foreign licences.

By the 1930s, however, Soviet designers were turning out respectable machines. An outstanding designer then, as now, was A. N. Tupolev, who had been with TsAGI since its establishment. Any listing of Soviet civil aircraft in the first two decades of Soviet aviation must include the Tupolev designation, *ANT*, with monotonous regularity. By 1924 Tupolev had produced the *ANT 1* and *ANT 2*, the latter being the basis for the military, all-metal *ANT 3* in 1925. This was followed by the *ANT 4* (called *TB 1* in the Red Air Force), an all-metal, twin-engine monoplane equipped with German *BMW* engines. In 1929 this type, under the name 'Land of the Soviets', flew from Moscow to New York. Probably the most successful Tupolev design was the *ANT 9*, a three-engine, nine-passenger monoplane. In 1936 a Tupolev plane, the *ANT 25*, flew across the Arctic to San Jacinto, California.

Tupolev's only real rival in those years was Kalinin, who worked for UKRVOZDUKHPUT in Kharkov. His single-engine fabric-metal *K 5* with room for eight passengers was ubiquitous on Soviet civil airlines. He also produced another best-seller, the *K 4*, a single-engine, high-wing monoplane which was used as a hospital plane. Kalinin disappeared in the maelstrom of the Stalin purges of the 1930s.

N. N. Polikarpov designed a utility aircraft, the *U 2*, that was first flown in 1927. This two-seat biplane with Shvetsov's *M 11* five-cylinder air-cooled engine became very widely used as a trainer, ambulance, and agricultural plane. On Polikarpov's death in 1944 this plane was renamed the *PO 2* in his honour.

In the 1930s the USSR went through a period that the Soviets now ruefully refer to as 'gigantomania'. This was an era of enormous plants and huge blast furnaces built more for the sake of bigness than for efficiency. Tupolev contributed to this obsession with his huge eight-engine *ANT 20*, more widely known under the name of 'Maxim Gorky', which was flown in 1934. But the Tupolev giant came to an abrupt end a year later in an air collision with a small plane. Another abortive giant of the period was the five-engine *ANT 14*.

The Soviets were far less original in the field of engine development in this early period. Most engines were copies of foreign makes produced under licence in Soviet plants. In the 1920s A. Shvetsov had started his five-cylinder air-cooled 100 hp engine, the *M 11*. Shvetsov and Klimov continued to plug away at their designs and by the time the second Five Year Plan was well under way a respectable number of Soviet-built engines in the 700 to 1,000 hp range began to roll off the assembly lines.

The increased speed and range of the aircraft facilitated a rapid expansion of the general length of airlines in the years of the second and third Five Year Plans. In 1932 the over-all length (including local lines and polar aviation) was 36,256 kilometres, in 1937 it was 93,300 kilometres, and by 1940 had risen to 138,700 kilometres.

Simultaneously freight turnover increased rapidly. I. Gorbunov in his *Aviatsiya v Narodom Khozyaystve* (Aviation in the National Economy) summarises this growth in the following table:

Year	Passengers Hauled	Mail Hauled (in tons)	Freight Hauled (in tons)
1928	7,000	64·8	85·3
1932	27,200	429·7	447·2
1937	183,245	6,075·0	35,967·0
1940	293,803	7,510·0	43,461·0

In 1939, at the 18th Party Congress, Stalin gave the following figures for civil aviation: in 1933 air transport had flown 3·1 million ton/ kilometres, and by 1938 this total had increased to 31·7 million ton/kilometres, or an increase of over 1,000 per cent. The Confidential Supplementary Plan for 1941, captured by the Germans, called for a total of 41 million ton/kilometres for civil aviation in that year.

The GVF, as has been stated, supervised all aviation outside that of the Red Army, and this was a tall order in the early days when ambitious plans far outran the equipment available. This mission embraced such diverse tasks as assistance to agriculture, forestry, geological surveys, and mapping services. In short, the Soviets were making every effort to overcome two of their biggest problems, enormous distances with their lack of adequate transport and technological backwardness, by an almost desperate use of civil aviation resources.

The story of GVF's little brother, polar aviation, may perhaps give a clearer concept of how widely the role of civil aviation was interpreted in the Soviet Union. As early as 1924 the Northern Hydrographic Expedition took along a two-seater *I 20* seaplane for reconnaissance and it proved to be so valuable that the use of aircraft in polar work became a *sine qua non*. By 1929 all Soviet activities in the Arctic regions were put under the Main Administration of the Northern Sea Route, GLAVSEVMORPUT in its Russian abbreviation. Polar aviation, although a branch of GVF, was also included under the activities subordinate to GLAVSEVMORPUT. These were the difficult years of polar aviation, the years when it was learning to live with, not fight against, the Arctic. It was also the period of an almost hysterical glorification of Arctic fliers. For instance, the fliers carrying out the air rescue of the survivors of the wreck of the *Chelyushkin* in 1934 were idolised, embraced by Stalin, and had a new order invented for them. Behind this façade of decorations and Red Square receptions, polar aviation was steadily chipping away at more mundane, but very important, problems such as standardising its equipment (more than twenty types of aircraft with their concomitant headache of spare parts), bringing repair facilities farther north, fuel storage, and polar navigation. Polar aviation really entered its adolescence when it flew logistic support for the drifting-ice station, North Pole 1, in 1937–8. During the second Five Year Plan (1933-7) polar aviation claims to have three-quarters fulfilled its planned 60,000 hours of flying. The Confidential Supplementary Plan for 1941 called for a total of 16,555 hours of flying and the hauling of 1,740,000 ton/kilometres of freight in that year alone.

Civil aviation also played an important role in Soviet agriculture during the pre-war years. One Soviet writer states that Soviet aviation was demonstrating the value of the aeroplane in agriculture as early as 1922 and its broad application dates from 1925. The basic use of the aeroplane in agricultural work in those days was to fight insect pests and plant diseases by dusting or spraying poisons, and in 1925 civil aviation sprayed over 6,000 acres of locust breeding grounds; anti-locust spraying had increased to over 1,000,000 acres by 1940. In that same year the total area sprayed and dusted by aircraft for pests and diseases had increased to around 2,300,000 acres.

The Second World War

The Soviet Union, even before the beginning of hostilities in the Second World War, or the 'Great Fatherland War' in Soviet parlance, had begun to incorporate the GVF into the over-all command of the Red Air Force. In the highly centralised structure of the Soviet Union this was not too difficult an undertaking, especially as both the military and civil air forces had been flying very similar aircraft.

Part of the militarised GVF continued to operate along the same lines as before the war, hauling passengers and freight. The difference was that all of its tasks were oriented towards backing up the military effort, and the efficacy of this back-up was ensured by military control of its work. The evacuation of numerous plants from European Russia to the Urals, Siberia, and Central Asia was facilitated by the GVF, which hauled key personnel and vital equipment. According to the statistics given in the *Great Soviet Encyclopedia* (Volume VIII, 1951 edition), the GVF carried 2,300,000 passengers and 300,000 tons of freight in the 1941-5 period.

The rest of the GVF equipment and personnel were incorporated directly into the military effort. Most of the aircraft were assigned to the VVD (Airborne Troops) and the ADD (Long Distance Air Force), although some aircraft and personnel were assigned to other

military units. The role of the militarised GVF in supporting
partisan warfare was outstanding. The Soviet authorities speak of
40,000 flights behind the enemy lines for contacts with the partisans
and air drops of food, ammunition, and equipment. This figure is
probably not too far off, as independent American studies, based
largely on German sources, hazard a guess of 30,000 flights as an
admittedly rough estimate. For a matter of fact, the ADD's main
contribution in the Second World War seems to have been flying
7,000 missions in support of the partisans inside and outside the
USSR, including Poland and Yugoslavia.

Partisan warfare has always been hard to manage when the
enemy lies between the partisans and the main military force that
they are attempting to help. But the Soviet experience seems to
demonstrate that partisan warfare entered a new era with the use
of the aircraft and radio communications. Officers to control the
partisan groups were flown in, and the dependence of the partisans
on air drops for their equipment, ammunition, and medicine
bolstered up the control of the Soviet military leaders. In August
1942, some of the leading partisan commanders were flown to
Moscow to meet Stalin and his commanders. Courier services were
established between the partisans and the headquarters of the army
groups nearest them, thus enabling the two forces to synchronise
their efforts much more effectively than in any previous conflict
utilising partisan forces.

The most frequently used plane for partisan support missions was
Polikarpov's old *U 2*, a single-engine biplane with a range of 300
miles and a maximum speed of 95 mph carrying a payload of around
300 pounds. The other type of plane most used was the two-engine
transport: the Russian-built *LI 2* and *PS 84* and the lend-lease
Douglas *C 47*. Actually, the word 'Douglas' in Soviet air parlance
came to mean any large plane used for partisan support. On
occasion four-engine aircraft were used, chiefly *TB 3s* of pre-war
vintage.

Civil transport fliers and equipment proved very valuable in
maintaining liaison between the headquarters of the various fronts,
especially when the Germans were retreating in the last half of the
war. Another task of the militarised GVF was assistance to what the
Soviets call the 'heroic cities', namely Leningrad, Odessa, and
Sevastopol, where the civil transports flew in vital supplies and

evacuated the wounded and children. In the case of Stalingrad, the closely organised air support of both military and transport aircraft proved very valuable. Not only was air supply to the beleaguered defenders facilitated, but the air transport of fuel to the Soviet tank columns in their counter-attack against, and encirclement of, the Germans made it possible for them to advance rapidly in spite of snow-blocked highways that left their ground supply vehicles stalled.

To sum up, even discounting some of the exuberance of the Soviet accounts of the GVF in the Second World War, the Soviets squeezed just about all that was possible out of their civil transport. Its close integration with the rest of the Red Army made the job of the Soviet strategist and commander much easier.

The Post-war Period

The first post-war Five Year Plan, the fourth, carried the title: 'The Restoration and Development of the National Economy of the USSR for 1946–50' and established the following targets for civil aviation: augmentation of the inventory of modern transport aircraft, an increase of the airline network to 175,000 kilometres, and a restoration and development of air communications between Moscow and the Union Republic capitals, the important cities, and the centres in the north, Siberia, and the Far East. According to Soviet statements, these tasks were fulfilled by 1949.

Immediately after the war the GVF was operating a very mixed collection of aircraft: the old *U 2 (PO 2)*, the wartime *SHCH 2*, a twin-engine ten-passenger light transport, and the Douglas *C 47* type, variously designated as *LI 2* or *PS 84*. In 1945 the GVF began to receive the new *IL 12*, a twin-engine transport developed by Ilyushin, which carried twenty-seven to thirty-two passengers at around 250 mph. This plane soon became the main support of AEROFLOT and to this day, along with its slightly modified brother, the *IL 14*, does most of the hauling along Soviet and satellite airlines. By 1948 a medium twin-engine, ten-passenger transport designed by Yakovlev was available. But this *YAK 16* never seems to have been a success with AEROFLOT. In the four-engine class things were less than prosperous. Tupolev's Chinese-copy of the *B 29*, the *TU 4*, had a transport version, the *TU 70*, and Ilyushin produced a four-engine transport for sixty passengers, but neither of them really caught on. Probably the most useful aircraft, outside of the *IL 12* and *IL 14*, to enter the inventory of AERO-FLOT service was Antonov's *AN 2*. This plane was designed specifically to replace the *PO 2* in forestry, agriculture, and local airline service, and thus had to be very rugged, land and take off in short, undeveloped fields, yet climb rapidly in mountainous areas. The *AN 2* fulfilled all these requirements admirably. It is a single-engine (*ASH 62*) biplane which can carry ten passengers or a ton of freight and still land and take off on sod areas of around 600 feet. It is the most versatile aircraft in AEROFLOT service and, since its inception in 1950, has become ubiquitous on feeder lines and in training parachutists.

The expansion of the airline network to 175,000 kilometres was stated to have been fulfilled by 1949 and this expansion has gone on steadily under the fifth and the now obsolescent sixth Five Year Plans. The major priority has always been to increase the mileage of domestic airlines in order to tie together ever more tightly the political and economic solidarity of the USSR. Although much work has gone into improving the facilities of local republic and *oblast* (district) airports, the Soviet planners are also realistic enough to carry in their inventory of aircraft a large number of planes that can operate from very primitive airfields. The *AN 2* is a prime example, crude though it may look parked next to the new giant four-jet *TU 114*; the new *Antonov Ukraina* (*AN 10*) turbo-prop giant can also operate off grass fields in spite of its enormous size.

Aviation has a number of advantages in a huge territory such as the USSR with its underdeveloped surface transport in many areas. Air travel is fast, it depends only slightly on topographical conditions except on landing and take-off points, an air route can be laid out much more quickly and cheaply than a railroad or motor highway, and in contrast to land transport in many areas it has a year-round capability. All these factors have encouraged the Soviet planners to emphasise local and republic airlines in tying together the disparate parts of their enormous territory.

The same motive is present in expanding air travel between the Soviet Union and the satellites since 1945 as well as building up air transport within the satellites. By the end of the fourth Five Year Plan the Soviet Union was able to make a beginning of supplying the satellites with *IL 12s*. During the fifth Five Year Plan the export of *IL 12s* and *IL 14s* increased considerably, and in late years they have become the work-horses on the satellite airlines.

Soviet expansion of airline operations in foreign (non-satellite) countries until very recently has been anything but hectic. Connections with foreign airlines in Sweden, Finland, and through the Czech airline with Paris were very limited. But with the entry of the GVF into the jet transport field in the last three years the pace is getting much hotter.

The Soviet Union, as we have seen, has always been very interested in the Arctic, mainly because so much of her area lies within the extreme northern regions. After the Second World War, however, there was a new reason for this interest, namely, the strategic significance of the polar routes between the USSR and the United States. Given the range capabilities of modern bombers, the most feasible route for Soviet aviation to reach the industrial and population centres of the United States lies over the polar area, and defence against American bombers over this route necessitated the building and supplying of interceptor and defensive missile bases in this region. Therefore, interest in the area was not confined merely to the exploitation of the wealth of Siberia. Since 1948 the Soviets have launched a number of scientific expeditions in the Arctic Ocean. Two techniques are used. One is to use aircraft as laboratories and fly from place to place making a series of scientific observations at each stop. The other, that of North Pole 1, is to set up a station on an icefloe and drift for months at a time. In 1957 the sixth of these postwar drifting stations, North Pole 7, was in operation using this technique. In either case the backbone of the operation is aircraft, and these are supplied and manned by a polar transport aviation organisation. The net result of these activities has been a greatly enlarged knowledge of the Arctic Ocean area and Soviet polar aviation now regards the task of flying logistic support to a drifting station in the Arctic Ocean as a 'milk run'. The busy scene at a modern drifting station such as North Pole 5 is a far cry from the primitive operations in support of North Pole 1. A steady stream of *IL 12s*, *IL 14s*, and *AN 2s* landing supplies is supplemented by *YAK* and *MIL* helicopters transferring the supplies from the ice land strip to the camp itself.

In 1955 AEROFLOT entered the jet age. In that year the Soviet

Union startled the West by unveiling its first jet transport, the *TU 104*, a twin-jet aircraft capable of carrying around fifty passengers. It was a sleek-looking job and seemed even more impressive because of the usual Soviet skill in springing a surprise on the world. The new *Tupolev* airliner was a civilian version of Tupolev's medium bomber, the *TU 16*, or *Badger* in NATO terminology, powered with *Mikulin M 209* axial-flow turbo-jets of around 15,000 lb thrust. The outstanding fact in connection with the *TU 104* was the speed with which it was produced: the design work was finished in 1954 and it was flying in pre-production form in 1955. The world had a chance to take a good look at it when it was flown to London in March 1956. Apparently the *TU 104* was put into production immediately and *Pravda* announced that it had gone into regular service on 15th September 1956 on the Moscow-Irkutsk run. The Soviets wrung every possible bit of publicity out of their new plane in 1956, the flights to Peking and New Delhi being the most sensational. In January 1957, the new aircraft began regular service between Moscow and Khabarovsk.

The *TU 104*, however, was only the first surprise AEROFLOT had for the aviation world. In April 1957, the flight test of Antonov's *AN 10*, the *Ukraina*, was publicised. The *Ukraina* is a turbo-prop four-engine plane capable of carrying 80 to 120 passengers, depending upon the seating arrangements and the fuel load needed. Probably the outstanding characteristic of the *Ukraina* is its capability of operating off short-run (2,000 feet) grass runways, thus giving AEROFLOT a large aircraft that can be used on its numerous underdeveloped airfields. Antonov has been generous in granting interviews concerning his new aircraft and has been very consistent in stressing the economy of operation of the *Ukraina*.

In July 1957, an improved *TU 104*, the *TU 104A*, was demonstrated. This is a lengthened version of the *TU 104* that can carry seventy passengers. In the same month, on the 10th, two new passenger aircraft were publicly demonstrated: the *TU 110* and the *IL 18*, the *Moskva*. The *TU 110* is a four-jet airliner which can carry either 78 or 100 passengers depending upon whether it is a luxury or tourist model. Its new *Lyulka* engines have less thrust than the *TU 104*'s *M 209s*, but are supposed to be more economical. It looks very much like the *TU 104*. The *IL 18 Moskva* is a four-engine turbo-prop transport very similar to the Lockheed *Electra*. It can carry seventy-five passengers or a payload of 8 tons and has a range of around 3,000 miles.

To bring 1957 to a climax, the Soviets displayed the latest Tupolev creation, the *TU 114 Rossiya*, a huge transport very much resembling the *Bear* bomber. It has four turbo-prop engines generating around 12,000 eshp each (i.e. the largest of their type in use in the world), and the aircraft weighs well over 300,000 pounds. It has a range of over 4,000 miles with a passenger load that varies with the seating and range: probably about 120 passengers for a very long range and up to 220 for very short hauls.

The GVF, which had to struggle along on a very mixed bag of obsolescent aircraft since its inception in 1932, has now apparently entered the age of plenty. With attention shifting more and more to missile development, the crack Soviet aircraft designers are now free to turn their attention to civil aircraft. Tupolev, Ilyushin, and Antonov are now household words signifying huge, glittering jet air transports. Marshal Zhigarev, head of Soviet civil aviation, in his Aviation Day speech on 30th June 1957, stated that GVF was scheduled, under the sixth Five Year Plan, to increase passenger turnover by 280 per cent and freight turnover was to double. If the figure of four million passengers carried by air be taken for 1956, then by 1960 AEROFLOT should be carrying over eleven million passengers if the goal is reached. Although the sixth Five Year Plan has been laid aside, it is probable that the same targets will hold for the GVF.

There is one aspect of AEROFLOT's new transport fleet, especially the turbo-props, which cannot be developed here, namely, the airlift capability this development gives to the VVS. In an age of mutual nuclear deterrence, limited war may become an all-important factor. The old military slogan of getting there with the most could swing the decision in many cases. The close integration of the GVF into the over-all military structure of the Soviet Union would make all aircraft immediately available for that purpose. This would be in accord with the thesis laid down by the Soviet military leader, Mikhail Frunze, in 1924 that all civil production should always have military use if at all possible.

Aeroflot Abroad

AEROFLOT began flying the Moscow-Warsaw and Moscow-Prague routes in 1946. By 1955 agreements had been signed with

China, Roumania, Hungary, Poland, Czechoslovakia, and Bulgaria. The civil air organisational pattern in each of these satellites was very similar to that of the GVF in the Soviet Union. The satellites were and are very dependent upon the USSR for aircraft, spare parts, and electronic navigational and landing equipment, thus simplifying Soviet control of their airlines. The satellites, however, showed a surprising amount of resistance to being entirely enmeshed in the Soviet GVF: they kept their own airline designations, uniforms, and so forth.

Late in 1955 AEROFLOT began to push beyond the satellite empire, and in that year agreements were signed with Yugoslavia and Austria which allowed AEROFLOT to fly into Vienna and Belgrade. In 1956 a bilateral agreement with SAS permitted AEROFLOT to establish direct service with Stockholm and Copenhagen; between 1954 and 1956 SAS passengers had changed to AEROFLOT at Helsinki.

In 1957 AEROFLOT began to seek bilateral agreements with western European countries very energetically. The reason for the long delay could easily have been a reluctance to display the rather obsolescent aircraft of AEROFLOT on the Western airlines. But with the advent of the *TU 104* and its shining new companions, the *IL 18*, *AN 10*, *TU 110* and *TU 114*, Soviet reluctance was transformed into an almost childish pride. The Soviet press and popular periodicals devoted a great deal of space to pictures of the new aircraft, interviews with the chief designers, and commentaries on how the Western countries had gazed with awe upon the newest achievement of Soviet technology. Therefore, it is not surprising that in late 1956 and through 1957 a series of overtures were made to France, Great Britain, the Netherlands, Belgium, etc. to negotiate bilateral agreements. Most of these negotiations are still in progress, but in December 1957 AEROFLOT opened a regular jet service, *TU 104A*, between Moscow and Copenhagen.

In the Middle East and Asia the pattern has been somewhat different. An opening gambit has often been to present the leader of the country with an *IL 14* for his personal use, for example Nehru, Nasser, U Nu, and Soekarno. Then comes a Soviet offer to sell aircraft at very low prices, accompanied by Soviet technicians to build airfields, install complex electronic navigational and landing equipment, and maintain the aircraft. Negotiations for bilateral agreements go on at the same time. By the end of 1957 few hard and fast agreements had been signed, but AEROFLOT's offensive in that field has hardly got under way as yet.

On the whole, it would seem that AEROFLOT operations on a world-wide scale are very probable in the immediate future. Two US air specialists, Stockwell and Miller, after their tour of AERO-FLOT, report that a 1,500 per cent increase in the satellite-bloc airlines is contemplated by 1960. The real break-through into western Europe was probably the preliminary agreement with British European Airways in December 1957, as there can be little doubt that other nations will follow this lead. The *TU 104A* and *TU 114* can compete successfully with the best of Western aircraft and Soviet pride will not suffer when these planes are parked opposite their European and American rivals on foreign airfields. With the transition to missiles for both offence and defence, the Soviet bomber aircraft plants and design bureaux can be converted to the building of commercial aircraft, and the West is probably going to see a sharp increase along this line. Some of the new production may be put on sale at prices well below that of the private companies in the West, and for political purposes the Soviets can make the price very low indeed.

The progress of civil aviation in the Soviet Union since the Second World War has been little short of phenomenal. Emerging from the war with an inventory of very obsolete aircraft and rudimentary communications equipment, the Soviet Union in a decade has not only caught up with the West in many aspects of civilian aircraft design and equipment, but in the not too distant future may surpass it in numbers of heavy transports. The tremendous output of engineers and technicians in the Soviet Union, many of whom began their first aeronautical studies in the flying clubs of the DOSAAF, should ensure adequate personnel for an all-out programme to surpass the West.

CHAPTER 18

THE AIR ALLIES OF THE USSR

Asher Lee

IN THE Second World War, the Soviet Air Force and aircraft industry had only to provide a slender proportion of their total resources to equip the Polish, Czech and French squadrons who helped to fight some of the air battles against the *Wehrmacht* on the eastern fronts of Europe. American generosity under Lend-Lease, a generosity which was militarily superfluous after 1943, though no doubt politically necessary, fed thousands of US fighters and light, and medium bombers into the Soviet pool of military planes. This flow of aircraft and supplies more than compensated for the minor drain on Soviet planes to the Czech, Polish and French squadrons.

But in the five years that followed the Second World War, there was a radical change. The USSR became the air arsenal of the Communist countries and undertook the considerable task of providing operational planes, training facilities and trainer aircraft, radio and radar equipment, fuel and flying instructors to modernise the air forces of Albania, Czechoslovakia, Poland, Hungary, Roumania, Bulgaria, Outer Mongolia, Northern Vietnam, North Korea, and China. Later, in the 1950s, the air forces of East Germany, Egypt, Afghanistan and Syria were added to her commitments though the last three were in a different political category and context from the others.

Between 1945 and 1950, the over-all air requirements of the various Communist countries outside the USSR must have involved an annual Soviet commitment of some 7,500 planes. Their combined front line operational strength in bomber, fighter, reconnaissance, and transport aircraft was between 4,000–5,000 planes and wastage and replacement with more modern aircraft called for an average annual intake in excess of that front line operational figure, particularly during the change over to jet fighters and fighter-bombers at the end of the period. To their total battle strength must be added the elementary, intermediate and advanced trainer machines and the requirements of the civil airlines of the Communist countries. In all an annual figure of 7,500 planes would appear to be a conservative estimate.

In the 1950s the picture has changed somewhat. The Soviet Union has continued to supply more modern jet fighters and light bombers. The *MIG 15s* and *YAK 23s* of the early 1950s are being replaced by *MIG 17s* with a top speed of over 700 mph. Soon there will be general re-equipment with supersonic *MIG 19* fighters and the twin-jet *IL 28* will be replaced by the more modern subsonic *YAK 25*. And the new machines will be fitted with airborne radar, radar gun-sights and, in a year or so, air to air guided missiles. But Czechoslovakia, Poland, Roumania, China, and Eastern Germany are developing their own jet aircraft, helicopter and radar production facilities and the drain on USSR air resources is being gradually reduced. Some of Russia's air allies, especially Poland and Czechoslovakia, will probably be providing most, if not all, of their own air resources by the 1960's.

The most important and powerful of the Communist Air Forces, apart from the Soviet Air Force itself, is the Chinese Communist Air Force, commanded by General Liu Ya-Lou. The Chinese Communist armies ousted Chiang Kai-Shek's ground forces from the mainland in 1949 without the help of air power. But since then, both during and after the war in Korea, the Soviet Union has poured a continual stream of her flying instructors, production engineers, ground technicians, radar equipment, military and civil aircraft, ammunition and fuel, and in fact everything she can spare, in an endeavour to give Communist China an air force commensurate with her military, political and strategic commitments as a great Asian power. By 1951, General Vandenburg, then the US Air Force Chief of Staff, had expressed the view that Communist China had 'blossomed overnight into one of the most powerful air forces in the world'. By 1955 General Nathan Twining, the next US Chief of Staff, revealed that the Korean War had not adversely affected the Chinese Communists' air ranking. In a statement subsequently carried by the press and radio of more than fifty countries, he told a Congressional Committee that the air force of Mao Tse-Tung was the fourth most powerful in the world. That statement is still true and is likely to remain true. Communist China probably has an operational strength, not all of it modern, of between 2,500 and 3,000 planes, including fighters, bombers, reconnaissance and transport units. Only the air forces of the USA, the USSR and Great Britain are larger.

No other modern air force of the post-war period has been developed so rapidly. Equally, no other air force has inherited such an aeronautical legacy and has such priority in air supplies from a major world power. The legacy came initially from United States and Japanese resources. Communist China inherited from the United States Army Air Forces of the Second World War a large number of well-equipped airfields in central and western China at such places as Liuchov, Hengyang, Lungling, Tanchuk and Paiching as well as a number of American-trained Chinese pilots and ground technicians, who originally fought with the United States and Chiang Kai-Shek but are now in the Communist Air Force. Then there were a useful number of trainer and transport planes which are, of course, now obsolete. Japan made Manchuria her chief overseas territory for aircraft production, air training and many basic air supplies for her war against China. All these facilities together with many Japanese engineers and technicians fell into the Communist aeronautical lap in 1950.

Despite the major legacies and the great help from the Soviet Union, the operational record of the Chinese Air Force showed all the signs of growing pains between 1950 and 1955. In the Korean War, Mao Tse-Tung's air force failed to defend adequately a small group of vital airfields, power stations and bridges in the Yalu River area, although they frequently enjoyed heavy local numerical superiority, had the tactical advantage of defending the same limited area day after day, and were backed by Soviet supplied and sometimes Soviet operated, early warning radar, and radar-controlled anti-aircraft fire and a generous supply of over 2,000 *MIG 15* fighters. This plane was roughly the technical equal of the best jet planes in the air squadrons of the United Nations and superior to many of the machines it met in combat over North Korea. Since the Korean War, Chinese air defences have not been impressive against the small-scale leaflet and bombing raids launched against Amoy, Shanghai and Canton by the US equipped Chinese Nationalist Air Forces based on Formosa. The Communist air attacks on the Tachen Islands launched early in 1955, with forces of fifty to seventy-five fighters and fighter-bombers, though irregular and spasmodic, showed the world that the Chinese Air Force, which in Korea had been almost entirely defensive, was capable of organised, though not sustained, offensive operations. In the same year came the news that an air regiment of some thirty to forty four-engined long range bombers, of an obsolescent Soviet design, the *TU 4*, was being formed. Strategic air power amongst the air allies of the Soviet Union was for the first time a factor to be reckoned with.

At a major Pekin Air Conference later that year, the Chinese Air Commander-in-Chief told his unit commanders that they must intensify training, avoid complacency and try to master the modern techniques of air power with a view to being ready to liberate Formosa and to defend China from air attack. It is the first of these two objectives which has been the lynch-pin of Chinese Communist Air Policy in the past two or three years. The second may never be feasible. The existing chain of airfields within 250 miles of Formosa has been strengthened. New or larger aerodromes have been constructed near Lungtien, Changtung, Kienow, Lukian, Foochow, Swatow and Wenchow as well as in the Shanghai, Canton and Shangsha areas. The primitive methods of airfield construction used a few years ago, during which, as one writer put it, 'the thirteenth and twentieth centuries met in the Chinese countryside', are a thing of the archaic past. The modern Chinese Air Force uses tractors, bulldozers and mechanical equipment to develop its airfields. In addition, the air training scheme in the USSR has been greatly expanded at Tashkent, Kiev, Vladivostok and Novosibirsk, and Chinese Communist air equipment has been modernised at a much greater rate than that of its most likely adversaries, the Chinese Nationalists on Formosa.[1] General Liu Ya-Lou has at his disposal some 1,500 single-seater jet fighters, most of them *MIG 17s* with a speed advantage of over 50 mph over the US-built *Sabres* which are the backbone of the National Air Force defences. It is almost certain that the Communists will have a few squadrons of Soviet supersonic *MIG 19s* long before Chiang Kai-Shek's units are fitted with the US counterparts, the *Super Sabre*. While the Communist radar equipment is all post-war, and nearly all post 1950 vintage, the Chinese Nationalists make do in part with Second World War

[1] In 1958 operations over Quemoy, however, the Chinese Nationalists successfully used US air to air guided missiles against them.

radar. Numerically the National Air Force would be outnumbered by at least three to one in any future air combat over Formosa. Clearly the defence of Formosa hinges on the presence of US Air Forces in that area.

What are the prospects for the future? Since 1954 Communist China has been making her own elementary trainer aircraft and recently has been assembling Soviet *MIG* fighters and *Ilyushin* twin-bombers at Manchurian factories at Moukden and Dairen. She is also beginning to manufacture these planes. Her expanding electronics industry will shortly be making her own radar equipment. She is utilising both man and woman power to modernise her air force. Some reports say that, like the Soviet Air Force, China has jet fighter squadrons manned by women pilots. Remembering the recent progress made by the USSR in developing long range rockets and using submarines as a platform for firing rockets of up to 1,500 miles fitted with an atomic warhead, it is at least likely that the USSR will soon be able to equip the long range bomber units of the Chinese Communist Air Force with *Tupolev* jet planes. And the recent emphasis on helicopter and jet transport production in the Soviet Union may result in the modernisation of the Chinese Communist air transport arm in the next two or three years. At present most of its transport aircraft are obsolescent, though it has recently acquired some *MI 4* helicopters and *IL 14* twin-engined transports.

To sum up, the Chinese Communist Air Force is more than ready to meet its local commitments in the Eastern Maritime Provinces against Chiang Kai-Shek's air forces but it has no means of defending Chinese metropolitan territory from major air assault, nor of supporting, by air power, any major military campaign in Asia outside its own territory. Prospectively, it can become, in the next decade, a major help or hindrance to the Soviet Union. Some of the latest reports from China do not augur well for the grand Communist alliance. Soviet air technicians are being treated as no more than equals and temporary guests. Soviet military intelligence must know as little as the West about what is going on in some parts of China.

Before China can be self-sufficient as a modern air power she has a long way to travel. Although oil is being produced in Manchuria and the Kansu province and, according to some reports, output will exceed two million metric tons per annum in the next year or so, this is totally inadequate for China's military and industrial needs. The mineral wealth of China must remain potential for many years. Currently there is a shortage of native produced aluminium for the aircraft industry. But China already makes most of her ammunition and bombs and manufactures engines for her trainer aircraft. She can now staff most of her own flying schools and also the radar, armament and engineering schools with Chinese personnel. Her progress as an air power will be stimulated by help not only from Communist Russia, for Poland, Czechoslovakia and East Germany have sent gliders, instructors and electronic equipment in order to make sure that Communist China remains a leading air power amongst the Far Eastern countries.

After the Chinese Air Force, the three Communist Air Forces of Central Europe probably constitute the most important of the allies of the USSR. But the Czechoslovak, Polish and Hungarian air forces, though similar in their military organisation and tactical air functions, vary enormously as potential allies. Czechoslovakia is the most important of the three, for it is probably the most stable politically, it has a well developed aircraft industry and valuable deposits of high grade uranium, which make a crucial contribution to the Soviet stockpile of atomic weapons.

Bases in Czechoslovakia, Poland, Hungary, Roumania, Bulgaria and East Germany constitute a vital part of the outer air defences of the USSR, for it is these territories which would take part of the first shock of any air attack which might come from the NATO forces based in Europe. It is, therefore, difficult to understand why the Soviet Supreme Command has had the air forces of these countries trained and organised primarily to support ground forces in the field. There are signs that fighter regiments of the Polish, Czech and Roumanian Air Forces are being gradually absorbed into the strategic air defence network of the USSR but for the first decade after the war this was not done. No doubt the Soviets knew that only their own aggression would spark off a world war and that they could bide their time in strengthening their air defences.

It is probably true to say that in terms of native production resources, Czechoslovakia is the most important air ally of the Soviet Union for she has a well organised modern aircraft industry making jet fighters and bombers as well as reasonably modern trainer, transport and helicopter planes. Long before the first Czech Communist air squadrons were formed on Soviet territory in 1943, Czech

pilots had given a good account of themselves fighting in the French
Air Force and the RAF. The Czech motto, 'our sea is the air', was
not just an empty phrase but was supported before the Second World
War by a rapidly growing modern aircraft industry which the
Luftwaffe used and expanded when Heinkel and Messerschmitt
production facilities were moved into Czechoslovakia, under the
growing threat of Anglo-American bombing, in 1943.

The immediate post-war Czech Air Force had a strange conglo-
meration of obsolescent German planes like the *Arado* and *Siebel*
trainer aircraft, a few *Spitfire* and *Mosquito* squadrons from Britain
and some *YAK* 9 and *IL* 10 fighter-bomber regiments from the
USSR. The Communist *coup d'état* early in 1948 changed the situation violently. There was a purge of officers in the Czech Air Force
on the scale of the Soviet military purges of 1937 and 1938. The
most notable victim was General Karel Janousak, the Czech Air
Commander-in-Chief, who had also been Inspector General of the
Free Czech Air Force in Britain from 1940 to 1945. Other senior
airmen of excellent calibre who were lost to the Czech Air Force
were Colonel Schneider, Colonel Nowak and Colonel Tarawi. In
1948 many Czech airmen began to leave their country by air with
the help of a well organised clandestine escape movement. Scorn-
ful of the individual escape by Polish pilots, the Czechs said at the
time: 'We get out wholesale in plane-loads.'

In the first years following the Communist coup, there was
emphasis on political reliability rather than technical progress. It is
not surprising that General Vicherek, General Janousak's successor
appointed by the Soviet, did not last long, but was purged and
replaced by General Josef Hanus who soon gave way to General
Vosahlo. The severe military discipline and political indoctrination
imposed by the Soviet authorities in the Czech Air Force between
1948 and 1952 have been documented by a number of Czech pilots
who escaped from Czechoslovakia during that period. Week-end
passes over a period of several months could be lost for a minor
offence such as bad bed-making, a dirty rifle or even inadvertently
failing to salute an officer. The Communist Party line on world and
Czech events was read out daily and provoked earthy hilarity from
young Czech airmen who were often punished for not listening.
Grim if fanciful lectures were frequent, warning pilots not to escape
and telling them about the minefields on the frontiers of Czecho-

slovakia and the gruesome treatment meted out to Czech escapees when they got into British, French or American hands in Germany and Austria. The food at flying training schools and air bases was not too plentiful and poor in quality. For breakfast a cup of poor coffee, black bread and a little butter or marmalade. For lunch there was meat only three or four times a week with soup and dumplings to fill the gaps. Supper consisted of more soup, dumplings, vegetables and black bread. This was inadequate for a working day which began at 5.30 am and went on with few breaks until the roll-call at 9.30 pm. For in the evening, there was the study of Soviet history and politics and failure to pass the examination in these subjects often meant loss of rank.

But in the last five years or so there has been greater stability and technical progress and the Czech Air Force is now probably the best of the air allies of the Soviet Union in central Europe, though East Germany may soon have a larger air force and better technical production facilities. Instead of sending Czech pilots to the USSR for operational training at the air schools at Kirovobad, Grozy, Dyagilevo, Moscow and other places, the Czechs now have elementary, intermediate and flying training schools of their own near Prague, Pilsen, Tabor, Pardubice and Bratislava. The *YAK 9* and *PE 2* obsolescent Soviet planes, which predominated in Czech air squadrons until 1952, have been replaced by modern jet planes, at first from the Soviet Union, but within a year or so from native aircraft production which had expanded at factories in northern Bohemia and near Prague. The Czechs by 1955–6 were ready not only to equip their own air regiments with native-built *MIG 15* and *MIG 17* jet fighters and *Ilyushin 28* bombers but to send jet planes to Egypt and Syria. During the last year or so they have been making helicopters of Czech design and non-jet transport machines of Ilyushin (Soviet) design.

What is their fighting strength and potential value as an air ally? Their front line tactical air force of about 800 planes is nowadays nearly all jet, but it should be regarded as part of the strategic air reserve of the Soviet Union, unlikely to play a major part in any vital early air battles of the atomic age. The practical lessons of Poland and Hungary in 1956 must have revealed to the Kremlin how potentially dangerous it would be to incorporate wholesale the air forces of central and eastern Europe into the over-all Communist strategic air defences in Europe or indeed any other major facet of Soviet air power planning. Clearly only politically picked Czech radar technicians and fighter pilots could be incorporated into the new Soviet strategic air defence command under Marshal Biryuzov. But some of the *élite* air squadrons probably will be: it is a sign of Soviet faith in Czechoslovakia that guided missile development has been reported within the last year or two. It is most unlikely that the Czech Air Force, or indeed any of the other European air allies of the USSR, will be fitted with long range rocket forces for some years yet; nor are they likely to have an atomic bomber force of their own.

The Hungarian Air Force enjoys the distinction of being the only one of Russia's present air allies that has carried out post-war air operations, minor as they were, against troops and armour of the Soviet Army. In the Second World War, Hungarian air squadrons were modernised from *Luftwaffe* resources and fought with the German air units against the Soviet Air Force and Army, mainly on the Ukrainian front. The Hungarian Air Force reached a peak operational strength of about 500 aircraft in the summer of 1944 and many of its squadrons were fitted with the latest German *Messerschmitt 109* fighters and *Junkers 88* bombers. But in the final mass air attacks of the Soviet Air Force on Hungary in 1945, the Hungarian air squadrons were decimated by Soviet air divisions flying the latest *Lavochkin 7* and *MIG 3* fighters.

With the Soviet military occupation of Hungary and the establishment of a communist regime, there were inevitably changes. The Kremlin ruled that the re-activation of the Hungarian Air Force was to be slow. The Soviet authorities allocated no really modern planes to their Hungarian satellite during the first post-war years. As a result of this go-slow policy, the equipment of the first line squadrons of the Hungarian Air Force, up to 1950, consisted mainly of obsolescent *Lavochkin 7* and *YAK 9* piston-engined fighters and *IL 10* and *IL 2 Sturmovik* light bombers. The Hungarian air transport units during this period flew *LI 2* planes equivalent to early Second World War versions of the US *Dakota*. The Hungarian trainer aircraft *PO 2* and *UT 2* were of similar obsolescence. During 1950 and 1951, the Kremlin gradually changed its air policy towards the Hungarian Air Force, no doubt because the Soviet authorities felt by then that all pro-Western elements had been eliminated from its ranks. The process of modernisation was cautious and slow. At first a few Hungarian squadrons were fitted with the obsolescent *MIG 9* Soviet jet fighter and fighter-bomber, and also some *YAK 15* jet fighters. Both these jet machines had been abandoned by Soviet Air Force front line squadrons two or three years previously because they were hopelessly out of date. However, by 1953 the *MIG 15* jet with a top speed of over 650 mph was beginning to replace the previous obsolescent Soviet jet planes in the Hungarian Air Force: again it was at a time when it was being phased out of Soviet first line units to be replaced by the 700–720 mph *MIG 17* fighters. During the same period, the tactical bomber regiments of the Hungarian Air Force were being fitted with twin-jet *Ilyushin 28* planes and the total front line strength in all categories was rising from 250 to some 300 planes. These air forces had two main functions. To do operational training preparing these units to act as close support to the Hungarian Army, if ever it were to go into action on the side of the Soviet Union. But of more immediate importance was the provision of auxiliary local air defence of such important objectives as the valuable Hungarian bauxite mines and the jet aircraft assembly factory near Gyor. The Hungarian Air Force had an air transport regiment of twin-engined *Lusinov* planes which could be used to lift part of the division of airborne troops it was then forming and a further regiment of *Antonov 2* biplane machines to help them. Like other Communist air allies of the USSR in Europe, the Hungarian Air Force had, and still has, neither long range bomber nor long range rocket units.

At the time of the Hungarian rising of October 1956, there was nothing to suggest that the Soviet authorities doubted the loyalty of the Hungarian Air Force: its Commander-in-Chief, Lieutenant-General Sandor Hazi, was a Soviet citizen; the leading officials of the Hungarian Defence Ministry were Moscow trained. And so, in the two to three years preceding the rising, the Hungarian Air Force had been further expanded and modernised. Total strength had risen to about 750 planes of which nearly 500 were front line operational aircraft. The jet fighter regiments were given a few squadrons of *MIG 17* planes. The non-jet fighter-bomber regiments of *IL 10* and *TU 2* planes were being replaced by the more modern twin-jet *Ilyushin 28s* and in the air transport regiment, the obsolescent *Lusinov* twin-engined transport planes were going out of service and the more modern *Ilyushin* twin-engine transports coming in. A few single-rotor *MIL* helicopters were also in service. Plans were being implemented to begin Hungarian production of Soviet-designed *MIG* and *Ilyushin* jets at the factories at Gyor and also at a newly-built aircraft plant at Adyliget.

A few days after the outbreak of the Hungarian revolt against Communist oppression, a few heroic pilots calling themselves and their aircraft the 'National Hungarian Air Force' struck some brave but futile blows for Hungarian freedom when they took off to attack Soviet anti-aircraft batteries near Budapest. And on the ground there was short-lived combat between Hungarian aerodrome servicing personnel and Red Army ground troops. This desperate resistance was inevitably abortive. Perhaps the most important aspect of the fighting in Hungary was the fact that despite the threat of the Soviet Union to use her Air Force against the Hungarian rebels it did not do so to any extent. Here surely was an interesting example of limited war in the atomic age in which air power had no place. This was a kind of civil war with street fighting predominating. Such a war could break out again, for instance between East and West Germany and might well call for some quickly flown in or parachuted shock troops as the only practical form of air intervention by the West or the East.

In 1957 Moscow and the Kadar regime went cautiously about the business of reviving the Hungarian Air Force, which was of course, with the above exception, grounded and heavily guarded during the revolt of October 1956. It is a matter of speculation to determine its future. The Soviet Air Force will probably increase its own strength of two air divisions of 300–400 aircraft in Hungary, perhaps by one or two further divisions. The Hungarian Air Force of some 500–600 front line planes will remain in being but is likely to be kept as part of the general strategic air reserve of the USSR. To use it in any advance into Austria or Yugoslavia would be to court trouble for the time being. To give it local responsibility for the first line outer strategic air defences of the USSR would be equally dangerous.

The Polish Air Force is essentially similar to the Czech Air Force in military composition. For different reasons, however, it is as unstable an element in Soviet Air Force plans as is the Hungarian Air Force. In 1956, following the departure of Marshal Rokosowski, General Turkiel, who was completely under Soviet influence, was replaced by General Frey Bielecki, a patriotic Pole. This year, which saw the Poznan riots and the emergence of Gomulka at the head of a new Polish Government, was a year in which Poland was modernising her aircraft industry and depending less and less on Soviet aircraft supplies and equipment. Having been assembling Soviet *MIG 15* jet fighters for three years or so, Poland was now beginning to manufacture the faster *MIG 17* fighters. She was also making her own primary trainer aircraft and abandoning the Soviet *Yakovlev* and *Polikarpov* machines, building *MIL* helicopters under Soviet licence, making her own medium range non-jet airliners and planning to build both jet helicopters and jet transport machines. Production facilities at Okencie near Warsaw developed by Heinkel during the Second World War were being further expanded and there was similar development at aircraft plants near Lublin and Lodz. The Polish aircraft industry like the Polish Air Force is gradually lifting Soviet control and supervision and becoming more national and more self-contained.

Between 1943, when the first Polish Communist air squadrons were formed in USSR territory, and 1954, Soviet control, through political and liaison officers and supply from factories in the USSR of most of the air equipment and aircraft, was virtually complete. In the last year or so there have been indications of relaxing of the Soviet control. Polish aircraft firms are now operating under pre-Second World War labels (eg the PZL factories) and are making most of their own aircraft, especially trainer aircraft and jet fighters, at Rzeszow and Mielec.

The Polish Air Force will probably remain essentially a tactical air force for some time to come. Its paper strength has made it seem larger than it is. The ten divisions of fighters and light bombers have theoretically two to three regiments each. This would give the Polish Air Force a front line strength of over 1,000 planes, mainly *MIG 15* and *17* jet fighters, and *Ilyushin 28* twin-jet fighter-bombers. In practice, however, the effective strength is only about 700 aircraft. Like the Hungarian Air Force, the Polish Air Force may be relegated to the strategic air reserves of the Communist camp. It is not likely to be given responsible work in the outer strategic air defences of the USSR. However the Poles have made important contributions to the development of Soviet rocket engines, guided missiles and the experimental atomic energy aero-engine and they may pull something advanced out of the bag in the field of jet-engined helicopters.

K

If political circumstances call for combat, the Poles will show their traditional skill and bravery which makes them produce outstanding pilots even in the best company. Whether they will ever be a fighting air asset to the USSR is something which Moscow must surely doubt.

Potentially, the most modern and powerful of Russia's European air allies is probably the East German Air Force. It is estimated to have about 1,200 modern jet planes, *MIG 15, 17* and some supersonic *MIG 19s* and twin-jet *Ilyushin* and *Yakolev* planes. Until 1955 its forces consisted of obsolescent transport and liaison machines, for the Soviet Union was not anxious to promote military flying in what had been enemy territory, and an enemy that had nearly brought about her downfall. And so East Germany provided aircraft production engineers, equipment and facilities from Heinkel, Junkers and Focke-Wulf factories to modernise the post-war factories in the USSR. Its factories also turned out electronic equipment for the Soviet Union.

But there was a great spurt in the military status of the East German Air Force between 1955 and 1957. The Soviet Air Force began to hand over some of its bases in Germany to the new East German air arm. The previous guise of regarding the German pilots as members of the civil *Volkspolizei* was abandoned when German pilots were seen doing military training on *Ilyushin 28* twin-jets at air bases near Berlin such as Oranienburg and Werneuchen. Other East German pilots were sent to Czechoslovakia and the USSR for jet conversion flying courses. East German aircraft factories which had been sending components and accessories to the aircraft industries of Poland, Czechoslovakia and China for the past two or three years (1953–6) now began to use them more for native production.

What will be the future role of Lieutenant-General Heinz Kessler's new *Luftwaffe* in the east? Will it clash with West German Air Forces? Will it develop the use of long range bombers and atomic weapons? The most likely operational purposes for which it is intended is to form part of the first line of defence for Marshal Biryuzov's strategic protective forces. It will probably manufacture much of the early warning radar equipment needed for local defence as well as the supersonic jet fighters and perhaps some of the guided missiles. East Germany is also manufacturing substantial numbers of transport aircraft. At first these will be mainly Soviet designed twin-engined non-jet *Ilyushins*. The main factory producing these machines is the Leipzig plant which formerly made *Junkers* bombers and *Messerschmitt* fighters. But the East Germans are also planning to make jet transport long range planes of their own design. At Genshagen near Berlin, previously a centre of Daimler Benz engine production, there is now production of a powerful axial turbo-jet engine which is to power the German designed transport planes of the future.

The *Volkspolizei* 'civil' German Air Force of the 1950–5 period with its obsolescent liaison planes, like the *YAK 11* and *18* and the *Antonov 2*, has become the German so-called *Luftstreitkraefte* of 1958. Its flying personnel strength has been more than doubled since 1955 from about 5,000 officers and other ranks to over 10,000. It remains to be seen if the Soviet policy of reviving the *Luftwaffe* in the East will be an air asset in Europe or not.

The other European air allies of the Soviet Union are the Albanian, Bulgarian and Roumanian Air Forces. Except to promote frontier or local mischief, it is difficult to see what kind of military asset they could be. Albania, of course, relies entirely on Soviet technical help for maintaining and training a small air force of about 100 *MIG 15* fighters. Roumania and Bulgaria have begun to make their own trainer planes and to assemble Soviet designed jets. They are, so to speak, the second quality European air allies, with small air forces of about 200–300 planes with a smaller proportion of *MIG 17s* and with smaller parachute forces and less modern radar equipment. Because of the continued importance of her oil production, and her more developed aircraft industry, Roumania may soon get a proportion of supersonic *MIG 19* fighters, if only because she may play a rather more prominent part in the strategic outer air defences of the USSR than Bulgaria.

But in an age in which rockets are playing a greater part in Soviet strategic defence and attack, one can scarcely attribute any great importance to the operational value of the European air allies of the USSR. Indeed the first sign that they are allies on whom the Soviet would rely in a major conflict would be the development in their air forces of guided missiles and long-ranged rocket units. As long as their modernisation is confined to subsonic and some supersonic jet planes, we can be sure that they will be air satellites in the fullest sense; that is following a Soviet pattern of development,

providing only a platform and a spring-board for Soviet armed
forces without becoming part of the spearhead of Soviet attack or
defence plans. Incidentally the standardisation of weapons and the
clash of national viewpoints present no problems of any dimension in
the military policy of the Warsaw Pact powers, as they do in NATO.

In considering the general political and military perspective of the
supply of Communist aircraft to the air forces of the Arab world,
two points might be made initially. It was Britain who first exported
aircraft to the air forces of Egypt, Syria, Jordan, Iraq and Lebanon,
and it was Czechoslovakia and not the USSR who first intervened
on behalf of the Communist world. In the first Arab-Israel war in
1948 she sent some obsolescent *ME 109* fighters to the Israeli Air
Force and in the year before the second Arab-Israel War, ie the 1956
Israeli attack on Egypt's forward forces in the Sinai desert, Czechoslovakia signed a three-year economic pact with Egypt in which she
agreed to supply the Egyptian Air Force with Czech built but Soviet
designed jet fighters and light bombers. By the end of 1955, Czech
built *Ilyushin 28* bombers arrived in Egypt. Early in 1956, *MIG 15*
fighters on board the Russian freighter *Stalingrad* put in at the small
port of Agami. These were the first of a total of some 200 *MIG 15s*
ordered and expected by the Egyptian Air Force.

It was clear now that the USSR intended to bolster Arab air
forces in the Middle East to supplement the Czech support of Arab
air power. In 1956 as she invited Egyptian naval crews to be trained
at the submarine base at Odessa so she sent aircraft instructors and
technicians to Egypt to supplement the existing air training and jet
conversion courses provided by Czechoslovakia in Egypt.

The war of October–November 1956 at first between Israel and
Egypt in the Sinai desert and then between Anglo-French forces and
Egypt in the Suez Canal Zone, provided few fresh pointers to the
Communist policy in the area or to the potential of the Egyptian
and other Arab air forces. Despite the broadcast threats of Com-
munist air force volunteers en route to help the Egyptians, the
Egyptian Air Force planes were not manned and fought by the
Soviet and Czech air instructors in the zone of combat in Egypt.
The Communists acted with great prudence and restraint. Their
pilots, who might have made devastating raids on Cyprus, where
British and French planes were jam-packed wing-tip to wing-tip,
confined themselves to ferrying as many *MIG* and *Ilyushin* jet

planes as they could to the safer confines of Luxor and to even safer air bases in Saudi Arabia, Jordan and Syria. Soviet prudence also confined the faster 700 mph *MIG 17* jets to their crates in the assembly shops at Alexandria.

The military events of the autumn of 1956 suggested that if the Communists do intend to infiltrate and exercise the maximum amount of military influence in the Middle East, they do not intend to provoke a major war in the course of their penetration. 'All mischief short of global war' seems to summarise their policy subsequent to the Second World War and their cautious support of the Egyptian Air Force illustrates this as much as anything.

By training and equipping the Egyptian and Syrian Air Forces, the USSR will contribute to maintaining the disturbed nature of the area. This is part of the Soviet 'termite' strategy, which consists of nibbling Western interests to death, without too much overt hostility on the part of the Communists. At the moment, Soviet and Czech support of Egypt is based on the desire to gain the favour of the most powerful of the Arab States.

But in Syria and Egypt the USSR has potential allies who may provide the first of the advanced bases in the Arab world. Syria, with Soviet-trained air squadrons, is a wedge in the soft underbelly of the Baghdad Pact powers. Syria can, and probably will, give the USSR the dominant position in the Middle East, which she has been seeking: a position which outflanks Turkey and is astride the important oil pipe-lines from the Persian Gulf. The present Syrian-Egyptian United Arab Republic may one day speed up a Soviet spring-board leap into North Africa and beyond.

Until 1956, the Syrian Air Force could muster an operational strength of about sixty aircraft. These were a mixture of British obsolescent jet planes, and of aircraft material from Italy, North America and France. Then came the first dispatch of Czech *MIG 15s* to Syria followed throughout that year by a steady stream of Russian air technicians, instructors and advisers flying in to Damascus from Sofia.

Near Homs, Latakiya and Baniyas, operational flying training under Soviet supervision began. Soviet radar engineers and maintenance personnel for the early warning system and the radar ground control of fighters were followed by other Soviet specialists for the radar controlled anti-aircraft guns. *YAK 11* and *YAK 18* trainer planes have been flown in to replace the British, American and

Italian trainer planes. Syrian air and ground personnel have gone to Poland, Czechoslovakia and the USSR for training.

During 1957 and 1958 some 100–150 *MIG 17s* were delivered to Syria from the USSR and there are also one or two squadrons of *Ilyushin 28* bombers flying from the modernised and extended air bases at Hama and Palmyra. There are some *MIG 17s* at Hama too and also at El Rasafa, the Mezze base near Damascus and at Sahl es Sahra. The Syrian Air Force in itself, however, is no threat to the Baghdad Pact powers, but with the Egyptian Air Force, it may well develop in a few years into a serious threat to Israel after due training and discipline under Communist tutelage. Its training and personnel standards over the last year or so have been poor. Even a squadron of *élite* Syrian pilots who had flown *Meteor* jets up to 1956 failed to qualify in a *MIG 15* jet conversion course held in Egypt. After ten months they were still flying the two-seater *MIG 15* trainer version under Soviet instruction.

But the major asset for the USSR is not the Syrian Air Force itself, any more than it is the Albanian, Hungarian or Czech Air Force in central Europe. Syria is now a permanent base and reception centre for advanced Soviet Air Forces and perhaps eventually rocket weapons. Soviet medium and light jet bombers could quickly neutralise US Strategic Air Bases in Tripoli and Saudi Arabia flying from Syria and the USSR could quickly reinforce from Soviet air regiments in the Caucasus. Like the Royal Afghan Air Force which now flies *MIG 15* fighters and is trained and equipped by the Soviet Air Force, the Syrian Air Force is a local trouble shooter and a provider of potential advanced bases.

Indeed these two main functions epitomise the main purpose of the air allies of the Soviet Union. China, whose future may be in any part of Asia, Afghanistan on the Pakistan border, and the group of Communist air forces in central and eastern Europe do not make any vital contribution to the integrated air policy of the Soviet Union. They provide the USSR with an infinite variety of ways of starting or inciting local limited wars to test the Western policy of the use of the limited deterrent. How far the Kremlin uses its air allies to this end may well be the measure of its intention to make war or keep the peace during the next few years, during which for the first time the USSR may have the advantage in the strategic offensive potential over the United States.

CHAPTER 19

THE FUTURE OF SOVIET AIR POWER

Asher Lee

WHEN GIVING A series of three lectures on military science at Trinity College, Cambridge, in the spring of 1956, Professor P. M. Blackett remarked that seldom in history can it have been more difficult than at present to formulate a defence policy. Professor Blackett speaking to a British audience was concerned chiefly with Western defence policy. It is doubtful if Soviet military leaders would confess to dilemmas in their present and future defence policy when speaking, say, to officers at the Zhukovski Air Engineering Academy or at the Voroshilov Higher Military Academy. Soviet military institutions have to maintain the façade and the fiction that the Soviet Union does not make strategic blunders and to propagate the legend that the USSR does not have any serious dichotomies in her air and rocket planning programmes. While the Western press almost heralds a crash, a rocket failure or an inter-service dispute as important head-line news, *Pravda* and *Izvestia* remain twin souls of discretion. In the course of reading Raymond Garthoff's interesting recent book on 'Soviet Strategy in the Nuclear Age'[1] one soon became aware of mixed and even confused lines of thought in Soviet military statements. The book, incidentally, is predominantly a series of quotations, with background comment by the author, taken from nuclear age pronouncements on military thinking made by a wide range of senior Soviet officers in the past three or four years.

Let us take the case of long range air attack by bombers or rockets. While one Soviet military leader holds the view that 'the objective of combat operations must be the destruction of the armed forces and not strategic bombing of targets in the rear', another declares that 'it is essential to select most carefully the targets for strategic attack so that the enemy cannot deal a retaliatory blow', and again, while

[1] Published in New York in 1958 by Frederick Praeger & Co. Inc.

one voice says that 'artillery, small arms, tanks and aviation remain the basic fire power of the army', other voices, including those of Vershinin, Commander-in-Chief of the Air Force, and of Mr Khrushchev himself, have said that the day of the manned fighter and bomber will soon be over, that they do not believe in limited nuclear war and that 'hundreds, thousands and even tens of thousands of nuclear weapons' may be used in a future conflict.

It seems clear from the utterances of Soviet military leaders of the past two or three years that they would, if they could, subscribe to Professor Blackett's view that present and future defence policy is difficult to formulate. Perhaps one will get a clearer view of Soviet strategy and planning if one looks at the present state of the Russians air and rocket forces and then considers some of the inevitable weapon and tactical changes which they must consider when formulating their future military potential.

The current estimates of Soviet aircraft operational strength range about the figure of 20,000 aircraft. If one were to include all types of military and civil transport planes and helicopters the figure might be about 25,000 machines. By far the largest air force in these totals is the tactical air forces. In fact if one takes account of tactical naval air forces they comprise some two thirds of all bomber and fighter units. The current strength of 'front aviation' (ie tactical air forces) given in such semi-official estimates as are published is believed to be about 10,000 machines. What are likely to be the future trends? It would seem logical to reduce the number of fighter and light bomber machines, such as the *MIG 15* and *17* and the *Ilyushin 28* and the *TU 14*, which will not be needed in such numbers as Soviet atomic artillery and ground to ground missiles of the *T 1* and *T 7* types increase in number. But it is doubtful if the number of supersonic fighter regiments will be substantially reduced, though a large number of them may be temporarily diverted to the Fighter Command of Marshal Biryuzov's PVO Strategic Air Defence System. With the increase in modern long range jet transport planes in the Soviet Union there is a need for fighters to be ready to escort them. There seems no reason why say 1,000–2,000 of the *MIG 21* (and possibly *MIG 23*) machines and the *Sukhoi* fighters of the next year or so should not be given dual operational training both in the interception of bombers over the USSR and in escort, patrol and interception work over regional battle fronts. As long as local air

superiority is needed to fly in troops, to ensure successful air reconnaissance, to prevent ground artillery, rockets and tanks from being
overwhelmed by enemy fire from the air or on the ground, it seems
that the modern jet and rocket-engined fighter will be a key factor in
any land campaign of the future. The Soviet Defence Ministry is
mindful of its great advantages over the West in fighting local land
battles and this is likely to be the situation as long as the West does
not introduce compulsory military service on a much wider scale
than hitherto. It may make good politics or even good democracy
to reduce national compulsory service in the armed forces, but it
does not enable NATO to compete on level terms in ground warfare with Communist forces, in an age in which the technical
differences between East and West are reaching the vanishing
point.

What about the future of Soviet strategic air defence? The PVO
command will clearly increase the number of its ground to air and
air to air missiles of *T 6*, *T 8* and *M 2* types and also their range
performance and efficiency. But all these developments will not
enable them to deal adequately with the growing threat of US long
range rocket attack from existing *Thor* and *Jupiter* bases in Europe,
and from the coming *Titan* and *Atlas* bases in North America, not to
mention the submarine-based *Polaris* rockets. Even if Soviet electronic scientists were to achieve a break-through by designing a long
range early warning system with a detection range of say 5,000 miles
and an automatic computer system which passed the details of the
incoming long range rocket tracks to anti-missile missile firing
points, it seems that the feints and stratagems of radio counter-
measures, the bewilderment of tracking incoming bombers flying at
different heights, of detecting incoming bombers not carrying atomic
bombs and doing feint runs, not to mention feint rocket firings and
rockets coming in simultaneously from different directions and
different ranges—it seems that all these things, which are to be expected,
will cause chaos amongst the Soviet early warning system. The USSR
has no reason to believe that she can effectively defend her territory
against an all-out nuclear attack, or by surprise Soviet nuclear
attack on NATO and US bases destroy the major part of the
Western deterrent forces which are, in part, so mobile. The carrier-
borne nuclear attack power for instance must first be detected by
armed reconnaissance or other means. The future submarine-

launched rocket forces of the West are likely to be detected only by the uncertain search operations of Soviet submarines.

It is the uncertainty about her air and rocket defence potential which has made the Soviet Union build up these forces since the early 1950s and makes her tread warily, without engaging in major military adventures in contemporary international diplomacy. At the moment her fastest experimental ground to air rockets probably have a speed of less than 5,000 mph and in most cases those in production and in service less than 2,000 mph. Against the *Titan*, *Atlas* or even the slower *Thor* and *Jupiter* they would have an enormous speed disadvantage. Against raiding bombers most of the current ground to air missiles of the *T 6*, *T 8* and *M 2* types are reported to have a range of fifty miles or less and so could not deal effectively with jet bombers using a stand-off bomb. Soviet ground to air missiles are probably ineffective against low flying bombers coming in at below say 500 feet. In short the preponderance of contemporary bomber and rocket air attack over the capabilities of air defence is the major strategic factor in keeping the present uneasy peace. Both sides can cause each other crippling damage. And the growing use of submarines on both sides for delivering long range rockets will serve to increase the preponderance of the rocket offensive against the rocket defensive.

To what extent will the current force of some 1,500 long and medium range bombers of the Soviet DA be maintained? This is perhaps the most difficult question for the Kremlin to decide. It will concentrate more and more on developing a long range rocket striking force of *T 3* and *T 4* types land-based missiles and of *Komet* and *Golem* submarine-based missiles. But despite inertial guidance and increasing accuracy with time, these missiles are unlikely to be the main weapon for containing the Western deterrent. The long range rocket is unlikely to become a precision instrument to attack air bases or submarines on the high seas or rocket bases on land. Estimates have put the present accuracy of long range missiles at from plus or minus one or two miles in the case of one-stage rockets to as much as plus or minus five to ten miles in the case of intercontinental ballistic missiles. As the West develops vertical take-off bombers, the problem of neutralising Western thermo-nuclear and nuclear attack will become increasingly difficult. Taking all the factors in an uncertain situation into account brings one to the conclusion that the Soviet DA strategic bomber force will remain in being for the next five years at least. It may transfer some of its air regiments to long range naval co-operation work with both Soviet submarines and cruisers, if only to do on the spot assessments of damage inflicted and to provide supplementary navigational aids which will be necessary for some of the less skilled submarine crews.

I think that, on balance, the Soviet Air Force is likely to go ahead and develop a supersonic bomber successor to the four-jet *Bison* and will also strive to be the first of the great powers to perfect an atomic-powered aircraft;[1] probably a flying boat developed from the present *Beriev* four-jet flying boat series adapted for nuclear conversion in the same way as the British Saunders Roe *Princess* flying boat may be or the US Navy's *P 6 M Martin Seamaster*. Some sources, however, prefer the view that Soviet nuclear conversion will be first tried in an adapted *Bison* jet bomber. No doubt both will be tried in the experimental stage.

It is now more than five years since the first reports of atomic-powered aircraft engine development in the USSR were received. These came from a Soviet atomic energy centre in the Altai mountains near Mongolia. The project was stated to have had the help of German and Polish rocket and nuclear scientists and the target was to construct an atomic-powered aircraft with a speed of about 1,000 mph, a ceiling of about 90,000 feet and an endurance of about a day and a half. The nuclear rocket motor used was stated to have a target thrust of about fifty tons. Since the first reports came in, there have been a number of others to suggest that the USSR is developing much more powerful nuclear-propelled rocket motors. There is no reason to think that the USSR has yet solved the problem of producing an airborne atom-powered engine unit with sufficiently light-weight shielding to protect the crew from harmful neutrons and gamma rays, though some reports say she has developed a relatively light material of which only five tons is required to build a shield. While one sees the value of a nuclear-powered patrol bomber or transport plane, used either as a missile carrier, or for reconnaissance, or as a radar or a radio counter-measures station, such an aircraft would appear to have more political propaganda than military significance at the present moment. A crash landing or a collision in flight would have danger-ous consequences. On balance it would seem that the Soviets are

[1] It may be the delta-winged bomber reported early in 1959.

more likely to use the nuclear-powered rocket for launching manned satellites or for eventual interplanetary travel.

The chief indication that the three existing Soviet long range bomber air armies are not likely to be expanded for the next year or so is the present emphasis on long range jet transport planes. Much of the manpower previously employed entirely on producing the long range four-jet turbo-prop *Tupolev 20* is now probably being used for making the more recent *TU 114* jet transport planes and the same must be true to some extent of the *TU 104* jet airliner based on the military medium range bomber, the *Badger TU 16*. Nor must one forget the current production of two other four-jet turbo-prop transport planes, the *Ilyushin 18*, and the *Antonov 10* and the four-jet *TU 110*. These must absorb manufacturing resources which could have been diverted to stepping up the output of Myasishchev's four-turbo-jet successor to the *Bison* bomber. The logical conclusion seems to be that the Soviet defence authorities are convinced that they have the edge of the West in long range rocket development and that in the future they propose to put greater emphasis on rocket firing submarines, on expanding their air transport arm both to improve their mobility and flexibility in ground battles and to make their airborne forces more effective than in the Second World War. Although the DA long range jet bomber arm is not likely to be expanded, it is also not likely to be seriously reduced in the next few years, certainly not before the Soviet Union has an adequate force of long range missiles with intercontinental range to replace it. She may wait not only until her ICBMs have greater accuracy and reliability but until they no longer need bulky liquid fuels difficult to store and transport. Perhaps by the time when nuclear-powered or solid fuel ICBMs are in general use, the Soviet long range jet bomber force will be being phased out of the strategic air and rocket striking power of the USSR, but this is not likely to be earlier than the late 1960s.

Parachute training is almost certainly carried out on a greater scale in the USSR than in any other country in the world. Navigational aids to make good use of parachute troop-carrying planes in night or long distance operations are now generally available. Marshal of Aviation N. S. Skripko, Commander-in-Chief of the aviation of Soviet airborne troops, will in the next year or so have a force of long range military jet transport planes comparable to any-

thing the West can assemble, and his force of jet and non-jet helicopters for operations in the battle zones will have a much greater
lift and stronger fighter escorts than any equivalent force which the
West could mount. The USSR will probably be able to mount a
force of say 500–1,000 medium and long range transport aircraft and
a similar number of helicopters by the early 1960s to support land or
air operations.

Apart from seizing such key bases as Iceland and Cyprus, Skripko
is already in a much better position than any of his predecessors to
bring swift help by air to the ground forces of the Soviet army or its
allies in almost any part of Europe, Asia or the Arab world. In
modern atomic warfare a strong force of parachute and airborne
troops would on occasion seem to be more important in ground
battles than even motorised infantry or tanks. They alone may be
able to by-pass areas of destruction and contamination which could
make planned outflanking and deep penetration movements by
ground forces virtually impossible by other means. The Soviet
defence authorities are readily aware of the importance of tactical
mobility in the atomic age. Apart from recent increased emphasis on
armoured forces, helicopters will assume more and more a large-scale
role in achieving this mobility. In the long run the Soviet Union will
almost certainly expand the production of transport aircraft and
helicopters at the expense of bomber production, in order to provide
air transport not only for her airborne forces, but also for reinforcing
infantry and artillery units. She has said again and again in
recent years that the best defence against atomic attack is to come to
close grips with the enemy and so limit his use of atomic weapons
against troop targets. In all forms of atomic attack in ground warfare, the mobility of Soviet ground forces can only be ensured locally
by strong forces of helicopter and transport planes. One wonders if
the transfer of Marshal Zhigarev to the post of head of civil aviation
in January 1957 was not in fact a recognition that Soviet air transport facilities were to be greatly expanded under the current Seven
Year Plan for aircraft production.

It is true to say that Soviet airborne forces will be vulnerable in
transit to attack by fighter planes and ground to air guided missiles,
in areas where they have not established local air superiority.
Despite Khrushchev's utterance that fighter planes can now be put in
museums the Soviet Air Force is likely to expand and modernise its

total fighter strength in the next few years. The *Sukhoi* delta-wing fighters which made their first flights in 1956 may well be powered with jet engines of 10,000–15,000 lb thrust and a rocket engine which will give them speeds of 1,500 mph and eventually much higher speeds. It would not be surprising if Yakovlev's design team produced a new fighter with this type of performance in the next few years. The Soviet Air Force has publicly declared its intention to produce fighters with a speed of Mach 3 or 4 and this is not likely to prove an idle boast.

The Soviet air planners must be very conscious of the vulnerability of their air bases, especially the advanced tactical air bases in central Europe. They have added a large number to the hundreds which they inherited from the *Luftwaffe*'s airfield construction work in the Second World War, in East Prussia, Poland, Czechoslovakia, Roumania, Hungary, Albania, East Germany and in western Russia itself. The obvious Soviet reply is to build more bases and to develop fighter and light bomber machines which can be launched from ramps and land on skids. There are a growing number of reports that developments proceed in both these fields. At the 1958 Soviet Air Day the VTO *Flying Table* said to be designed by Raphael-yantz was on public display before a crowd of 250,000. This was a year or so at least after comparable British and US VTO machines had been developed for public display and there is no reason to believe that the Soviet Air Force is ahead of the West in the vertical take-off field which will become more crucial in the 1960s. The US *Bell X 14*, the French *Coleopter C 450* and the British *Short SC 1* form a stronger group of experimental VTO machines than any group of similar machines which the Soviet authorities are thought to have developed so far. The same probably applies to ramp-launched fighter and bomber aircraft such as the US *F 84 G Thunderjet* and the French *SE 5000 Baroudeur*. But there have been recent reports that the Soviet Air Force is experimenting with ramp-launched *MIG* fighter and fighter-bomber planes because it is aware of the vulnerability of its tactical air bases which must be maintained fairly close to the battle area. Because of the vulnerability of these advanced bases it would be surprising if the Soviet Air Force did not increase the extent of in-flight refuelling training not only of the fighter units in the tactical front aviation, but also of those of the PVO strategic air defence. In the event of a large-scale local war in western Europe for instance, large numbers of reinforcing fighters would be needed if permanent local air superiority over the battle areas is to be maintained. These planes might have to be sent from the Crimea or from east of Moscow and clearly in-flight refuelling may well be essential if they are to arrive in time. This process might be even more essential in long range escort of air transport planes bringing troop reinforcements from say 2,000–3,000 miles away. The fact that little has been published to suggest that large-scale use of in-flight refuelling exists in the Soviet Air Force may be misleading.

The importance of securing local air superiority has been underlined in a number of recent Soviet pronouncements by leading military writers. 'Supremacy in the air has the purpose not only of enabling the air force to carry out its operations, but above all of creating favourable conditions for the operations of ground forces.' 'Without air superiority, one cannot quickly seize the strategic initiative in the beginning of a war and so successfully develop operations on land or sea.' These are typical quotations which in effect support the view stated earlier in this book that the Soviet will retain large forces of high speed fighters for supporting local land operations. In ground combat in the atomic age the high speed fighter is still a key element. This is true not only to ensure the safe arrival of airborne troops, but also to ensure adequate air reconnaissance and observation.

The Soviet Air Force of the Second World War was not particularly strong in either tactical or strategic reconnaissance work. Its air leaders are well aware of the extra importance of reconnaissance in the nuclear weapons age. Two likely developments in the coming years are the stepping up of the use of light helicopters for tactical reconnaissance work, probably those designed by Kamov, and the development of television apparatus for showing the effects of atomic weapon strikes in the battle area and for detecting troop movements. In addition the recent advances in airborne radar equipment and VHF radio voice equipment will make Soviet tactical reconnaissance more efficient than in the past. But the Russians have the same dilemma which affects all tactical reconnaissance operations. To use light helicopters such as the *Kamov 15* or *18* or the *MIL 3* means using machines vulnerable to fighter interception or to attack by long range ground to air guided missiles. To use fast fighter-type supersonic jet planes such as the *MIG 19* or *MIG 21* must mean travelling too fast to pick up the vital details of what is going on in closely knit ground combat. The Soviet Air Force is likely to use a combination of the supersonic, the subsonic and the slow vertical take-off machine and to train some of its tactical air regiments more intensively than in the past in army reconnaissance work. The key here, as in the case of the use of airborne troops, will be the establishment of local air superiority. The extra importance of reconnaissance is yet another key reason why the Soviet Air Force will probably maintain a large force of high speed jet fighters in the foreseeable future. To know whether one can use atomic weapons with safety in a closely locked ground battle will be one of the major problems of any future combat. The combination of strong fighter protection and the use of tactical reconnaissance helicopters may be the best air combination to meet this particular problem.

The launching of the first earth satellite, the Soviet *Sputnik*, in the autumn of 1957 and the subsequent launching of more powerful *Sputniks* by the USSR have posed the question of the future effect of manned or unmanned space platforms on military strategy. It is thought for instance that special reconnaissance of enemy rocket launching might be made and its initial radar guidance equipment jammed. Alternatively space platforms might be used to launch missiles against targets on earth. It is suggested that long range television from satellites could detect the firing of large numbers of long range rockets and so give immediate warning of a major attack by these weapons to earth-based anti-missile missiles.

Before assessing the potential strategic military advantages of manned or unmanned space platforms, it should be stressed that any 1957–9 assessment of the relative progress of the USSR and USA in this field may well be misleading. Current *Sputniks* or *Explorers* are only the first generation forerunners of much more powerful rocket-driven earth satellites in which solid fuels, atomic power and ion propulsion will probably be in use. Though the USSR may have the edge in 1959 in the production of ICBM and IRBM missiles, this advantage could easily be lost in the 1960s. The same applies to the objective of manning a space platform for military purposes. The USSR, because she has launched heavier *Sputniks*, may seem to have a temporary advantage. But the USA has yet to use her most powerful rocket motors from the *Titan* and *Atlas* ICBMs, as the USSR appears to have done, to launch her earth satellites. The development of the US *Polaris* and *Pershing* IRBM solid fuel rockets as opposed to the present liquid fuel rockets may also change the balance of rocket power to some extent.

The President of the Californian Institute of Technology is reported to have said that from a military view-point the space platform was not a very great advantage. Dr Wernher von Braun, the US rocket designer, on the other hand is convinced that guided missiles from orbit bases have a very great military potential and that reconnaissance from an orbit could discover the exact location of Soviet industry and would be of value against moving surface targets when the ICBM would not be. He also said that he believed that space-launched rockets could intercept high flying bombers from their vantage point.

Even if von Braun's views are correct, the space platform is scarcely a place to hunt submarines from or to interfere with the course of local limited wars and these two aspects of modern strategy are likely to be predominant by the 1970s or later, i.e. the earliest date when military space platforms are likely to be in use. Nor will space platform weapons be effective against low flying bombers or for detecting local troop movements. It also seems that if it is feasible to shoot at the moon and hit it, a space platform can scarcely claim immunity from an earth-launched rocket, nor can it hope to hide very effectively. It is surely easier to aim a rocket at a satellite platform 1,000 miles up than at the moon which is over 200,000 miles from the earth. One wonders too if the reconnaissance information sent from an earth satellite would not be interfered with and whether underground production and local camouflage will not reduce the value of observations made from space platforms. In short it is not thought that space platforms will have a major influence on modern strategy in the next decade or two and that the advent of the rocket-firing atomic-engined submarine is far the most important new element in the international military scene.

The view has been expressed earlier in this book that the USSR's military policy is all mischief short of war. It has also been suggested that she may well use her allies, for instance in Eastern Germany or in the Arab world, to initiate local military action rather than do so themselves. Moreover because of their great advantage in conventional weapons, i.e. armoured divisions and jet fighter, fighter-bomber and light bomber planes, she is not likely to initiate the use of tactical atomic weapons either artillery and ground-launched rockets or tactical atomic bombs. She is likely to proceed by what Air Chief Marshal Sir John Slessor has called 'termite tactics', that is gradually extending the Communist empire by local military-political action, e.g. by making more of the Arab world dependent on the USSR for military weapons, by political propaganda work and by economic penetration of Asia and Africa.

If this is so, is one to take any of the Soviet proposals for international inspection or for ending atomic weapon tests at more than face value? This is perhaps the most crucial problem of contemporary history and unless a disarmament solution is found in the course of the next decade or so, more and more countries will stock-pile atomic weapons and the prospects of a general settlement will become remote. It would seem that the best approach would be to accept one of the recently proposed plans for disengagement in central Europe. In the long run no one can predict the future military intentions of a United Germany, whether unity is achieved before or after a disengagement plan is accepted. Any links between NATO and West Germany would have to be re-forged.

As things are likely to be in the next decade or so, the most important aspect of the East-West strategic situation is the need to formulate a serious programme of mutual inspection which must precede any general disarmament programme. It is unlikely that any initial inspection agreement would take in the USA or the USSR. Therefore Germany and perhaps Poland, Hungary, and Czechoslovakia are the territories in which the machinery of international inspection must be worked out. It is hard to see what important disadvantages would accrue to the West from any existing disengagement plan. Certainly there are not likely to be any serious military disadvantages. NATO ground and tactical air forces might even be better placed outside Germany. Surely there is the danger of the advanced forces in West Germany being overrun and destroyed in the early days of a major conflict in western Europe? Surely NATO relies in western Europe on the retaliatory power of its tactical atomic weapons and could not many of these be used more flexibly and more reliably if operated in the first place from outside Germany?

But much more important is the need to know if the Soviets mean what they say about disengagement or mutual inspection and the only way is to put the matter to the test. Presumably the details of any worked-out plan would be on a day to day basis. If the USSR did not co-operate in the first few days, it would at least be clear that her inspection and disarmament proposals were not serious. No great harm would have been done, but important facts, if only of a negative kind, could be ascertained. The United Nations could be used to act as neutral observers and though they would not influence Soviet intentions, they could at least help to clarify them.

I think the time has come when the Soviet Union realises that any conflict between herself and the USA will almost certainly involve the large-scale use of atomic weapons and that it will not be practical to try to limit the areas in which these weapons can be used. In such a conflict she cannot be sure of the result. However, she has reached the stage of achieving strategic parity in long range weapons and superiority in the use of conventional weapons or in other means of fighting local wars. It has become very popular to say that the Western use of the deterrent is a negative strategy because it prevents the West taking positive action locally, as for instance in the case of Hungary in 1956. But the existence of thousands of atomic missiles on both sides imposes a cautious military policy on the USSR and her military action in the case of Suez and the 1958 events in Lebanon and Jordan was negative. Nor did the USSR react, except with words, to US action on behalf of the Chinese Government in Formosa when the offshore islands of Quemoy and Matsu were attacked by Communist China. If there were a dispute between East and West Germany, the Soviet has the same problem about intervention as the United States. It is to know to what extent intervention would extend the area of conflict and at what stage thermo-nuclear weapons would be brought into use. This situation applies to any other local conflict, e.g. in the Arab world or in Asia.

I think the time has come when military action is no longer a major instrument of political strategy either Soviet or Western. The potential large-scale use of atomic weapons on both sides has brought this about. It will probably take a decade or more to work out a scheme of mutual inspection and disarmament but there is no practical alternative to this. I doubt if a single Soviet military leader (or Western leader) can tell how long a future war would last and how far a central military or political machine of any kind could continue to function in the face of atomic attack. Clearly maximum nuclear hitting power must remain the major plank in Western defence policy. In the face of it, how can the Soviet really know in detail how to fight their tank and airborne forces? Can they assess the effect of Western radio counter-measures or the striking power of US carrier forces in the first week of a war? How effective will their communications be in the face of large-scale atomic attack? Without consecutive communications how can the Soviet General Staff give orders and know what is going on? How effective will be Soviet flight refuelling in time of war? How will they know in time what damage their bombers and the long range rockets have achieved? War between USA and the USSR is no longer the continuation of politics by other means, but the creation of haphazard chaotic circumstances over which neither side can exercise political control.

The Soviet Marxists believe that they have a superior and more flexible economic system than the capitalist West. They have built up armed forces to the pitch when they need not fear attack from the West unless they themselves do something to stimulate it. In the long run they may believe that they can cripple the crucial overseas markets of the Western powers and show the superiority of their economic system. That is why I think their proposals for eventual disarmament may well be genuine.

BIOGRAPHICAL NOTES ON CONTRIBUTORS

BALDWIN, Hanson W.

Hanson Baldwin is the military editor of the *New York Times*. He graduated from the US Naval Academy at Annapolis in 1924. For the next three years he served first as an ensign and later as a junior lieutenant in battleships and destroyers but then resigned from the navy. Within two years he was working as a journalist for the *New York Times*, a paper he has served for some thirty years. During this period his articles, books and radio and television programmes have earned him a growing reputation and he is now probably the doyen and most influential of US defence commentators. Apart from writing for the *New York Times* he has contributed to a wide range of US and foreign periodicals and his military views are widely quoted. He has lectured to the US National War College, Naval War College and Air War College. His writing awards include a Pulitzer Prize and the medal of merit of the school of journalism at Syracuse University. His books include *The Price of Power*, *Great Mistakes of the War* and *United We Stand*. He has been awarded honorary degrees by two United States Universities and has twice visited the Soviet Union, in 1937 and in 1956.

GARTHOFF, Dr Raymond L.

A graduate of both Princeton and Yale Universities, Dr Garthoff has come to be recognised as one of the leading US authorities on Soviet military and political affairs. He has lectured on these subjects to the United States National War College, the Army War College, the American Military Institute and the Air University at Maxwell Air Base. His first major book on *Soviet Military Doctrine* was published in the United Kingdom under the title *How Russia Makes War*. His second major work on *Soviet Strategy in the Nuclear Age* was published in 1958. He has published a number of articles on Soviet Air Force strategy and organisation in such periodicals as the *US Air University Quarterly* and the *Royal Air Force Flying Review*.

GREEN, William

Aged thirty-two, Green is the youngest contributor to this volume. During the Second World War he was a member of the editorial staff of the *Air Training Corps Gazette* and then, after eighteen months as a journalist, had three and a half years in the Royal Air Force. After being demobilised he began a career as a free-lance international aviation journalist and made an immediate success of his writing. In the last few years he has earned a growing public for his aeronautical articles and books all over the world. He writes for both British and

Continental air reviews and has been a major contributor to the *Royal Air Force Flying Review*, in which he has published many articles on technical and other developments in the Soviet Air Force. In addition he has written on almost every air force in the world for one or other periodical and has also published a number of books. Two of the best known are *Jet Aircraft of the World*, which has been translated into Russian and published in the USSR and *Air Forces of the World*, which has been widely read in both the United States and the United Kingdom. There can be few aeronautical writers in the world with a wider knowledge of international aviation.

JOUBERT DE LA FERTÉ, Air Chief Marshal Sir Philip

After serving in the First World War in France, Egypt and Italy, Sir Philip Joubert was successively between the two World Wars RAF instructor at the Imperial Defence College, Commandant of the RAF Staff College at Andover, Air Officer Commander-in-Chief of RAF Coastal Command and then of the RAF in India. In the Second World War he attained the rank of Air Chief Marshal and was Assistant Chief of Air Staff in 1941 and once again Commander-in-Chief of Coastal Command from 1941 to 1943. He was Inspector-General of the RAF in 1943 and Deputy Chief of Staff of the South-East Asia Command from 1943 to 1945. After being Director of Public Relations at the Air Ministry from 1945 to 1947 he reverted to the retired list.

During the Second World War Air Chief Marshal Sir Philip Joubert achieved fame both as an air leader and as a broadcaster and writer on air affairs. He says that once he started to write he could not stop and a flow of broadcasts, articles, critiques, short stories and books came literally from his pen. He has to write in longhand for he can neither type nor dictate his manuscripts. His publications include three post-war books, all widely read on both sides of the Atlantic—*The Fated Sky*, published in 1953, *The Third Service*, two years later, *Rocket* in 1956, and *Birds and Fishes*, to be published shortly.

KUBAN, Boris

Born thirty-six years ago in the Soviet Union. After spending ten years at school he spent two years in an aircraft training college learning to be an aircraft designer. When the German War broke out in June, 1941, he was a member of the *Komsomol* and was sent to a military school for training artillery officers. His war service was not, however, with the artillery but with the infantry, where as a commissioned officer he commanded divisional reconnaissance troops, was then a company commander and later temporarily a battalion commander. He was twice wounded and then ceased front line duties. He was sent to another officers' training school catering for the military diplomatic service, and on completing the course was attached to the Northern Group of Soviet armies in the capacity of 'special duties officer' to the air forces in that group. He later transferred to the Ministry of Foreign Affairs was on the staff of the political adviser to the C.-in-C. of the Northern Group of Soviet Armies. He then decided to come over to the West and has been working as a journalist for the past few years.

LEE, Asher (Wing Commander)

Born Plymouth, 1909. Prior to the Second World War studied literature and philosophy at the Universities of London and Paris.

In the Second World War he served in RAF intelligence at the Air Ministry and was the senior British air intelligence officer at the Cairo Conference. He also served with the United States Army Air Forces and the 1st Allied Airborne Army. His post-war publications include *The German Air Force*, *The Soviet Air Force* and *Air Power*. All three appeared both in the United Kingdom and the United States, and *Air Power* has been translated into Russian and published in the USSR. He has written articles on air power in general and the Soviet Air Force in particular for the *Economist*, the *Royal Air Force Flying Review*, the *US Air University Quarterly*, the *New York Herald Tribune*, *Figaro*, *Réalités* and *Wehrkunde*.

MACKINTOSH, J. M.

Born in 1921, on Christmas Day. When he joined the Army in 1941, he was a student of history at Glasgow University. During the Second World War, he served in the Royal Scots and the Intelligence Corps. After appropriate parachute training he became part of the forces which maintained contact with the Balkans and in 1944 he became a liaison officer to the Soviet Armies in the Balkans. In 1946 he returned to Glasgow University and took a First in History in 1948. He has specialised in the study of East European Affairs for the last ten years, speaks Russian and Bulgarian fluently and has also specialised on Soviet Army organisation and strategy. He contributed notably to Liddell Hart's book on *The Soviet Army* and has lectured on Soviet military affairs at the Royal Institute of International Affairs in London.

SCHATUNOWSKI, George (Lieutenant)

George Schatunowski was five years of age when the first Soviet Air Squadrons were formed in 1917. As a junior air lieutenant in the Soviet Air Force in the Second World War he was shot down three times, once during the Battle of Stalingrad. He says that he joined a local flying club when at school, against strong family opposition. At the club he did little flying and found he was afiaid of parachute jumping. He had two years of scrappy aeronautical education between his studies in science at the University. The Canadian Army liberated him from a German prisoner of war camp in April, 1945. In 1947 he came to England as a volunteer coal miner and is now a journalist. He says that he never realised till too late the fascination that aviation has for him.

SCHWABEDISSEN, Walter (General)

Born in 1896, General Schwabedissen saw service in both World Wars. At the beginning of the First World War he was an artillery officer, but from July, 1915, he served as an observer in German air units operating over France, Flanders, Roumania and Macedonia. He received high decorations for his part in these air operations, Between the two World Wars he served at first in the *Reichswehr* both as an artillery specialist and as a general staff officer. In the recreated German Air Force he was at first a major in the Air Ministry, then Colonel and Commanding Officer of a bomber wing and on the eve of the Second World War was chief of staff of one of the chief air administrative districts (*Luftgau* 3 covering Berlin).

In the Second World War he was successively chief of staff of an anti-aircraft corps, a general on the *Wehrmacht* staff in Holland, held two separate commands each with the rank of lieutenant-general, in Germany's strategic air defences in 1942 and 1943, was General commanding German Air Forces in Denmark in 1944, and at the end of the Second World War was the *Wehrmacht*'s senior officer working with the Hungarian Air Force on the Eastern Front.

Before the Second World War began, General Schwabedissen had achieved a growing reputation as a military writer on air matters. He wrote articles for a number of air periodicals and his textbook on bomber operations was published in Germany under the sponsorship of the German Air Ministry. He has specialised in the past few years in writing on Soviet Air operations during the Second World War as well as on the problems which confronted the German Air Force through its multi-air-front commitments.

STOCKWELL, Richard E.

Richard Stockwell was born near Neilsville, Wisconsin, USA, in 1917. After graduating from the University of Wisconsin in bio-chemistry, he took a post-graduate degree in economics at the University of Minnesota. He began his professional career in radio, working as a news editor for the Wisconsin Radio Network and then for the Columbia Broadcasting System. His work in this field earned him a Niemen Fellowship at Harvard University. After the war he transferred to printed journalism and from 1949 to 1952 was editor of *Aviation Age*, a New York magazine. This publication issued a lot of information about the growing technical strength of aviation in the USSR when Stockwell was in the editorial chair. Although he later moved into industry with the Aircraft Gas Turbine Division of General Electric, and now is with the Crossley and Nashville Divisions of Avco Corporation, his interest in Soviet Air and Rocket Forces grew and in 1956 his book on *Soviet Air Power* was published and widely reviewed in both the United States and the United Kingdom.

Since writing the book he has twice visited the Soviet Union, in 1957 and 1958, staying in Leningrad, Sochi, on the Black Sea, Stalingrad, Kiev, Rostov, Tiflis and Moscow. He was able to see at first-hand something of the latest developments in AEROFLOT organisation, in turbo-jet engines, in aviation training and, as well, the machine tool industry of the USSR. Mr Stockwell is an associate member of the Institute of Aeronautical Sciences and the American Rocket Society and is also a member of the Wings Club of New York.

WHITING, Kenneth R.

Dr K. R. Whiting was born in 1913 at Somerville, Massachusetts, USA. He studied at Boston University, specialising in the history of Latin America. During the Second World War he served in the United States Army Air Force and was engaged in the campaigns in the South-West Pacific. Following a period of university history teaching, he took a doctorate degree in Russian history and language at the University of Harvard in 1951. Since 1951 he has been on the staff of the US Air University at Maxwell Air Force Base, engaged mainly in research on Soviet studies. He has published material on Soviet military doctrine, Soviet nationality problems, on Soviet economic resources and on Soviet-Turkish relations.

WILLIAMS, Peter

As a specialist in radio communications, Peter Williams had a varied career in the Second World War. He served with British, Dutch, Polish and United States forces. He was in action in the Battle of the Atlantic and saw service for twelve months with the US Navy in the Pacific against the Japanese. He was also based in Burma, India, Australia and Egypt at various stages of the war and was liaison officer with the Polish forces in the allied invasion of Normandy in the summer of 1944.

Since the end of the war his reputation as an author and a journalist has grown. He says he gained his first love of flying in the early 1930s. In the last ten years he has written widely on aviation subjects, for example on the heat barrier, the fighter aces of the Second World War and on the Egyptian Air Force.

Since 1956 he has been Editor of the *RAF Flying Review*. This monthly magazine has prospered under his leadership. Williams is a keen student of Soviet air and military affairs and his journal has become one of the most authoritative on aviation behind the Iron Curtain. He is also the author of a farce which was staged in the United Kingdom last year and has written for both radio and television.

INDEX